Post-colonial Translation

This outstanding collection brings together eminent contributors to examine some crucial interconnections between post-colonial theory and translation studies.

As English becomes an increasingly global language, so more people become multilingual and translation becomes a crucial communicative activity. Whereas traditional thinking about translation saw it as a poor copy of an original, today translation is viewed as an act of invention that produces a new original in another language. The essays in this book, by contributors from Britain, the US, Brazil, India and Canada, explore new perspectives on translation in relation to post-colonial societies. The essay topics include: links between centre and margins in the intellectual domain; shifts in translation practice from colonial to post-colonial societies; translation and power relations among Indian languages; Brazilian cannibalistic theories of literary transfer.

Examining the relationships between language and power across cultural boundaries, this collection reveals the vital role of translation in redefining the meanings of cultural and ethnic identity.

Susan Bassnett is Professor at the Centre for British and Comparative Cultural Studies, University of Warwick. She has published extensively in the fields of Translation Studies and Comparative Literature. She is author of *Translation Studies* (Routledge 1991) and of *Studying British Cultures* (Routledge 1997).

Harish Trivedi is Professor of English at the University of Delhi. He is author of *Colonial Transactions: English Literature and India*, and co-editor of *Interrogating Post-colonialism*. He has also published English translations of Hindi poetry and short fiction.

Translation Studies

General editors: Susan Bassnett and André Lefevere

In the same series:

Post-colonial Translation

Theory and practice

Edited by
Susan Bassnett
and Harish Trivedi

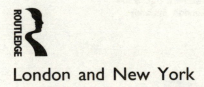

London and New York

First published 1999
by Routledge
11 New Fetter Lane, London EC4P 4EE

Simultaneously published in the USA and Canada
by Routledge
29 West 35th Street, New York, NY 10001

© 1999 Susan Bassnett and Harish Trivedi, collection and editorial
matter; © the contributors, individual contributions

Typeset in Baskerville by
The Florence Group, Stoodleigh, Devon
Printed and bound in Great Britain by
Clays Ltd, St Ives plc

British Library Cataloguing in Publication Data
A catalogue record for this book is available
from the British Library

Library of Congress Cataloging in Publication Data
Post-colonial translation: theory & practice / [edited by]
Susan Bassnett & Harish Trivedi.
  (Translation studies)
  Includes bibliographical references and index.
  1. Translating and interpreting–Social aspects.
  2. Postcolonialism.   3. Intercultural communication.   I. Bassnett,
  Susan.   II. Trivedi, Harish. III. Title: Post-colonial translation
  theory   IV. Series: Translation studies (London, England)
  P306.2.P67   1998
  418'.02–dc21   98–12969
                 CIP

ISBN 0–415–14744–1 (hbk)
ISBN 0–415–14745–x (pbk)

To André Lefevere (1945–1996), who was a dear friend to many of us and an inspiration to all.

Contents

Acknowledgements

The editors wish to thank all those friends and colleagues who have helped in the production of this book. A number of the papers have been tried out with students in different parts of the world and their responses have been gratefully noted. We would like particularly to thank Talia Rogers and Sophie Powell for their forbearance, patience and wise editorial advice. Grateful thanks to Mrs Maureen Tustin who has kept the lines of communication between editors and contributors open throughout.

Contributors

Rosemary Arrojo is Associate Professor of Translation Studies at the Universidade Estadual de Campinas in Brazil. She has published two books in Portuguese: *Oficina de Tradução: A Teoria na Prática* (1986) and *Tradução, Desconstrução e Psicanálise* (1993). In recent years, samples of her work have been published in English and in German.

Ganesh Devy is the author of *After Amnesia: Tradition and Change in Indian Literary Criticism* (1992), *In Another Tongue* (1993) and *Of Many Heroes* (1998), and is engaged in the documentation and study of the languages and literature of tribal communities in India. He was formerly Professor of English at the Maharaja Sayajirao University of Baroda. At present he is the Chairman of Bhasha Research and Publication Centre, Baroda, and Director of National Literary Academy's Project on Tribal Literature and Oral Traditions.

Vinay Dharwadker is Associate Professor in the Department of English at the University of Oklahoma. He is the author of *Sunday at the Lodi Gardens* (1994), a book of poems; and the editor, with A.K. Ramanujan, of *The Oxford Anthology of Modern Indian Poetry* (1994). He has co-edited *The Collected Poems of A.K. Ramanujan* (1995), and is the general editor of *The Collected Essays of A.K. Ramanujan* (1998). He is currently completing *The Columbia Book of Indian Poetry* (forthcoming, 2000). His recent essays have appeared or are forthcoming in *New National and Post-Colonial Literatures* (1996), *Language Machines* (1997) and *Self as Image in Asian Theory and Practice* (1998).

André Lefevere (1945–1996) was one of the leading figures in translation studies. His books include *Translating Poetry* (1975),

Translating Literature: The German Tradition (1977), *Translation, History, Culture* (1992) and *Translation, Rewriting and the Manipulation of Literary Fame* (1993). He began his academic career in Belgium, taught in many countries including Hong Kong and South Africa and was Professor of Germanic Languages at the University of Texas at Austin from 1984. His final essays are included in *Constructing Cultures* (1998), written jointly with Susan Bassnett.

G.J.V. Prasad is Assistant Professor at the Centre of Linguistics and English, Jawaharlal Nehru University, New Delhi, India. He is also a writer and has published a novel, *A Clean Breast* (1993), and a book of poems, *In Delhi Without a Visa* (1996).

Sherry Simon directs the Humanities Doctoral Programme and teaches in the French Department of Concordia University in Montreal. She is the author of *Le Trafic des langues: traduction et culture dans la littérature Québecoise* (1994) and *Gender in Translation: Cultural Identity and the Politics of Transmission* (1996), and editor of *Culture in Transit: Translating the Literature of Quebec* (1995). She is currently preparing a volume provisionally entitled *After Translation: The Esthetics of Cultural Hybridity*.

Maria Tymoczko is Professor of Comparative Literature at the University of Massachusetts, Amherst. She has published extensively on Irish literature and on translation studies. She is the author of *The Irish 'Ulysses'* and writes about James Joyce as a post-colonial writer. Her most recent book, *Translation in a Postcolonial Context: Early Irish Literature in English Translation*, is in press.

Else Ribeiro Pires Vieira is an Associate Professor of the Postgraduate School of Comparative Literature and of the Department of Anglo-Germanic Languages at the Federal University of Minas Gerais, where she is also the Convener of Postgraduate Studies in Literature and Linguistics. Her major field of interest is translation as intercultural transfer on which she has published widely in many countries. At present, she is the co-ordinator in Brazil of an international project on the interface between critical and cultural studies. Her most recent book is *Teorizando e Contextualizando a Tradução* (1996).

Vanamala Viswanatha teaches translation studies, Indian literatures and English language teaching in the Department of English,

Bangalore University, India. Winner of the KATHA award for Best Translator from Kannada into English in 1994, Vanamala Viswanatha is currently translating into English a novel by Sara Aboobakkar, a Muslim woman writer, for Macmillan (India) as well as a collection of short stories by Lankesh, a modernist writer in Kannada, for Sahitya Akademi. She is also the Kannada language editor for a British Council project, 'Representations of the Occident in short stories from South India'.

Introduction

Of colonies, cannibals and vernaculars

Susan Bassnett and Harish Trivedi

I

Once upon a time, in the sixteenth century, in what is now Brazil, members of the Tupinambà tribe devoured a Catholic priest. This act sent shudders of horror through Portugal and Spain, representing as it did the ultimate taboo for a European Christian. The very term 'cannibal' was associated with the Americas; originally referring to a group of Caribs in the Antilles, it entered the English language definitively in the *OED* of 1796 meaning 'an eater of human flesh' and subsequently passed into other European languages. The name of a tribe and the name given to savage peoples who ate human flesh fused into a single term.

The eating of the priest was not an illogical act on the part of the Tupinambà, and may even be said to have been an act of homage. After all, one does not eat people one does not respect, and in some societies the devouring of the strongest enemies or most worthy elders has been seen as a means of acquiring the powers they had wielded in life. Nor was it unknown in Europe; we need only think of Portia, the noble Roman widow who drank her husband's ashes in a glass of wine, declaring her body to be his fittest resting place. And, of course, no doubt confusingly for the Tupinambà tribe that the priest was seeking to convert, Christianity rests on the symbolism of devouring the body and blood of Christ, the Saviour. In vain to protest that the symbolic eating of the Eucharist needed to be distinguished from the actual eating of Father Sardinha's flesh – the Tupinambà concept of eating and taboo came from very different sources.

Now what, we may ask, does this narrative have to do with translation? A great deal, in fact, but before considering the question more fully, it is important to establish certain premises. First, and very obviously: translation does not happen in a vacuum, but in a continuum; it is not an isolated act, it is part of an ongoing process of intercultural transfer. Moreover, translation is a highly manipulative activity that involves all kinds of stages in that process of transfer across linguistic and cultural boundaries. Translation is not an innocent, transparent activity but is highly charged with significance at every stage; it rarely, if ever, involves a relationship of equality between texts, authors or systems.

Recent work in translation studies had challenged the long-standing notion of the translation as inferior to the original. In this respect, translation studies research has followed a similar path to other radical movements within literary and cultural studies, calling into question the politics of canonization and moving resolutely away from ideas of universal literary greatness. This is not to deny that some texts are valued more highly than others, but simply to affirm that systems of evaluation vary from time to time and from culture to culture and are not consistent.

One problem that anyone working in the field of translation studies has to confront is the relationship between the text termed the 'original', or the source, and the translation of that original. There was a time when the original was perceived as being *de facto* superior to the translation, which was relegated to the position of being merely a copy, albeit in another language. But research into the history of translation has shown that the concept of the high-status original is a relatively recent phenomenon. Medieval writers and / or translators were not troubled by this phantasm. It arose as a result of the invention of printing and the spread of literacy, linked to the emergence of the idea of an author as 'owner' of his or her text. For if a printer or author owned a text, what rights did the translator have? This discrepancy has been encoded into our thinking about the relationship between translation and so-called originals. It is also significant that the invention of the idea of the original coincides with the period of early colonial expansion, when Europe began to reach outside its own boundaries for territory to appropriate. Today, increasingly, assumptions about the powerful original are being questioned, and a major source of that challenge comes from the domains of the fearsome cannibals, from outside the safety of the hedges and neat brick walls of Europe.

Octavio Paz claims that translation is the principal means we have of understanding the world we live in. The world, he says, is presented to us as a growing heap of texts,

each slightly different from the one that came before it: translations of translations of translations. Each text is unique, yet
at the same time it is the translation of another text. No text
can be completely original because language itself, in its very
essence, is already a translation – first from the nonverbal world,
and then, because each sign and each phrase is a translation of
another sign, another phrase.

(Paz 1992: 154)

This is a radical view of translation, which sees it not as a marginal
activity but as a primary one, and it fits in with similar comments
made by writers such as Gabriel García Márquez, Jorge Luís Borges
and Carlos Fuentes. Indeed, Fuentes has gone so far as to say that
'originality is a sickness', the sickness of a modernity that is always
aspiring to see itself as something new (Fuentes 1990: 70). It is
fair to say that a great many Latin American writers today have
strong views about translation, and equally strong views about the
relationship between writer/reader and translator. To understand
something of this change of emphasis, we need to think again about
the history of translation, and about how it was used in the early
period of colonization.

Vicente Rafael describes the different significance translation had
for the Spanish colonizers and the Tagalog people of the Philippines:

> For the Spaniards, translation was always a matter of reducing
> the native language and culture to accessible objects for and
> subjects of divine and imperial intervention. For the Tagalogs,
> translation was a process less of internalizing colonial-Christian
> conventions than of evading their totalizing grip by repeatedly
> marking the differences between their language and interests
> and those of the Spaniards.

(Rafael 1988: 213)

He pinpoints the profoundly different meaning that translation held
for different groups in the colonization process. For it is, of course,
now recognized that colonialism and translation went hand in hand.
Eric Cheyfitz has argued that translation was 'the central act of
European colonization and imperialism in America' (Cheyfitz 1991:
104). Tejaswini Niranjana goes even further, and suggests that translation both shapes and takes shape 'within the asymmetrical relations
of power that operate under colonialism' (Niranjana 1992: 2).

The figure of La Malinche, the native American woman taken as mistress of the conquistador Hernán Cortés who was also the interpreter between the Spaniards and the Aztec peoples, serves as an icon to remind us that a dominant metaphor of colonialism was that of rape, of husbanding 'virgin lands', tilling them and fertilizing them and hence 'civilizing' them (Hulme 1986). So in this post-colonial period, when, as Salman Rushdie puts it, the Empire has begun to write back, it is unsurprising to find radical concepts of translation emerging from India, from Latin America, from Canada, from Ireland – in short, from former colonies around the world that challenge established European norms about what translation is and what it signifies.

Let us return at this juncture to cannibalism. The Tupinambà ate their priest; and in the 1920s a group of Brazilian writers returned to that story in an attempt to rethink the relationship which they, as Latin Americans, had with Europe. For Europe was regarded as the great Original, the starting point, and the colonies were therefore copies, or 'translations' of Europe, which they were supposed to duplicate. Moreover, being copies, translations were evaluated as less than originals, and the myth of the translation as something that diminished the greater original established itself. It is important also to remember that the language of 'loss' has featured so strongly in many comments on translation. Robert Frost, for example, claimed that 'poetry is what gets lost in translation'. Students of translation almost all start out with the assumption that something will be lost in translation, that the text will be diminished and rendered inferior. They rarely consider that there might also be a process of gain. The notion of the colony as a copy or translation of the great European Original inevitably involves a value judgement that ranks the translation in a lesser position in the literary hierarchy. The colony, by this definition, is therefore less than its colonizer, its original.

So how were the colonies, emerging from colonialism, to deal with that dilemma? How might they find a way to assert themselves and their own culture, to reject the appellative of 'copy' or 'translation' without at the same time rejecting everything that might be of value that came from Europe? Oswald de Andrade's *Manifesto Antropófago*, which appeared in 1928, was dated 374 years after the death of Father Sardinha, the cannibalized priest, and proposed the metaphor of cannibalism as a way forward for Brazilian culture. Only by devouring Europe could the colonized break away from what was imposed upon them. And at the same time, the devouring could be perceived as both a violation of European codes and an act of homage.

The cannibalistic metaphor has come to be used to demonstrate to translators what they can do with a text. Translation, says the great Brazilian translator Haraldo de Campos, whose work is discussed in detail by Else Vieira in her chapter in this book, may be likened to a blood transfusion, where the emphasis is on the health and nourishment of the translator. This is a far cry from the notion of faithfulness to an original, of the translator as servant of the source text. Translation, according to de Campos, is a dialogue, the translator is an all-powerful reader and a free agent as a writer. This is a vastly different view of translation from that described by George Steiner as involving the 'penetration' of the source text (Steiner 1975).

At this point in time, post-colonial theorists are increasingly turning to translation and both reappropriating and reassessing the term itself. The close relationship between colonization and translation has come under scrutiny; we can now perceive the extent to which translation was for centuries a one-way process, with texts being translated *into* European languages for European consumption, rather than as part of a reciprocal process of exchange. European norms have dominated literary production, and those norms have ensured that only certain kinds of text, those that will not prove alien to the receiving culture, come to be translated. As Anuradha Dingwaney and Carol Maier point out, translation is often a form of violence (Dingwaney and Maier 1995). Moreover, the role played by translation in facilitating colonization is also now in evidence. And the metaphor of the colony *as* a translation, a copy of an original located elsewhere on the map, has been recognized.

This shameful history of translation that is now being exposed has led to some extreme reactions. There are those who maintain that translation into European languages should be restricted, even curtailed, that texts should not be translated into dominant linguistic and cultural systems because this perpetuates the colonizing process. They have a point, of course. But to restrict translation is to tread perilously close to other forms of censorship. A ban on translation can lead one down the same pathway that ends with the burning of books judged unacceptable by a tyrannous regime. Much more productive is the approach proposed by such writers as Homi Bhabha, and many of the Canadian women translators discussed by Sherry Simon in her chapter, who argue persuasively for a new politics of in-betweenness, for a reassessment of the creative potentialities of liminal space. As Homi Bhabha puts it:

> we should remember that it is the 'inter' – the cutting edge of translation and renegotiation, the *in-between* space – that carries the burden of the meaning of culture. It makes it possible to begin envisaging national anti-nationalist histories of the 'people'. And by exploring this Third Space, we may elude the politics of polarity and emerge as the others of our selves.
>
> (Bhabha 1994: 38–9)

The editors of this volume of papers by translation specialists, writers and translators share the desire to eschew a politics of polarity. The basic premise upon which all the chapters are based is that the act of translation always involves much more than language. Translations are always embedded in cultural and political systems, and in history. For too long translation was seen as purely an aesthetic act, and ideological problems were disregarded. Yet the strategies employed by translators reflect the context in which texts are produced. In the nineteenth century, an English translation tradition developed, in which texts from Arabic or Indian languages were cut, edited and published with extensive anthropological footnotes. In this way, the subordinate position of the individual text and the culture that had led to its production in the first place was established through specific textual practices. The Arabs, Edward Lane informed readers in notes to his popular translation of *The Thousand and One Nights*, were far more gullible than educated European readers and did not make the same clear distinction between the rational and the fictitious (Lane 1859). In similar vein, Edward Fitzgerald, author of one of the most successful translations of the nineteenth century, *The Rubaiyat of Omar Khayyam*, could accuse the Persians of artistic incompetence and suggest that their poetry became art only when translated into English (Bassnett 1991). Both these translators were spectacularly successful, but when we start to examine the premises upon which their translation practice was based, what emerges is that they clearly saw themselves as belonging to a superior cultural system. Translation was a means both of containing the artistic achievements of writers in other languages and of asserting the supremacy of the dominant, European culture.

II

When Sir William Jones (1746–96) translated the Sanskrit romantic play *Abhijnanashakuntalam* into English as *Sacontala, or the Fatal Ring: An Indian Drama* (1789), a major departure he made from the original was to stop the tender lovelorn heroine from breaking into sweat every now and then. Having lived in Calcutta as a judge of the Supreme Court there since 1783 he could not but have noticed that the climate was appreciably warmer, but he still felt obliged to mitigate this essential bodily function in the interests of his Western notion of the aesthetic. He would not have known, with the *Kama Sutra* yet to be 'discovered' and translated, that to sweat was traditionally known and appreciated in India also as a visible symptom of sexual interest and arousal (in contrast with England, where one sweats when one is 'hot, ill, afraid or working very hard'; Collins 1987: 1477), nor could he have taken recourse to the English euphemism, which probably was invented somewhat later, that while horses sweat and men perspire, women glow. Anyhow, his act of prim and proleptically Victorian censorship neatly points up the common translatorial temptation to erase much that is culturally specific, to sanitize much that is comparatively odorous.

Sir William Jones was, of course, universally acclaimed till the other day as 'Oriental Jones' (Cannon 1964), in pre-Saidian innocence and even reverence. He pioneered translations into English of Indian (specifically Sanskrit) as well as Arabic and Persian texts, and helped bring about a new awareness of oriental literature which initially caused such tremendous excitement among some of the best and most creative European minds of that age as to have precipitated nothing less than an 'Oriental Renaissance' – or so it then seemed (Schwab 1984: 4–8). What is notable here is that now, as for some decades afterwards, the traffic in translation between the East and the West remained decidedly one-sided, from the East to the West. However, through the nineteenth century and well into the twentieth, even when a regular flow of translations from English into the Indian languages had been inaugurated, nearly as many works from Sanskrit continued to be translated into the modern Indian languages as from English, and often by the same multilingual Janus-faced Indian translators.

Throughout this period, the Indian literary space was a vigorously contested terrain, with the impulse for an eager reception of the new Western modes of literature being counterpointed by a tendency to resist such influence, often through reasserting the older indigenous forms of Indian writing. Eventually, however, the resurgence of native traditions gave way to a hegemony of Western literary culture even as the British colonial dominance grew more entrenched all round. A striking instance of the new literary climate was a flurry of about a dozen translations into Hindi in the 1920s and 1930s of the *Rubaiyat of Omar Khayyam*. These were, of course, translations of a translation, an instance indeed of orientalism translated, and perhaps even a foreshadow, so to say, of the Empire translating back. For several of these translations were strongly modified Indian adaptations, while a couple had been done straight from Persian, which had been the elite court-language of India for several centuries before English supplanted it under the Macaulay-Bentinck diktat from 1835 onwards, and in which many cultured Indians were still well versed a century later. Thus, while multiple translations into Hindi of Edward Fitzgerald's *Omar Khayyam* may have underlined the condition of colonial dependence in which Indians now gained access to Persian literature through English, the translations undertaken at the same time direct from Persian can be seen as a resolute act of resistance to the English intervention. In any case, the most successful of all these translations (or new and inspired versions), *Madhushala* (i.e. The House of Wine; 1935), by the most popular romantic poet in Hindi this century, Harivansha Rai Bachchan (1907–   ), was a wholesale appropriation of the *Rubaiyat* to the local cultural and even topical nationalist context (Trivedi 1995: 29–52). Thus, if the Persian poets such as Khayyam and Attar needed to be supplied with 'a little Art' by Fitzgerald before they could become acceptable in English, Fitzgerald in turn needed to be fairly comprehensively modified and even subverted before he could be metamorphosed into successful Hindi poetry.

If Bachchan's *Madhushala* is at all translation, it is translation as rewriting, as André Lefevere has called it, or translation as 'new writing', as Sujit Mukherjee has named it in the Indian literary context (Mukherjee 1994: 77–85). In India, with its long history of oral composition and transmission, and the dominant early phase of *bhakti* or devotional poetry in all its modern languages in which the poet surrendered to and sought to merge his individual identity with his divine subject, the distinction between different composers of poetry within the same tradition or between an original writer and a translator was never half as wide as it has been in the West. Indeed, Gayatri Chakravorty Spivak's uncharacteristically tender plea that a translator should adopt a procedure of 'love' and 'surrender' towards the original, as she herself claims to have done when translating from the Bengali some devotional poetry as well as the contemporary fiction writer Mahasweta Devi, may be seen as a vestigial persistence of these traditional Indian practices (Spivak 1993: 180–1). It is relevant in this regard that the printing of books started in India on any significant scale only towards the end of the eighteenth century. Charles Wilkins, an early orientalist and translator from Sanskrit, also designed and cast the first font of Bengali characters and founded in 1778 in Calcutta a printing press which was generously patronised by the East India Company (Brockington 1989: 96); the Indian incunabulum thus may be said virtually to comprise books published before 1801. The rise of print capitalism in India was thus a modern-colonial phenomenon, as was the birth of the individual copyright-holding 'author', whose 'death' and 'function' have lately been debated in the West by Roland Barthes and Michel Foucault. Such an author could no longer be simply and silently rewritten; he needed to be scrupulously, even faithfully, translated.

The word for translation in Sanskrit, which persists unchanged in most of the modern Indian languages, is *anuvad*, which etymologically and primarily means 'saying after or again, repeating by way of explanation, explanatory repetition or reiteration with corroboration or illustration, explanatory reference to anything already said' (Monier-Williams 1997: 38). (One of the early Sanskrit uses of the word in this sense occurs in the *Brihadaranyaka Upnishad* in a passage which T.S. Eliot picked up for use in the last section of *The Waste Land*; Eliot's 'What the Thunder Said' is, in the Sanskrit source, strictly speaking What the Thunder Translated/ Repeated – for the syllable DA had already been first uttered by the god Prajapati.) The underlying metaphor in the word *anuvad* is temporal – to say *after*, to repeat – rather than spatial as in the English/Latin word translation – to carry *across*. Thus, 'imitation' in the neo-classical sense was in India a form of translation as being a repetition of something already written, and formed the staple of the pre-colonial literary tradition with those two great source-books of Indian culture, the *Ramayana* and the *Mahabharata*, being worked and reworked by countless writers in Sanskrit itself as well as in all the modern Indian languages, with various shifts of emphasis and ideology through which gaps in the original were inventively filled in, silences were rendered poignantly articulate, and even some of the great heroes turned into villains and villains into heroes.

The most outstanding examples of literature as an accumulative endeavour constantly to make it new are the standard versions of these two great epics in nearly every one of the modern Indian languages. Each of these versions, which were done on the whole sometime between the tenth and the sixteenth centuries AD, is clearly and substantially based on the Sanskrit original it repeats or retells, but with sufficient indisputable originality for it to be regarded by everyone as an autonomous free-standing creative work of the first order. For example, Tulsi Das (1532–1623) is still regarded as the greatest poet ever in Hindi for having (re-)written the *Ramayana*. Such was his own poetic genius that he enjoys the status in Hindi, incredible as it may sound, of both Shakespeare and the Authorised Version of the Bible put together in English.

Tulsi Das was by birth a brahman. Even as he brought this scriptural epic to the 'vernacular' masses by releasing it from the monopolist custody of Sanskrit pundits, by whom he was predictably derided and harassed, he remained, as decreed by religious tradition and caste, entirely nonviolent and a vegetarian. His reformational act of the appropriation of the *Ramayana* could thus hardly be called an instance of Brazilian cannibalism; it marked, rather, a natural process of organic, ramifying, vegetative growth and renewal, comparable perhaps with the process by which an ancient banyan tree sends down branches which then in turn take root all around it and comprise an intertwined family of trees: *quot rami tot arbores*. Such symbiotic intermingling of the original with the translation, of the tradition with the individual genius, still persists, and is seen as sanctioning the practice, fairly widely prevalent in contemporary India, of 'transcreation' (Lal 1996). Indeed, this word is listed in a new supplement of 'Indian English' words in the *Oxford Advanced Learner's Dictionary of Contemporary English* (5th edn, 1996), along with such exotically incomprehensible terms as *tota* and *trishul* – unmindful of the fact that transcreation is a term which has independently been used also on the other side of the globe, by Haroldo de Campos in Brazil (as shown in Else Vieira's chapter in this volume).

A crucial disjuncture between the older pre-colonial translational practice in India (of which different aspects are highlighted in this volume in the chapters by G.N. Devy and by Vanamala Viswanatha and Sherry Simon) and the present post-colonial phase is that now, translations from the various Indian languages into English, whether done by foreigners or by Indians themselves, have attained a hegemonic ascendancy. The widely shared post-colonial wisdom on the subject is that the Empire can translate back only into English, or into that lower or at least lower-case variety of it, english, according to some pioneering and influential theorists of the subject (Ashcroft et al. 1989: 8). To any counter-claims that literature especially with a post-colonial thrust is being written equally or even more abundantly in languages other than English, especially in countries such as India where only a small elite (variously estimated to constitute between 2 and 10 per cent of the population) knows any English, the usual sceptical Western retort is: But show us – in English translation! (Trivedi and Mukherjee (eds) 1996: 239). Yet, in inveterately multilingual countries such as India, not only is most literature being written now in the indigenous languages but the majority of translations being done are from one Indian language into the others. In 1996, when Mahasweta Devi, translated, introduced and theorized in English by no less a post-colonial authority than Gayatri Chakravorty Spivak, received India's highest literary award, the Jnanpeeth (at a ceremony at which a special guest was Nelson Mandela) and acknowledged in her acceptance speech the role played by translation in gaining her a wider audience beyond Bengali in which she writes, she mentioned with gratitude the role played not by Spivak or any others of her translators into English but rather by Arvind Kumar, the then director of the National Book Trust of India, and earlier a Hindi publisher himself, who had for many years facilitated the translation and dissemination of her works into Hindi and other Indian languages. There are thus two Mahasweta Devis, the one addressing the political and cultural realities on her native ground in her native language as these have evolved over a long stretch of both colonial and post-colonial times (right from her first novel, which had for its heroine Rani Lakshmi Bai, one of the most valiant fighters against the British during the 'Mutiny' of 1857, to her more recent works describing the present-day struggles of the tribals and Marxist revolutionaries against the independent Indian nation-state), and the other the author of a few selected short stories which through English translation have been borne across and co-opted within the post-colonial agenda set by the Western academy. And there are many Mahasweta Devis in each of the Indian languages whose writings engage with a whole range of post-colonial issues but who are yet untranslated into English and therefore unknown to post-colonial discourse.

The question to be asked here is: can one be thought to be a post-colonial even before or without being translated into English? Does s/he even exist before so translated? It is an understandable urge for simple self-assertion which in a large measure accounts for the great translation boom currently on in India in which any number of Indians have taken it upon themselves to translate works of Indian literature, both ancient and modern, into English, to show the world (including anglophone Indians) that such works do exist. A.K. Ramanujan, probably the most outstanding Indian translator in the half-century since Independence, set an example in this regard through his own informed and conscientious practice, as Vinay Dharwadker's chapter on him in this volume demonstrates.

Symptomatically, Salman Rushdie, probably the most eminent of all post-colonial writers, writes in English in the first place and therefore does not need to be translated. And yet, this is because (as G.J.V. Prasad shows in his chapter with reference to Rushdie and several other older Indian novelists in English) he has already translated himself into becoming an English-language writer, through a transformation of which signs are deliberately and transparently (or for most Western readers opaquely?) strewn all over his work in the form of Hindi/Urdu words and phrases. This is the magic bilingualism which paradoxically authenticates him as a post-colonial writer. There is another sense, of course, in which Rushdie himself has claimed to be a 'translated' man, for the reason as he explains it that he has physically been 'borne across the world' from India/Pakistan to England (Rushdie 1991: 17). In his formation as a post-colonial writer, the fact of his having abandoned both his native language and his native location has played a crucial constitutive role. With him as with numerous other Third World writers, such translingual, translocational translation has been the necessary first step to becoming a post-colonial writer.

Indeed, if one is to go by a characteristically homophonous formulation by Homi Bhabha, offered specifically in connection with Rushdie's fiction, there is now a conceptual near-synonymity between the 'transnational' and the 'translational', and the translated hybridity of the 'unhomed' migrant now inhabits a 'Third Space' (Bhabha 1994: 5, 224) – which presumably becomes accessible only after one has left the Third World. But even when one is firmly located on colonial ground, one is no less 'in a state of translation', as Tejaswini Niranjana argues in her complex conflation of colonial history with post-structuralist theory; for her, translation is an overarching metaphor for the unequal power relationship which defines the condition of the colonized (Niranjana 1992).

The colonial subject fixed to his native site as well as the unsited migrant post-colonial are thus equally translated persons.

In current theoretical discourse, then, to speak of post-colonial translation is little short of a tautology. In our age of (the valorization of) migrancy, exile and diaspora, the word translation seems to have come full circle and reverted from its figurative literary meaning of an inter-lingual transaction to its etymological physical meaning of locational disrupture; translation itself seems to have been translated back to its origins. As André Lefevere suggested, 'the time may have come to move beyond the word as such, to promote it to the realm of metaphor, so to speak, and leave it there' (Lefevere 1994: vii).

Meanwhile, however, the old business of translation as traffic between languages still goes on in the once-and-still colonized world, reflecting more acutely than ever before the asymmetrical power relationship between the various local 'vernaculars' (i.e. the languages of the slaves, etymologically speaking) and the one master-language of our post-colonial world, English. When the very first translation from Sanskrit into English was published in 1785 (the only one to precede Jones' *Sacontala*), of the *Bhagavad-gita* by Charles Wilkins, the then Governor-General Warren Hastings remarked that 'works such as this one will survive when the British dominion in India shall have long ceased to exist' (quoted in Brockington 1989: 97). He could not have foreseen the post-colonial turn in world history, through which the *Bhagavad-gita* now augurs to circulate and survive rather better in English translation than in the original language – perhaps even within India in the decades to come.

III

The contributors to this volume are concerned in many different ways with both the theory and practice of translation in a post-colonial context. In her chapter, 'Post-colonial writing and literary translation', Maria Tymoczko suggests that there are strong simi-larities between these two types of textual production. Both are concerned with the transmission of elements from one culture to another, both are affected by the process of relocation, hence it is hardly surprising that so many post-colonial writers have chosen to use the term 'translation' metaphorically. Tymoczko focuses on the way in which African writers such as Ngũgĩ wa Thiong'o have consciously chosen to import African words into their writing, which creates variations in the standard language and highlights the hybridity of the text. She points out that in translation studies a distinction is always made between whether to take an audience to a text, or to take a text to an audience, and argues that the same distinction applies also to post-colonial writing. By defamiliarizing the language, post-colonial writers can bring readers face to face with the reality of difference, and call into question the supremacy of the standard language.

G.J.V. Prasad, in similar vein, considers the case of the Indian English novel, starting with the views of the novelist Raja Rao, who sees the act of writing as a struggle for a space created by the transformation of the Indian text, the context and the English language. He points out that Indian English writers do not so much translate Indian language texts into English, but rather use different strategies to make their works sound like translations. This conscious 'thickening' or defamiliarization of English makes the act of reading more difficult, but proclaims the right of Indian writers to translate the language for their own purposes. A complex web of translations results, and a new space is opened up in which bilingualism becomes the norm.

In 'Translating and interlingual creation in the contact zone: border writing in Quebec', Sherry Simon argues that bilingualism leads to the dissolution of the binary opposition between original and translation. Following Mary Louise Pratt, she uses the notion of the 'contact zone', the place where previously separated cultures come together. Traditionally a place where cultures met on unequal terms, the contact zone is now a space that is redefining itself, a space of multiplicity, exchange, renegotiation and discontinuities. Simon looks at the work of three Quebec writers, Jacques Brault, Nicole Brossard and Daniel Gagnon, showing how these writers play on language relationships in radically innovative ways. Their work, she claims, is deliberately, self-consciously provocative, blurring boundaries of cultural identity and writing against a cultural tradition that has, as she puts it, 'been deeply suspicious of the work of translation'. Simon also points out that more and more writers, from James Joyce and Samuel Beckett through to Salman Rushdie and Derek Walcott, claim that they are never 'at home' in any language. Neither culture, nor language in today's world offer themselves as unifying forces, sharing a universe of references. Contemporary understanding of translation both as reality and as ideal, Simon suggests, has more to do with discontinuity, friction and multiplicity.

André Lefevere takes up similar lines of argument in his chapter, in which he proposes the notion of a 'conceptual grid' and a 'textual grid' that underpin all forms of writing. These grids, which he sees as inextricably intertwined, derive from the cultural and literary conventions of a given time. So, for example, the epic, once the great literary form of European cultures, has virtually ceased to exist, and has become strange and distant for contemporary readers. Any translator wishing to translate an epic has therefore to deal with the fact that this form is alien to readers, even though they may be aware of its historical significance. In contrast, with a form like the Arabic quasida, which has no precedent in Western literatures, the reader's resistance may effectively block its translation altogether. Lefevere argues that translators need to keep in mind a double set of conceptual and textual grids, in both source and target systems, but points out also that Western cultures 'translate' non-Western cultures into Western categories, imposing their own grids regardless. To illustrate his argument, he considers three Dutch texts, written between 1740 and 1820, that construct an idea of Dutch India (now known as Indonesia) specifically for Dutch readers. These are texts produced in a colonial context, for consumption at home, and Lefevere shows how the three writers, in different ways, used forms that reinforce their attitude to the Dutch colonizing venture.

Else Vieira moves us from epics of colonialism to the cannibalistic undertaking of the twentieth century in her chapter on the Brazilian translator Haroldo de Campos. She draws attention to the wealth of metaphors he has used to define what he perceives as a new kind of post-colonial translation: 'transcreation', 'transluciferation', 'translumination', 'transtextualization', even 'poetic reorchestration' and the profoundly significant 'reimagination'. De Campos' translation practice, which is as radical as is his theory, derives from the deliberate intention to define a post-colonial poetics of translation. Translation, says de Campos, is a form of patricide, a deliberate refusal to repeat that which has already been presented as the original. Vieira looks at the importance of the metaphor of cannibalism in twentieth-century Brazil, and shows how de Campos presents cannibalism as both a break with monological (colonial) truth and a form of nourishment. Translation, she claims, disturbs linear flows and power hierarchies, and unsettles the logocentrism of the original.

The unsettling power of translation is also the subject of Vinay Dharwadker's chapter on A.K. Ramanujan's translation theory and practice. He examines the work of the great Indian translator, showing how Ramanujan voiced the idea that the task of the translator was to 'translate' the foreign reader into a native one, and argues that Ramanujan's work effectively demonstrates the eurocentrism of Walter Benjamin's and Derrida's theories of translation, by offering an alternative Indian translation poetics. In the second part of his chapter he defends Ramanujan against his critics, seeking to show that he was not, as has been suggested, a colonialist translator.

The case against dominant European models is also the theme of Rosemary Arrojo's chapter on Hélène Cixous' versions of the work of Clarice Lispector. Although recognizing that Cixous has an authentic passion for Lispector's writing, Arrojo argues that Cixous uses this as a device for appropriating Lispector's work to serve her own ends. Cixous' discovery of Lispector has, as she points out, been perceived as a reversal of traditional colonial, patriarchal encounters, with a European writer worshipping the work of a woman from a colonized continent. But Arrojo suggests that the outcome of this relationship is merely a reinforcement of the colonial model, with Cixous in the dominant position, deliberately ignoring, disregarding or even destroying Lispector's own ideas. Ultimately, Arrojo believes, Cixous does nothing more than repeat the model of oppressive, masculine patriarchy that she claims to oppose.

Vanamala Viswanatha and Sherry Simon, who also started out from very different places, collaborate in a chapter significantly entitled 'Shifting grounds of exchange'. They point out that in both India and Canada, their homelands, translation is a particularly sensitive indicator of cultural tensions. Translation practice, they suggest, is always grounded in a set of assumptions about ways in which linguistic forms carry cultural meanings – in short, in an implicit theory of culture. A post-colonial perspective foregrounds the asymmetrical relationships between cultures that are also evidenced in the translation of literary texts.

Understanding the complexities of textual transfer through translation is of especial importance at the present time, for multilingualism, and the cultural interactions that it entails, is the norm for millions throughout the world. European languages, once perceived as superior because they were the languages of the colonial masters, now interact with hundreds of languages previously marginalized or ignored outright. Translation has been at the heart of the colonial encounter, and has been used in all kinds of ways to establish and perpetuate the superiority of some cultures over others. But now, with increasing awareness of the unequal power relations involved in the transfer of texts across cultures, we are in a position to rethink both the history of translation and its contemporary practice. Cannibalism, once the ultimate taboo of European Christians, can now be put into perspective, and the point of view of the practitioners of cannibalism can be put through the medium of translation.

References

Ashcroft, B., Griffiths, G. and Tiffin, H. (1989) *The Empire Writes Back: Theory and Practice in Post-colonial Literatures* (London: Routledge).

Bassnett, S. (1991) *Translation Studies* (London: Routledge), citing Edward Fitzgerald, Letter to Cowell, 20 March 1851.

Bhabha, H. (1994) *The Location of Culture* (London and New York: Routledge).

Brockington, J.L. (1989) 'Warren Hastings and Orientalism', in *The Impeachment of Warren Hastings: Papers from a Bicentenary Commemoration*, eds G. Carnall and C. Nicholson (Edinburgh: Edinburgh University Press).

de Campos, H. (1981) *Deus e o diablo no Fausto de Goethe* (San Paolo: Perspectiva).

Cannon, G. (1964) *Oriental Jones: A Biography of Sir William Jones (1746–1794)* (London).

Cheyfitz, E. (1991) *The Poetics of Imperialism: Translation and Colonization from The Tempest to Tarzan* (New York and Oxford: Oxford University Press).

The Collins-COBUILD English Language Dictionary (London: Collins, 1987).

Dingwaney, A. and Maier, C. (eds) (1995) *Between Languages and Cultures: Translation and Cross-Cultural Texts* (Pittsburgh and London: University of Pittsburgh Press).

Fuentes, C. (1990) *Aura* (London: André Deutsch).

Hulme, P. (1986) *Colonial Encounters* (London and New York: Routledge).

Lal, P. (1996) *Transcreations: Seven Essays on the Art of Transcreation* (Calcutta: Writers' Workshop).

Lane, E. (1859) *The Thousand and One Nights* (London).

Lefevere, A. (1994) 'Introductory comments II', in *Cross Cultural Transfers: Warwick Working Papers in Translation* (University of Warwick: Centre for British and Comparative Cultural Studies).

Monier-Williams, Sir Monier (1997 [1899]) *A Sanskrit–English Dictionary Etymologically and Philologically Arranged* (Delhi: Motilal Banarsidass).

Mukherjee, S. (1994 [1981]) 'Translation as new writing', in his *Translation as Discovery and Other Essays on Indian Literature in English Translation* (Hyderabad: Orient Longman).

Niranjana, T. (1992) *Siting Translation: History, Post-Structuralism and the Colonial Context* (Los Angeles: University of California Press).

Paz, O. trans. Irene del Corral (1992) 'Translations of literature and letters', in R. Schulte and J. Biguenet (eds) *Theories of Translation from Dryden to Derrida* (Chicago: University of Chicago Press), pp. 152–63

Rafael, V. (1988) *Contracting Colonialism: Translation and Christian Conversion in Tagalog Society under Early Spanish Rule* (Ithaca, NY: Cornell University Press), p. 213.

Rushdie, S. (1991) *Imaginary Homelands: Essays and Criticism 1981–1991* (London: Granta Books).

Schwab, R. (1984) *The Oriental Renaissance: Europe's Rediscovery of India and the East 1680–1880* (New York: Columbia University Press; orig. pub. in French, 1950).

Spivak, G.C.(1993) 'The politics of translation', in her *Outside in the Teaching Machine* (New York: Routledge).

Steiner, G. (1975) *After Babel: Aspects of Language and Translation* (Oxford: Oxford University Press).

Trivedi, H. (1995 [1993]) *Colonial Transactions: English Literature and India* (Manchester: Manchester University Press).

Trivedi, H. and Mukherjee, M. (eds) (1996) *Interrogating Post-colonialism: Theory, Text and Context* (Shimla: Indian Institute of Advanced Study).

Chapter 1

Post-colonial writing and literary translation

Maria Tymoczko

Analysis of literary texts emerging from peoples who have been colonized or oppressed invites metaphor: the criticism of such texts speaks, for example, of voices silenced, margin and centre, and epistolary exchange.[1] Perhaps this is so because of cognitive processes themselves. In speaking of unfamiliar or new phenomena, humans often adapt the language of similar though disparate objects and action. Figurative language is used: in English, for example, the newly invented vehicle propelled by an internal combustion engine was sometimes known as *the horseless carriage*.[2] The penchant for metaphorical speech about post-colonial literature suggests that critics view it as a new literary phenomenon about which we do not as yet know how to speak directly, a type of writing for which we do not as yet have an adequate vocabulary. Because metaphoric speech is cognitively pervasive, a normally harmless and time-honoured linguistic practice, the approach could be extended; metaphors are to hand. Mirrors come to mind as appropriate figures, for example: the writing of post-colonial authors or those from subaltern cultures as a house of mirrors in which the reader and writer alike risk being lost in the tangle, confusion and redundancy of reflections; as the mirror in St Paul's trope, in which one as yet sees only darkly rather than face to face; or, to adapt Joyce's aphorism about Irish art, as the cracked looking-glass of a servant. And let us not forget the mirroring in the well-used figure of Caliban's rage.

Translation might be used as such a metaphor, but this is not what I am about here. Translation as metaphor for post-colonial writing, for example, invokes the sort of activity associated with the etymological meaning of the word: translation as the activity of *carrying across*, for instance, the transportation and relocation of the bones and other remains of saints. In this sense post-colonial writing might be imaged as a form of translation (attended with much ceremony and pomp, to be sure) in which venerable and holy (historical, mythic and literary) relics are moved from one sanctified spot of worship to another more central and more secure (because more powerful) location, at which the cult is intended to be preserved, to take root and find new life. There is, of course, much in this metaphor that bears reflection (mirroring again) in relation to many works emanating from former colonies, and the metaphor is suggestive of certain perils faced by writers in these circumstances.[3]

However that might be, in this enquiry I am not using translation as a metaphor of transportation across (physical, cultural or linguistic) space or boundaries: instead, interlingual literary translation provides an *analogue* for post-colonial writing. The two types of intercultural writing are essentially distinct, but they have enough points of contact that exploration of the two in tandem and comparison of the two – investigation of the commonalities and the differences – results in new insights about both. Moreover, because literary translation is a phenomenon that can be charted for more than two millennia with an almost coeval critical and theoretical literature about it, many of the workings of literary translation are reasonably well understood. Thus, the comparison of literary translation and post-colonial writing is particularly apt to shed light on the latter more recent literary phenomenon, an understanding of which can benefit from the body of knowledge that has been built up in translation studies.

Significant differences between literary translation and post-colonial literature are obvious and should be addressed from the outset. The primary difference is that, unlike translators, post-colonial writers are not transposing a text. As background to their literary works, they are transposing a culture – to be understood as a language, a cognitive system, a literature (comprised of a system of texts, genres, tale types, and so on), a material culture, a social system and legal framework, a history, and so forth. In the case of many former colonies, there may even be more than one culture or one language that stand behind a writer's work. A translator, by contrast, has seemingly a much more limited domain, only a single text to transpose. As perspectives from general systems theory and semiotics suggest, however, this difference is more apparent than real, for the same cultural complexity facing a post-colonial or minority-culture author is implicit in any single text of the same culture: Ivir (1987: 35) goes so far as to claim that translation means translating cultures not languages.[4] Thus, a literary translator is *de facto* concerned with differences not just in language (transposing word for word, mechanically), but with the same range of cultural factors that a writer must address when writing to a receiving audience composed partially or primarily of people from a different culture. The culture or tradition of a post-colonial writer acts as a metatext which is rewritten – explicitly and implicitly, as both background and foreground – in the act of literary creation. The task of the interlingual translator has much in common with the task of the post-colonial writer; where one has a text, however, the other has the metatext of culture itself.

A more significant difference in the two literary activities has to do with the parameters of constraint. A translator is faced with a fixed text (one usually freely chosen, to be sure, but fixed nonetheless); such a fixed text includes cultural and linguistic elements that are givens for the translator and that typically involve factors that are particularly problematic for the receiving audience. Thus the translator is faced with the dilemma of faithfulness: to be 'faithful', such problematic factors must be transposed despite the difficulties they might cause to the sensibilities or cognitive framework of translator or audience; in obscuring or muting the cultural disjunctions, the translator ceases to be 'faithful' to the source text. This constraint of a text with cultural givens in a fixed ordering is a major factor behind the discourse regarding literalism that has been part of discussions of translation for some centuries.[5] A post-colonial writer, by contrast, chooses which cultural elements to attempt to transpose to the receiving audience.

An author can choose a fairly aggressive presentation of unfamiliar cultural elements in which differences, even ones likely to cause problems for a receiving audience, are highlighted, or an author can choose an assimilative presentation in which likeness or 'universality' is stressed and cultural differences are muted and made peripheral to the central interests of the literary work. Similarly, linguistic features related to the source culture (such as dialect or unfamiliar lexical items) can be highlighted as defamiliarized elements in the text, or be domesticated in some way, or be circumvented altogether. The greater element of choice in the construction of an original literary text means that in the hands of a skilled writer it is easier to keep the text balanced, to manage the information load, and to avoid mystifying or repelling elements of the receiving audience with a different cultural framework. Because a translator begins with a text intended for an audience in the source culture, however, it is not uncommon that elements that are difficult for the receiving audience will cluster; a translated text more than an original piece of literature thus risks losing balance at critical moments, making the information load too great for comfortable assimilation by the receiving audience. These differences are somewhat mitigated in practice by the choice actually exercised by translators in deciding which elements of a text to preserve in translation (Tymoczko 1995); at the same time writers are not necessarily so free as might be imagined, constrained as they are by history, myth, ideology, patronage and affiliation, which set bounds on the presentation of the source culture in the literary work. Thus, the two types of writing converge on the shared limit defined by cultural interface.[6]

It is tempting to identify the greater range of paratextual commentary permitted to the translator as another difference between literary translation and post-colonial writing. In the form of introductions, footnotes, critical essays, glossaries, maps, and the like, the translator can embed the translated text in a shell that explains necessary cultural and literary background for the receiving audience and that acts as a running commentary on the translated work. Thus, the translator can manipulate more than one textual level simultaneously, in order to encode and explain the source text. This, too, is a distinction that may be more seeming than real between these two types of intercultural writing. Particularly in contemporary literary works aimed at intercultural audiences, it is not uncommon to find maps, glossaries, appendices with historical information, or introductions describing the cultural context of the work, while experimental formal techniques and multilayered textual strategies may even permit the use of embedded texts, footnotes and other devices constituting more than one textual level. Authors also frequently provide introductions and postscripts, write critical essays commenting on their own texts, or facilitate 'authorized' commentaries on their work.[7] Indeed, we better understand why post-colonial authors embrace such textual types and such literary strategies by considering the functions of similar elements for translators.

Thus, although there are differences between literary translation and post-colonial writing, such differences are more significant *prima facie* than they are upon close consideration. The two types of textual production converge in many respects; as the metaphor of translation suggests, the transmission of elements from one culture to another across a cultural and/or linguistic gap is a central concern of both these types of intercultural writing and similar constraints on the process of relocation affect both types of texts. To these constraints let us now turn. It is abundantly clear from the theory and practice of translation that no text can ever be fully translated in all its aspects: perfect homology is impossible between translation and source.[8] Choices must be made by the translator; there are additions and omissions in the process, no matter how skilled the translator. Some of the differences between text and translation have to do with incompatibilities between the substance of any two linguistic systems, and it is for this reason that J.C. Catford defines translation as 'a process of substituting a text in one language for a text in another', involving the replacement of source-language meanings with alternate receptor-language meanings (Catford 1965: 1, 20, 35–42). Many of the differences between source text and translation are inescapable, resulting from the shift from the obligatory features of one language to the obligatory features of another. Other shifts have a cultural basis; the translator must decide how to handle features of the source culture (e.g. objects, customs, historical and literary allusions) that are unfamiliar to the receiving audience, adapting and modifying the source text in the process, if only through the process of explanation.[9] Still other differences have to do with information load: in trying to adapt the multiple layers of information in a text to a new reception environment, a translator will almost inevitably produce a longer text. Even that eventuality does not result in a full capture and transposition of all the coded information.[10]

A translator's refractions of a source text have analogues in the choices a minority-culture writer makes in representing the home culture, for no culture can be represented completely in any literary text, just as no source text can be fully represented in a translation. Selectivity is essential to the construction of any piece of literature, particularly when the intended audience includes readers who are unfamiliar with the cultural subject.[11] Not everything in a post-colonial cultural metatext can be transposed in a literary format; just as literary translations are typically simpler than their source texts, so post-colonial authors of necessity simplify the cultural fields they write about. Like translators, they will be criticized accordingly. The greater the distance between an author's source culture and the receiving culture of the author's work, the greater will be the impetus to simplify. A minority-culture or post-colonial writer will have to pick aspects of the home culture to convey and to emphasize, particularly if the intended audience includes as a significant component international or dominant-culture readers; similarly, a literary translator chooses an emphasis or privileges an aspect of the text to be transposed in translation (e.g. linguistic fidelity, tone, form, cultural content, or some combination thereof). Another name for the choices, emphases and selectivity of both translators and post-colonial writers is *interpretation*. Judgement is inescapable in the process; 'objectivity' is impossible. And just as there can be no final translation, there can be no final interpretation of a culture through a literary mode. There is no last word.[12]

Such a process of selectivity and interpretation is ideological and will inevitably invite controversy. The political censure that post-colonial writers are subject to from their fellow citizens can be given an intellectual context in the proverbial denigration of translation as a process; the Italian aphorism about translation, 'traduttore, traditore', says it succinctly. The ideological valences of post-colonial literature are spectacularly obvious in cases where feelings run so high about the portrait of the source culture that the very life of an author is in jeopardy, but the case of Salman Rushdie is only a limiting example of the way in which post-colonial literature can become the battleground of ideological disputes. Many post-colonial writers choose to live abroad, writing about their culture of origin from the vantage point of another nation, in part because of the ideological pressure and censure – both implicit and explicit political constraint – that they are subject to within their native framework. Joyce is an example of such a writer, and he was outspoken about the impossibility of writing freely about his culture from within Ireland, making explicit the necessity he saw of exile if he was to be an artist.[13] Translation is generally a less heated affair at present, but the process of translating texts from minority cultures can in fact become fraught for ideological reasons (Simms 1983), while in the past translation has produced its own martyrs to ideology.[14]

Various well-known problems of translation can be related to marked features of post-colonial writing. There are, for example, often perturbations in the lexis of a translation. In source texts to be translated translators are presented with aspects of the source culture that are unfamiliar to the receiving audience – elements of the material culture (such as foods, tools, garments), social structures (including customs and law), features of the natural world (weather conditions, plants, animals), and the like; such features of the source culture are often encoded in specific lexical items for which there are no equivalents in the receptor culture or for which there are only extremely rare or technical words. In the face of such a crux, a translator has a variety of choices: to omit the reference or pick some 'equivalent' in the receptor culture on the one hand, and on the other to import the word untranslated (with an explanation in a footnote perhaps), add an explanatory classifier or an explicit explanation, use a rare or recondite word of the receiving language, extend the semantic field of a word in the receptor language, and so on.[15] The use of rare or untranslated words in translations and the inclusion of unfamiliar cultural material are not necessarily defects of translated texts: translation is one of the activities of a culture in which cultural expansion occurs and in which linguistic options are expanded through the importation of loan transfers, calques, and the like. The result is, however, that translations very often have a different lexical texture from unmarked prose in the receptor culture.

Similar features are to be found in the lexis of post-colonial texts as writers struggle to translate the cultural metatext, and similar lexical solutions can be discerned as well. In *A Grain of Wheat*, Ngũgĩ wa Thiong'o imports without explanation words for plants (e.g. *Mwariki*, p. 125), tools (e.g., *panga* and *jembe*, pp. 6, 8), garments (e.g. *Mithuru, Miengu*, p. 180), and dances (p. 205), among others, where the category of the words is made clear by context or collocation. In *A Man of the People* Chinua Achebe also imports African words into English (e.g. *lappa*, a garment), but more typically uses established English equivalents for African cultural concepts that are part of his English dialect (e.g. *head tie, pit latrine, highlife*). Another tactic is exemplified by Buchi Emecheta, who introduces African words, for which she then provides explicit explanations: 'he ... paid ten shillings towards his *esusu*, a kind of savings among friends whereby each member of the group collected contributions in turn' (*Joys of Motherhood*, p. 147). The same technique is found in Bapsi Sidhwa's introductions of '*bijli*: a word that in the various Indian languages, with slight variations stands for both electricity and lightning', '*Choorails*, witches with turned-about feet who ate the hearts and livers of straying children', or 'a plump, smiling bowlegged Sikh priest, a *granthi*' (*Cracking India*, pp. 30, 31, 63). In *Midnight's Children* Rushdie takes an assimilative approach to lexis in a key metaphor, using *pickle* where he might have chosen *chutney* as representing the source culture concept more precisely.[16]

Other lexical anomalies can also be identified in both literary translations and post-colonial writings. Features of the source language or the source culture in both types of intercultural transposition are associated with variant semantic fields for words, with non-standard frequency distributions of particular lexemes, and with non-standard patterns of collocation. These aspects of translation have been discussed extensively in the literature about translation (cf. Nida 1964: 137–40), and similar features are found in post-colonial writing. Thus, for example, Ngãugãi uses the term *ridge* in a non-standard sense to refer to villages and their territory; his use of the English *taste* is also non-standard: 'Did he himself taste other women, like Dr Lynd?' (*Grain of Wheat*, p. 157); 'Come, man. You must have tasted her. How do her goods taste?' (*Grain of Wheat*, p. 160).

In both cases the sense is clear, though the English is non-standard; the usage seems to represent the semantic fields of words in Ngãugãi's language which have been represented by literal English equivalents. By contrast, in the following sentences, spoken by a woman in Achebe's *A Man of the People*, it is the unusual collocation that strikes the reader: '. . . she is our wife . . .' (p. 36); 'We are getting a second wife to help me' (p. 36); '. . . our new wife . . .' (p. 88). In standard English the word *wife* does not collocate with the first-person plural unless the speaker is royalty and, moreover, only lesbian women refer to their wives, but neither of these conditions obtains in Achebe's text. In both respects, then, Achebe's usage is non-standard: the Nigerian custom of multiple wives forces the linguistic variation in his text, much as it might in a translation.

For various reasons such as these, therefore, the metatext of an unfamiliar culture in a post-colonial text is a factor in the wide range of lexical items in some post-colonial works, many unfamiliar to the ordinary reader in the dominant culture. The size of James Joyce's vocabulary in *Ulysses* stands as an early example of the phenomenon in English; it results in part from Joyce's transposition of lexemes referring to Irish culture, his use of words that derive from Irish, and his representation of Irish dialects of English speech which include archaic words, imports, loan translations and words with lexical meanings, semantic fields or semiotic values that differ significantly from those of standard English (Wall 1986; Tymoczko 1994: 229–30). Salman Rushdie is a contemporary writing in English who has an unusually varied lexis, particularly in *Midnight's Children*; as in the case of Joyce, Rushdie's rich word-hoard is not simply attributable to his wit and literary sensibility, but to the cultural substratum of his work as well.

Often unfamiliar cultural information does not simply reside in lexical items, but is a more diffuse presence in a source text. A translator may be faced, for example, with a myth, custom or economic condition presupposed by a text, but not located explicitly in it. If such implicit information is to be made accessible to the receiving audience, it must be presented either through explicit inclusion in the translation or through paratextual devices.[17] In post-colonial texts parallels are apparent, and many tactics used by contemporary minority-culture writers to deal with such problems are familiar to literary translators. Customs, beliefs and myths are frequently explained explicitly in post-colonial literature, much as they must be in translations, and the following is illustrative:

> The feast of the New Yam was approaching and Umuofia was in a festival mood. It was an occasion for giving thanks to Ani, the earth goddess and the source of all fertility. Ani played a greater part in the life of the people than any other diety. She was the ultimate judge of morality and conduct. And what was more, she was in close communion with the departed fathers of the clan whose bodies had been committed to earth.
>
> The Feast of the New Yam was held every year before the harvest began, to honor the earth goddess and the ancestral spirits of the clan. New yams could not be eaten until some had first been offered to these powers. Men and women, young and old, looked forward to the New Yam Festival because it began the season of plenty – the new year. On the last night before the festival, yams of the old year were all disposed of by those who still had them. The new year must begin with tasty, fresh yams and not the shriveled and fibrous crop of the previous year. All cooking pots, calabashes and wooden bowls were thoroughly washed, especially the wooden mortar in which yam was pounded. Yam foo-foo and vegetable soup was the chief food in the celebration. So much of it was cooked that, no matter how heavily the family ate or how many friends and relatives they invited from neighboring villages, there was always a large quantity of food left over at the end of the day. The story was always told of a wealthy man who set before his guests a mound of foo-foo so high that those who sat on one side could not see what was happening on the other, and it was not until late in

the evening that one of them saw for the first time his in-law
who had arrived during the course of the meal and had fallen
to on the opposite side. It was only then that they exchanged
greetings and shook hands over what was left of the food.

(Achebe 1991: 37–8)

Similarly in a minority-culture text, mythic allusions may require
an explicit presentation of the myth at some point in the text, as in
translations (where such allusions are typically explained in the footnotes or prefatory material). Thus, when Toni Morrison wishes to
use the myth of the African slave who flies away home to Africa,
she cannot suppose that most of her white American or international audience will know the tale, so she must provide a version
explicitly in the text (Morrison 1978: 326–7; cf. Lester 1970:
147–52). The same is true about information related to historical
events and historical figures which is frequently made explicit in
post-colonial literature, as in literary translations. It is probably for
this reason that in chapter 2 of *A Grain of Wheat* Ngũgĩ gives a
version of the colonial history of Kenya, and he makes the historical background explicit at other points as well where necessary for
an uninformed international audience. Although Rushdie has left
the myth of Shiva largely implicit in *Midnight's Children*, thus risking
its being missed by non-Indian readers, he is explicit about corresponding historical information having to do with the formation of
the states of India and Pakistan.[18]

When a literary work is intended for an audience that shares the
culture of the text, such customs, myths and historical information
can and generally do remain implicit, whether that audience is from
a dominant or marginalized culture, because the audience can be
counted upon to recognize the allusions and to have the requisite
cultural background. It is telling that translators moving from
a dominant-culture source text to a minority-culture audience often
leave dominant cultural materials implicit, presupposing knowledge
of the mythic allusions, historical events or customs of the dominant
culture: such a stance is part of the assertion of hegemony. A text
produced in this way participates in the assertion of cultural dominance, defining what constitutes the domain of knowledge necessary
for public discourse. Thus, in both literary translations and original
literary works, the necessity to make cultural materials explicit and
to foreground potentially unfamiliar cultural materials affects primarily the movement of a cultural substratum from a marginalized

culture to a dominant culture and it is associated with a negative cline of power and cultural prestige. In post-colonial writing the amount of cultural material that is explained explicitly serves as a kind of index of the intended audience and of the cultural gradient between the writer/subject and the audience, with greater amounts of explicit material indicating that a text is aimed at the former colonizers and/or a dominant international audience. In such cases cultural background is, so to speak, explicitly 'frontloaded' for the reader.[19]

Prevailing Western standards of literature, however, exclude instructional or didactic literature; although such a posture is by no means universal in literature, with many oral traditions combining instruction and entertainment easily, it has been an aesthetic standard in the West since the Romantics. Thus 'frontloading' cultural information or foregrounding material that is normally presupposed in an intracultural text – resulting in the more highly explicit quality of both post-colonial literature and translations – potentially compromises the literary status of a text *per se*. The text begins to read more like an instructional or didactic work, rather than a piece of imaginative literature. When such a text is also full of specialized or unfamiliar words, unusual grammar and other linguistic anomalies, the explicitly informative elements of the text combine with the dense information load from the language itself to work against other features of the text that are perceived as literary. These are risks shared by both translators and writers of post-colonial and minority-culture literature. Yet both translators and post-colonial writers are caught in the dilemma of producing texts with large amounts of material that is opaque or unintelligible to international readers on the one hand or having large quantities of explanation and explicit information on the other hand. Either choice threatens to compromise the reception of the text as literature. A third alternative – suppressing the distinctive qualities of the writer's culture and language – compromises the writer's own affiliation with his or her culture and probably the very reasons for writing, just as a translation which is highly assimilated or adapted to the standards of the receiving culture raises questions of 'fidelity'.

In translation studies a distinction is often made between 'bringing the text to the audience' and 'bringing the audience to the text'. The same type of distinction can be projected with respect to post-colonial writing: some texts make more severe demands on the audience, requiring the audience to conform to the beliefs, customs, language and literary formalism of the source culture, while other works conform more to the dominant audience's cultural, linguistic and literary expectations, as we have seen. In translations the greater the prestige of the source culture and the source text, the easier it is to require that the audience come to the text. In post-colonial writing there is an analogue in the prestige of the author: the greater the international reputation of an author, the greater the demands that can be placed upon an international audience. One avenue of research that suggests itself, accordingly, is to test post-colonial writing to see if there is a correlation between the success of the writer and growing demands on the audience to conform to the ways, beliefs and language of the culture being portrayed.[20]

The problem of information load in both translations and post-colonial writing is not restricted to unfamiliar cultural material such as customs, history or myth, and material culture. Even proper names if they present unfamiliar phonemes or foreign phonemic sequences can cause problems for the receptor audience of both post-colonial literature and literary translations, while finding ways to transpose the semantic meanings of names may be of concern to both the writer and translator.[21] Similarly, transposing the literary genres, forms, proverbs and metaphors of the source culture will be equally problematic to translators and post-colonial writers alike. Each will struggle with the question of naturalizing material to the standards of the receiving audience; each will consider whether to adopt representations that tend towards formal or dynamic standards.[22] Such dilemmas influence the representation of the largest elements of text (e.g. genres, character types, plot materials) down to the smallest (phonemes, lexis, idiom, metaphor).

Indeed, in Gideon Toury's terms, both types of intercultural writing involve norms: preliminary norms involving general principles of allegiance to the standards of the source culture or the receptor culture, as well as operational norms guiding the myriad small choices that are made in textual and cultural transposition (Toury 1995: 53–69; cf. Holmes 1994: 81–92). The discernment of such norms is essential to any analysis of a translation, but it is essentially impossible to determine from the vantage point of the receptor culture alone; typically judgements about translations are made by people who know both the source language and the receptor language, and can evaluate the adaptations and adjustments in the transposition on the basis of both languages and cultures. This situation should strike a cautionary note about criticism of post-colonial works: detecting the norms governing cultural transposition in a piece of post-colonial writing is an equally important point of departure for an evaluation of the aims and achievements of the work, but at the same time it is difficult to do without a standpoint in both cultures that permits comparison.[23]

Recent work on translation theory and practice indicates the importance of patronage as a determinant of translation practice, and this is another area that bears on post-colonial writing. Patrons – once wealthy aristocrats – now take the form of presses and publishing houses, universities and granting agencies, which are in turn dependent on such groups as a readership, a critical establishment or government officials. Patrons determine the parameters of what is translated just as they determine parameters of what is published; that the effects of patronage are currently achieved largely through self-censorship does not invalidate the point. Studies of translation are increasingly alert to the circumstances under which books are chosen for translation and translations are published,[24] and similar questions are relevant to post-colonial writing. Literary merit, though not insignificant, is rarely the only or even the chief issue to consider in answering such questions. Here it is germane that many – perhaps most – post-colonial writers who have achieved an international reputation also reside in foreign metropolitan centres; the risk of such a choice is, of course, that the demands of international patronage will compromise the form, content and perspective of the post-colonial works themselves.[25]

The demands of patronage are intertwined with questions of audience, which is an important element in translation norms and strategies. Not only will factors such as the belief system or the values of an audience affect the translation strategy, but the nature of the audience itself will determine translation norms.[26] Issues about intended audience are often deceptive; for example, paradoxically translations are at times produced for the source culture itself when, say, a colonial language has become the lingua franca of a multicultural emergent nation or of a culture that has experienced a linguistic transition of some sort. The most efficient way of addressing such a nation after a colonial period may be through translation into the colonizers' language. A translation of this type, however, is produced within an ideological climate that is quite different from a translation oriented primarily at an international audience, and the translation strategies are, accordingly, divergent (cf. Simms 1983). In recent years translation studies have turned increasingly to such issues of audience, opening up profitable lines of investigation, and they are no less relevant to post-colonial texts. Reception theory has indicated the central importance of the audience or implied reader in the production of literary texts, of course. But even more basic economic and ideological questions about audience must be asked that have close parallels to the questions asked about the audiences of translations. Who is a writer writing for? Is the audience primarily an audience within the post-colonial culture? Is the work addressed primarily to the former colonizers or is the audience an international culture, neither primarily the former colony nor the former colonizer? Writing strategies will differ considerably depending on the audience, and critics must be alert to such factors.

In the case of post-colonial writers, the question of an international audience – neither primarily former colony nor colonizer – is in turn related to a marked trend at present towards the internationalization of literature. It becomes increasingly hard to define national traditions of the modern novel, for example, for more and more the novel has become an international genre with writers influenced by and influencing other writers from different linguistic traditions. Thus, Faulkner has influenced García Márquez, who in turn influences writers in English. Borges speaks of himself as an English writer who happens to write in Spanish. At the same time American cultural and economic hegemony means that to succeed as writers, many authors feel an imperative either to write in English or to be translated into English: being marketed in the United States is often seen as an essential index of international success which in turn augments an author's reception at home. Thus the international audience of a post-colonial writer might be, in fact, first and foremost an American audience, with the drama of colony and colonizer – or of author and cultural establishment – being played out for arbitration on an American stage. Where Tagore – through auto translation – turned for acceptance to the literary world of the colonizing power (Sengupta), contemporary post-colonial writers have a different set of priorities. The ways in which such considerations impact on text production have been partially explored with reference to translation; the intersection of literary systems, their symbiotic and dependent relations, have been productive avenues of enquiry that can offer models for the study of post-colonial and minority-culture writing.[27]

The case of Ngãugãi is instructive with respect to these issues of internationalization, patronage, audience, and the extent to which

an audience is 'brought to the text'; Ngãugãi also illustrates the fine
line between post-colonial writing in a metropolitan language and
literary translation. In 1977, after writing several successful novels
in English, Ngãugãi turned to writing in his native language, Gĩkũyũ;
since then his literary works have been accessible to international
audiences only through literary translation. Ngãugãi's linguistic shift
was prompted in part by a crisis having to do with audience:

> I came to realise only too painfully that the novel in which I
> had so carefully painted the struggle of the Kenya peasantry
> against colonial oppression would never be read by them. In
> an interview shortly afterwards in the *Union News* . . . in 1967,
> I said that I did not think that I would continue writing in
> English: that I knew *about* whom I was writing, but *for* whom
> was I writing?
>
> (Ngãugãi 1993: 9–10)

Influenced also perhaps by his growing international reputation (cf.
ibid.: 5), in *A Grain of Wheat* Ngãugãi already exhibits a growing
confidence in the demands he can place upon his international
readers: he uses 'resistant' strategies of writing, embedding without
explanation Gĩkũyũ words and phrases in his text. Through these
means he implicitly shifts to the standards of his own culture, even
while writing in English. In *Moving the Centre* Ngãugãi writes that his
shift of language was related to his desire to make connections with
the forms and modes of oral literature in his culture (Ngãugãi 1993:
21), but issues having to do with the ideology of language are central
for Ngãugãi, including his belief that languages should meet as
equals (ibid.: 35, 39). The politics of post-colonial writing, thus,
brings Ngãugãi to the importance of translation; he writes, 'Through
translations, the different languages of the world can speak to one
another. . . . Interlanguage communication through translation is
crucial' (ibid.: 40).[28]

Translation is frequently a source of formal experimentation in
receptor cultures, as translators import or adapt the genres and
formal strategies of the source text into the receptor system. Because
translation is at times one locus in a literary system where formal
experimentation is more easily tolerated, translation can even
become an 'alibi' for challenges to the dominant poetics. Translation
was used by modernists in this way, and Pound is one of the foremost examples. When translation acquires prestige, in part because

it is associated with literary innovation, one even finds the phenomenon of pseudo-translation, in which an innovative, original literary work masquerades as translation.[29]

There are analogues in post-colonial and minority-culture writing. In twentieth-century literature formal experimentation is widespread, but, even so, formal innovation is a notable characteristic of these forms of intercultural writing. Indeed, post-colonial and minority literatures are literary domains in which challenges to dominant standards of language, poetics and culture are frequently advanced, where literature is expanded through new mythic paradigms and archetypal representations, new formal resources and paradigms, and revitalized language, including new mythopoeic imagery. As with translations, innovative formalism often reflects the literary system of the post-colonial or minority culture itself, and the writer may introduce various forms of indigenous formalism to the dominant culture. Joyce does this in *Ulysses*, importing the standards of Irish epic, elements of Irish poetic form, characteristics of Irish prose, and structures of Irish narrative genres into his English-language masterwork.[30] The dramatic forms of Wole Soyinka stand as another example of innovative formalism that is indebted to the indigenous literature of a post-colonial culture, while even the most superficial reading of Amos Tutuola's *The Palm-Wine Drinkard* must come to terms with its Yoruba poetic sensibility (cf. Thelwell 1994: 188 ff.).

But formal experimentation may also have to do with other aspects of the interface of two cultural systems. As an author strives to represent the experiences or beliefs of a minority culture that differ from those of the dominant culture, it may be necessary to develop new forms which are not part of the dominant receptor system in order to signal or encode such alternate experiences or beliefs. Thus, Zora Neale Hurston in *Their Eyes Were Watching God* uses a divided narrative voice, shifting between a literate voice in standard English and a highly idiomatic black voice. The unreconciled tension between the two forms of narration are 'a verbal analogue of her double experiences as a woman in a male-dominated world and as a black person in a non-black world, a woman writer's revision of W.E.B. Du Bois's metaphor of "double-consciousness" for the hyphenated African-American'; her voice captures, as well, the fragmentation of modernity (Gates 1990: 193–4). At the same time, Hurston's narrative voice is also collective rather than individualistic, thus representing the 'collective spirit of African-American oral tradition' (Washington 1990: xii).

The appropriation of a dominant language for the aims of a former colony or an oppressed group and the shift of dominant poetics towards the standards of a minority or post-colonial people are potent means of realigning power structures in a shared cultural field and of asserting an independent world-view. In the Spanish-speaking culture area, the authors of the former Spanish colonies of Latin America have pioneered important formal strategies, including those of Magic Realism, and they have expanded the linguistic resources of literary Spanish in this century so as to express specifically the hybridity and specificity of Latin-American historical and cultural experience. In the English-language world this process has been in the making for 200 years as former colonies, including the United States and Ireland, have developed literatures in their own versions of English. In this linguistic sense, post-colonial literature like translation is subversive, and Heaney, speaking of Joyce's use of Dublin's demotic English, claims that Joyce turned English from 'an imperial humiliation' to 'a native weapon' (Heaney 1978: 40).

One of the most challenging features of writing about post-colonial and minority-culture literature is constructing a standard of judgement, for it is difficult to sort out the creativity of the writer from the deautomatization associated with the importation of new cultural materials, new poetics and new linguistic patterns derived from the cultural substratum of the author's culture itself. It is easy to overread such features as metaphor, linguistic transpositions of obligatory features of a native language, or shifts in frequency distribution associated with a variant dialect; a critic may take the cultural givens of a post-colonial writer as authorial creativity. While it is clear that the author exercises mastery in selection, the extent to which the author creates may be less clear. How is the critic to evaluate such neologisms as Ngãugãi's 'birth-motions' or 'love-mates' (Ngãugãi 1986: 203), or Achebe's 'cowrie-shell eye'[31] (Achebe 1989: 14)? Is Tutuola's *drinkard* an 'error', a lexeme from his dialect of English, or a brilliant, innovative portmanteau word? An author may even have a vested interest in concealing the debt of a text to the native culture, fearing that his or her own authorial status may be compromised.[32] Paradoxically, even when the innovative elements of a specific text may not be personally invented by the author, post-colonial authors nonetheless remake the languages and literatures of their former colonizers through the importation and adaptation of native mythos, mythopoeic imagery, an alternate lexis, vibrant textures of idiomatic speech and new formalisms, as we have seen. It is ironic that the rich presence of these elements confers prestige in contemporary post-colonial literature while the same elements have been so often rejected in translations.

Most literary phenomena are defined by more than their content. Though certain types of the novel – such as the picaresque or the Bildungsroman or anti-Utopian literature – are defined primarily with reference to their subject matter, this is rarely done with larger literary categories: American literature is not defined as being about America, nor is every work of literature written by an American relevant to American literature *per se*. Similarly, post-colonial literature as a literary phenomenon is more than just literature about a former colony or by a citizen of a former colony. Criticism about post-colonial literature and minority-culture literature will benefit from a clearer sense of the parameters that are characteristic of post-colonial and minority-culture literatures; several such parameters have emerged through the comparison of these bodies of literature with literary translations, an analogous form of intercultural writing. Comparisons of the type suggested here help to define the boundaries of these cohesive groups of literary works, indicating commonalities of linguistic texture and form, as well as challenges of the artistic task. Just as descriptive approaches to translation avoid the pitfalls of certain vicious circles having to do with normative standards, so a stronger sense of the ways in which post-colonial literature is a self-standing type of writing will help move the criticism beyond repetitive ideological debate or a sophisticated form of assimilative cannibalism in which post-colonial works are appropriated or swallowed whole into hegemonic canons of world literature.

Notes

1 See Ngãugãi 1993; Ashcroft, Griffiths and Tiffin 1989. Strictly speaking the purview of this investigation is broader than post-colonial writing *per se* and includes minority-culture writing that involves the negotiation of significant cultural and / or linguistic boundaries, as, for example, is the case with African-Americans and Irish writers. Thus, examples from such writers as Zora Neale Hurston and Toni Morrison, as well as James Joyce, are relevant to some of the points raised here.

2 Jakobson (1959: 234–5) gives other examples of this type of metaphorical speech about new phenomena; see also Lakoff and Johnson 1980.

3 Cf. Bhabha 1990: 292–3, 314–20, and sources cited for instances of the use of translation as a metaphor for post-colonial writing.

4 See also Pym 1992; Lefevere 1992b: 51–8; Even-Zohar 1990: 74 ff.; Snell-Hornby 1990: 81–2, and sources cited.

5 Nida discusses literalism in 1964: ch. 2; cf. 184 ff., 213 ff. See also Bassnett 1991: ch. 2.

6 The question of information load as a controlling factor in the construction of intercultural writing – particularly in the shaping of the fictive world – should be closely attended to in the analysis of any specific literary work. Post-colonial texts, like literary translations, can also be examined for places at which they risk becoming opaque to an international audience, such spots revealing pressure points of cultural constraint on the writer.

7 Joyce is an early example of the latter strategy; he facilitated the 'authoritative' studies of both Stuart Gilbert and Frank Budgen, both of which introduced important cultural and textual contexts to readers.

8 See, for example, the discussions in Bassnett 1991: ch. 1 and Jakobson 1959.

9 On the differences that result from shifts between obligatory features of different languages, see the examples in Catford 1965: chs 3, 5, 12; on shifts having to do with cultural differences, see the examples in Nida 1964: 215–18, 228–9, 235–7. See also Bassnett 1991: ch. 1.

10 Discussions are found in Nida 1964: chs 4–6. Note especially the ways in which referential meanings are language-bound insofar as semantic fields are inherently related to contrasting words, linguistic hierarchies, and so forth *within* any single language.

11 The creation of all literary worlds involves selection, not merely representation. Both the inclusions and omissions of post-colonial authors are significant; indeed the silences are as revealing as the subjects spoken of in these literary texts.

12 Bhabha 1990 attempts to displace the discourse of historicism which has dominated critical approaches to post-colonial authors in favour of seeing them as interpreters of the nation as metaphor, open-ended as the image of the past is projected into the performative world of the present and future. See esp. pp. 292–3, 303–7 and sources cited. Cairns and Richards offer a case study of the ways in which over time authors create shifting symbolic images of their people and their nation within the changing political and ideological contexts of colonization and decolonization. Literary translations can similarly be viewed as metonymic refractions of original literary works and, ultimately, ideological representations of the underlying source cultures of those literary works; see Tymoczko 1995.

13 The question of exile and post-colonial writing is taken up and reappraised by Brennan 1990, esp. pp. 60–6; note Brennan's assessment of the relationship between exile and patronage.

14 See, for example, the history of Bible translators discussed by Bassnett 1991: 45–50; Nida 1964: 14 ff.

15 Nida 1964: ch. 10 offers examples.

16 There are, of course, symbolic reasons for his choice of *pickle*.

17 Examples of such problems can be found in Lefevere 1992a: 22–9. Other complex types of diffuse cultural material that both translators and writers struggle to communicate include elements of the habitus (see Bourdieu 1977), as well as pervasive cultural metaphors (see Lakoff

and Johnson 1980); these issues are, however, beyond the scope of this essay.

18 In this discrepancy we see Rushdie's priorities for communication with his readers; at the same time the ironizing of history and the unreliable historical narration in the text are probably obscured for most international readers whose ignorance hampers recognition of Rushdie's rhetorical strategies.

19 A writer like Joyce who does not provide explanation (of customs, beliefs, social structure, politics, history, geography, language, and so forth) for his international readers assumes a political stance resistant to hegemony (cf. Sommer 1992), but also risks alienating the international readership.

20 An example suggesting this trajectory is Achebe's careful explanation of the kolanut ceremony in *Things Fall Apart* (Achebe 1991: 9–11) which contrasts markedly with his later treatment of the same ceremony in *A Man of the People* (Achebe 1989: 91) in which no explanation is provided. One can also project an alternative trajectory in which growing international success leads an author to a somewhat cynical accommodation to the standards of the dominant-culture audience.

21 For examples, see Ngãugãi 1986: 14; Emecheta 1979: 11. Nida discusses issues in translating names (1964: 193–5, 233–4).

22 Types of translation strategies are discussed in Bassnett 1991: 23–9 and Nida 1964: ch. 8.

23 Consider, for example, the problems of interpreting Rushdie's versions of history discussed above; see also the discussion in Tymoczko 1994 of the skewed readings of Joyce produced by critics with inadequate knowledge of his Irish cultural context.

24 For a discussion of patronage and translation, see, for example, Lefevere 1985 and 1992b.

25 As, for example, Brennan claims (1990: 63 ff.).

26 Thus, for example, translators must take into account the literacy levels of their audience (Nida 1964: 129 ff., 143–4).

27 See, for examples, the essays in Even-Zohar 1990; Hermans (ed.) 1985; and Lefevere and Jackson (eds) 1982.

28 On resistant strategies of writing and translation see Sommer 1992; Venuti (ed.) 1992 and Venuti 1995.

29 These points are taken up in Even-Zohar 1990: 45–51; Kálmán 1986; Lefevere 1979; Toury 1985: 20 ff. and 1995: 40–52; Venuti 1995.

30 See Tymoczko 1994: chs 3, 5 and 6.

31 Referring to a cataract.

32 Joyce, for example, seems to have deliberately suppressed his debt to Irish formalism for both intrapsychic and practical reasons pertaining to patronage (Tymoczko 1994: chs 1, 9). Conversely in judging a translation, a reader may be deceived into overreading a text as 'universal' by a translator's assimilative strategies of rendering the text; Fitzgerald's infamous translation of Omar Khayyam's *Rubaiyat* comes to mind.

References

Achebe, C. (1989 [1966]) *A Man of the People* (New York: Doubleday).
—— (1991 [1959]) *Things Fall Apart* (New York: Fawcett Crest).
Ashcroft, B., Griffiths, G. and Tiffin, H. (1989) *The Empire Writes Back: Theory and Practice in Post-colonial Literature* (London and New York: Routledge).
Bassnett, S. (1991) *Translation Studies* rev. edn (London: Routledge).
Bhabha, H.K. (1990) 'DissemiNation: time, narrative, and the margins of the modern nation', in Bhabha (ed.) 1990, pp. 291–322.
—— (ed.) (1990) *Nation and Narration* (London and New York: Routledge).
Bourdieu, P. (1977) *Outline of a Theory of Practice* trans. R. Nice (Cambridge: Cambridge University Press).
Brennan, T. (1990) 'The national longing for form', in Bhabha (ed.) 1990, pp. 44–70.
Cairns, D. and Richards, S. (1988) *Writing Ireland: Colonialism, Nationalism and Culture* (Manchester: Manchester University Press).
Catford, J.C. (1965) *A Linguistic Theory of Translation: An Essay in Applied Linguistics* (London: Oxford University Press).
Emecheta, B. (1979) *The Joys of Motherhood* (New York: George Braziller).
Even-Zohar, I. (1990) *Polysystem Studies, Poetics Today* 11 (1), special issue.
Gates, H.L., Jr. (1990) 'Afterword: Zora Neale Hurston: "A Negro Way of Saying"', in Hurston (1990), pp. 185–95.
Heaney, S. (1978) 'The interesting case of John Alphonsus Mulrennan', *Planet: The Welsh Internationalist* 41 (Jan.): 34–40.
Hermans, T. (ed.) (1985) *The Manipulation of Literature: Studies in Literary Translation* (New York: St Martin's Press).
Holmes, J.S. (1994) *Translated! Papers on Literary Translation and Translation Studies* 2nd edn (Amsterdam: Rodopi).
Hurston, Z.N. (1990 [1937]) *Their Eyes Were Watching God* (New York: Harper & Row).
Ivir, V. (1987) 'Procedures and strategies for the translation of culture', *Indian Journal of Applied Linguistics* 13: 2.35–46.
Jakobson, R. (1959) 'On linguistic aspects of translation', in R. A. Brower (ed.), *On Translation* (Cambridge, Mass.: Harvard University Press), pp. 232–9.
Kálmán, G.C. (1986) 'Some borderline cases of translation', *New Comparison* 1: 117–22.
Lakoff, G. and Johnson, M. (1980) *Metaphors We Live By* (Chicago: University of Chicago Press).
Lefevere, A. (1979) 'Slauerhoff and "Po Tsju I": three paradigms for the study of influence', *Tamkang Review* 10: 67–77.
—— (1985) 'Why waste our time on rewrites? The trouble with interpretation and the role of rewriting in an alternative paradigm', in Hermans (ed.) 1985, pp. 215–43.
—— (1992a) *Translating Literature: Practice and Theory in a Comparative Literature Context* (New York: Modern Language Association).

—— (1992b) *Translation, Rewriting, and the Manipulation of Literary Fame* (London: Routledge).

—— and Jackson, K.D. (eds) (1982) *The Art and Science of Translation, Dispositio* 7, special issue.

Lester, J. (1970 [1969]) *Black Folktales* (New York: Grove Press).

Morrison, T. (1978 [1977]) *Song of Solomon* (New York: Signet).

Ngāugāi, wa T. (1986 [1967]) *A Grain of Wheat* rev. edn (Oxford: Heinemann).

—— (1993) *Moving the Centre: The Struggle for Cultural Freedoms* (London: James Currey).

Nida, E.A. (1964) *Toward a Science of Translating: With Special Reference to Principles and Procedures Involved in Bible Translating* (Leiden: E.J. Brill).

Pym, A. (1992) *Translation and Text Transfer: An Essay on the Principles of Intercultural Communication* (Frankfurt: Peter Lang).

Rushdie, S. (1991 [1980]) *Midnight's Children.* (New York: Penguin).

Sengupta, M. (1990) 'Translation, colonialism, and poetics: Rabindranath Tagore in two worlds', in S. Bassnett and A. Lefevere (eds), *Translation, History and Culture* (London and New York: Pinter), pp. 56–63.

Sidhwa, B. (1991 [1988]) *Cracking India* (Minneapolis: Milkweed).

Simms, N. (1983) 'Three types of "touchy" translation', in N. Simms (ed.), *Nimrod's Sin, Pacific Quarterly Moana* 8 (2) (special issue): 48–58.

Snell-Hornby, M. (1990) 'Linguistic transcoding or cultural transfer? A critique of translation theory in Germany', in S. Bassnett and A. Lefevere (eds), *Translation, History and Culture* (London and New York: Pinter), pp. 79–86.

Sommer, D. (1990) 'Resistant texts and incompetent readers', *Latin American Literary Review* 20: 40.104–8.

Thelwell, M. (1994) 'Introduction', in A. Tutuola [1984] *The Palm-wine Drinkard and My Life in the Bush of Ghosts* (New York: Grove Press), pp. 177–90.

Toury, G. (1985) 'A rationale for descriptive translation studies', in Hermans (ed.) 1985, pp. 16–41.

—— (1995) *Descriptive Translation Studies and Beyond* (Amsterdam: John Benjamins).

Tymoczko, M. (1994) *The Irish 'Ulysses'* (Berkeley and Los Angeles: University of California Press).

—— (1995) 'The metonymics of translating marginalized texts', *Comparative Literature* 47: 1.11–24.

Venuti, L. (ed.) (1992) *Rethinking Translation: Discourse, Subjectivity, Ideology* (London: Routledge).

—— (1995) *The Translator's Invisibility: A History of Translation* (London: Routledge).

Wall, R. (1986) *An Anglo-Irish Dialect Glossary for Joyce's Works* (Gerrards Cross: Colin Smythe).

Washington, M.H. (1990) 'Foreword', in Hurston 1990, pp. vii–xiv.

Chapter 2

Writing translation
The strange case of the Indian English novel

G.J.V. Prasad

In 1982, Salman Rushdie, having shown the way to a whole generation of Indian English writers, set down the challenges to the Indian
English writer and reiterated that 'all of us share the view that
we can't simply use the language the way the British did; and
that it needs remaking for our own purposes' (Rushdie 1991: 17).
He quickly answered the (unasked) question as to why Indians
should then choose to write in English (assuming that they are
creatively bilingual or that they could choose not to write), stating
that the Indians who do, write 'in spite of our ambiguity towards
it, or because of that, perhaps because we find in that linguistic
struggle a reflection of other struggles taking place in the real
world, struggles between the cultures within ourselves and the
influences at work upon our societies' (ibid.). Rushdie's interest is
particularly in the Indo-British writer who cannot reject English,
who must, in fact, embrace it. He added in a famous aside that
British Indians are 'translated men' and opposed the commonly
held view 'that something gets lost in translation', believing 'something can also be gained' (ibid.). This gain is mirrored in the
pollinated and enriched language (and culture) that results from
the act of translation – this act not just of bearing across but of
fertile coming together. Thus it is not only in the case of Indo-
British writers but in that of all Indian English writers that the texts
they create are 'translated', the very act of their writing being one
of translation.

Raja Rao recognized and articulated this fifty-four years before
Rushdie, in the foreword to his first novel, *Kanthapura* (1938). The
basic problem in writing in English, he says, is that '[O]ne has to

convey in a language not one's own the spirit that is one's own' (Rao 1971: 5). This is a difficulty any translator will admit to facing; one has to decide how 'to convey the various shades and omissions of a certain thought-movement that looks maltreated in an alien language' (ibid.). But, as Rao hastens to add, English is not an alien language to Indians. Most educated Indians are bilingual, with 'many of us writing in our own language and in English' (ibid.). Like Rushdie later, Rao states that '[W]e cannot write like the English. We should not. We cannot write only as Indians' (ibid.). Thus Rao posits a struggle for space, between colonial English and the native Indian languages. The act of writing in English is not 'merely' one of translation of an Indian text into the English language, but a quest for a space which is created by translation and assimilation and hence transformation of all three – the Indian text, context and the English language. Thus the English that each Indian writer uses is partly the message as well as the medium, and is important in itself. Rao advocates in his foreword both Indian narrative strategies and Indianization of the English language. He is also aware of the nature of power – he compares English to Sanskrit and Persian, the two languages that were used for communication across the sub-continent in earlier times, both having predominated over other Indian languages. Writing in either language, as in the case of English, would have been an act of translation into and a transformation of (as well as by) a more powerful language.

It must be noted that Raja Rao does not claim to be writing in Indian English. He is not writing in British English either. He is creating a language as well as creating in it. His attempt in *Kanthapura* is to create a 'rough' text, one that will underscore the otherness of the language used as well as the culture depicted. Many of his characters in this novel, including the narrator, would not speak any kind of English and yet the novelist has to bring out the rhythm of their expression, the tempo of their speech and the configurations of their world-view in his English novel. Thus, in Meenakshi Mukherjee's words, there is a 'double complication' involved in Indian English fiction, because it 'is written in a language that in most cases is not the first language of the writer nor is it the language of the daily life of the people about whom the novels are written' (Mukherjee 1971: 24). Though writing here about Indian English fiction in general she pinpoints the particular challenges that Raja Rao faces and overcomes in *Kanthapura*:

Technically the problem becomes most acute in the writing of
dialogue and presenting conversation . . . . But apart from
dialogue, even in description, narration and reflection, the Indo-
Anglian novelist is dealing with modes of thinking, manners of
observation, and instinctive responses of people whose awareness has been conditioned by a language other than English.

(ibid.: 174)

She says that the Indian English writer has to deal with non-English-
speaking people in non-English-speaking contexts and 'has to
overcome the difficulty of conveying through English the vast range
of expressions and observations whose natural vehicle is an Indian
Language' (ibid.: 173). The choices the writer has to make are those
of a translator: 'literal translation is not always the answer because
he has to make sure that the translated idioms or images do not go
against the grain of the English language' (ibid.: 173–4).

The writer has then to ensure that the English s/he writes conveys
the spirit of the Indian region s/he is depicting: 'the quality of that
particular area, the characteristics of its speech, its typical responses
and its distinctive spirit' (ibid.: 174). Thus each writer has to find
her/his own answers, style(s) and English. Braj Kachru, in his study
of Indian English, points out collocations which 'are *author-oriented*
and may be present only in the works of creative Indian English
writers who write about typically Indian contexts' (Kachru 1983: 76).
He cautions that these features may be text-specific rather than characteristic of 'the total literary output of a writer . . . the style of
Kanthapura cannot be generalized as the style of Raja Rao' (ibid.: 77).
In other words the writers do not write in an Indian English or even
in their own English but in an English intended to approximate the
thought-structures and speech patterns of their characters and not to
betray the Indian text and context by an easy assimilation into the
linguistic and cultural matrices of British English. Hence when
Kachru himself uses a passage from *Kanthapura* to illustrate the differences between 'educated' Indian English and '"educated" native
varieties of English', claiming 'that Indian English has a tendency
toward using complex noun and verb phrases and rather long sentences' (ibid.: 78), he cannot but be immediately aware that this is
Rao's strategy to convey the rhythms of spoken Kannada, a Kannada
spoken by the narrator who is an old woman. The passage he quotes
is thus no example of Indian English, 'educated' or otherwise.
Kachru admits that '[O]ne cannot generalize, since R.K. Narayan's

style is the opposite of Raja Rao's' (ibid.). The following passage
which he cites from *Kanthapura* is not illustrative of Raja Rao's style
as much as of his successful translation of the Kannada speech of his
narrator:

> The day rose into the air and with it rose the dust of the
> morning, and the carts began to creak round the bulging rocks
> and the coppery peaks, and the sun fell into the river and
> pierced it to the pebbles, while the carts rolled on and on, fair
> carts of the Kanthapura fair . . .
>
> (Rao 1971: 60)

It is this individual effort to translate local speech rhythms, idioms
and culture-specificities that Meenakshi Mukherjee refers to when
she says that 'Mulk Raj Anand at his best manages to convey a
Punjabi flavour through his English' and that R.K. Narayan 'depicts
the customs and manners of the Tamil people accurately . . . [and]
what is more important, through skilful use of the English language
he delineates people whose actions, behaviour and responses are
shaped by a language different from English' (Mukherjee 1971: 174).
What is even more important however is that, as she points out,
Narayan's characters are shaped by a language 'not only different
from English, but also markedly different from Punjabi which is the
language of Anand's most successful fictitious characters, or Bengali,
the normal mode of speech of characters created by Bhabhani
Bhattacharya' (ibid.). The Englishes that these writers create (in)
are not unintentional, and are not merely or wholly illustrative of
varieties of Indian English. As stated earlier, many of their characters would not speak English at all, and people who belong to the
particular regions concerned may speak English quite differently.
The aim of the authors is not to reproduce the specific characteristics of the English spoken in the regions they depict but to create
an English that fulfils their translational-creative aims. The text-
specificity of these authorial styles is immediately evident if we
compare the Kannada-ness of the language of Raja Rao's *Kanthapura*
with the language he uses in *The Serpent and the Rope*. S. Nagarajan
suggests that in the latter novel Raja Rao 'has tried to adapt his
style to the movement of a Sanskrit sentence' (cited in Mukherjee
1971: 183). In each individual novel the Indian English writer has
to write an English suitable for the task at hand, to convey the
particularities of the situation and region portrayed. Each writer is

aware of this task and makes a conscious attempt at it through various linguistic experiments as well as the use of imagery.

Mulk Raj Anand, who along with Raja Rao and R.K. Narayan forms the great trinity of Indian English fiction, records that he chose to write not in Urdu but in English with Mahatma Gandhi's permission. He is aware of the politics of his choice and that English is not the natural national medium for his social novel. He describes his process of creation thus:

> I found, while writing spontaneously, that I was always trans-lating dialogue from the original Punjabi into English. The way in which my mother said something in the dialect of central Punjabi could not have been expressed in any other way except in an almost literal translation, which might carry over the sound and the sense of the original speech. I also found, that I was dreaming or thinking or brooding over two-thirds of the prose narrative in Punjabi, or in Hindustani and only one-third in the English language. This happened usually while I was writing stories and novels.
>
> (Anand 1979: 36)

Anand says that he decided 'to consciously introduce translation of Punjabi, Urdu and Hindi words into all my writing' (ibid.). R.K. Narayan, who had the 'benefit' of Graham Greene's editorial inter-vention, still manages to write an Indian English capable of negotiating the terrain between Tamil, and possibly Kannada, and English. He has to make the choices that translators are forced to consider: what to translate from Tamil, which Tamil words to retain, whether to render in English certain styles of speech, etc. Narayan says of his generation of writers that 'often the writing seemed . . . an awkward translation of a vernacular rhetoric, mode or idiom. But occasionally it was brilliant' (Narayan 1979: 22). This process of transmutation of English, he says, has served his 'purpose admirably, of conveying unambiguously the thoughts and acts of a set of personalities, who flourish in a small town named Malgudi (supposed to be) located in a corner of South India' (ibid.)

Khushwant Singh, another writer who has experienced this need to create a new language, calls this Indian English by the quaint term 'Indish' (Singh 1986: 36). He writes that 'Anglo-Indian' writers like Thackeray had already 'introduced the English literati to Indian words and proverbs'. Indian English writers carried the process further and 'experimented with literal translations of Indian words into English' (ibid.: 37). He identifies Raja Rao and Mulk Raj Anand as the writers who took the lead in this and goes on to state that 'Salman Rushdie's use of Indian vocabulary is altogether more natural and sophisticated . . . [and he] uses the kind of Indish that the jet-set of Bombay do today' (ibid.: 37). Drawing our attention to the bilingual contexts of the writers as well as their own bilingualism, Singh even quotes a dialogue from his childhood based entirely on the English alphabet but with a distinct meaning in Punjabi: 'BBG T POG, PK I C' (Bibiji, tea peeoji / Peekay ai see) – where a lady is asked to have tea and replies that she has already had some (ibid.). Bilingualism gives rise to what Singh calls 'kichdi language' in the popular press. This permeation of one language by another is a natural by-product of the bilingual situation, but not everyone sees it as desirable or even inevitable. Ketaki Kushari Dyson, who writes in both Bengali and English, makes a distinction between a writer who is creatively bilingual and one who is creatively monolingual however many languages s/he may know. Her standpoint is clear in her chastisement of Rushdie:

> Salman Rushdie interlards his English with Urdu words and phrases as a naughty teenager interweaves his speech with swearwords, but he cannot write a book in Urdu . . . . He may be a cosmopolitan, but he is a monolingual writer. His use of Urdu adds colour to his texts, but does not lead us to an Indian intellectual world. Had he been an artist in Urdu, I doubt if he would have used the language to pepper his English in the facetious way he does now.
>
> (Dyson 1993: 178–9)

Dyson seems to hold the view that a true bilingual would have perfect control over two or more linguistic systems and manage to keep them separate from each other. Her objection to the use of Urdu words in an English text is similar to that of monolinguals and implies that languages can be kept pure and inviolate. A further implication is that there is no serious artistic intent in Rushdie's use of Urdu, 'only a desire to add local colour'. A bilingual may be defined as a person who has two linguistic systems which s/he uses for communication in appropriate situations. In a bilingual or multilingual situation 'transfer' or 'interference' is inevitable. This transfer will work both ways, each language influencing the other. One system may be more dominant than the other in the relationship of give and take but this may be as much a question of the relative competence of the speaker's as of the social prestige or power of the languages. On the other hand, a person may use English terms while speaking Tamil not because her/his English is stronger but because English is the language of prestige and power and may also signal a context (e.g. a formal situation or official business). As Elizabeth Tonkin says, 'language is always a part of human culture, and its use is alike a lived practice, coercive, and a means of choice' (Tonkin 1993: 188).

The choice of one language variety over another as much as of one language over another 'signals social meanings to listeners and readers'. Hence it is important to examine 'acts and choices: on shifts between different languages, between a standard and non-standard dialect or a mixture of all these, according to the social situation' (ibid.). Tonkin adds that 'many shades of social meaning' can be conveyed by people 'by their choice of sound, word or grammar, and it is common for them to code-switch, that is move from one variety to another, even in the course of a sentence' (ibid.: 188–9). Code-mixing and code-switching are both communicative strategies and can have various motivations. Code-switching, for example, may be used to reveal to the listener the regional identity of the speaker, thus enabling the speaker to establish kinship if the listener belongs to the same region. Code-switching can also be used to reveal class and religion. Conversely, code-switching can also be resorted to in order to conceal the speaker's region, class or religion. Thus code-switching may be used in a conversation to establish affinity with one or more persons while excluding others who do not belong to this linguistic or class or religious group. Code-mixing plays a similar role and often marks the context of the conversation. Code-mixing in English while speaking an Indian language, for example, may mark a professional or academic context. Code-mixing in a 'neutral' language like English will reveal rather than conceal region, class, religion, caste and gender. It may alert us to a local register or may define a concept or term, keeping alive the Indian nuances. A bilingual writer of English (and this category includes almost all Indian writers in English) walks this tightrope of choices carefully and consciously.

Further, the contexts of these Indian English writers are often multilingual and multicultural; certainly the dominant culture around them is not British or Western. Hence even when there may be nothing unintelligible or seemingly translated in a piece of Indian English writing, a reader from a different culture may have difficulty in fully understanding or interpreting the text. Using examples from Nayantara Sahgal, R.K. Narayan and Bharti Mukherjee, Yamuna Kachru demonstrates how

> they are fully interpretable only in the context of conventions of a community that uses kinship terms as instruments of politeness, has a belief system that accommodates astrology as relevant to human endeavours, has an institution of arranged marriage, and sharply demarcates the spheres of domestic activities of each spouse in a marriage. A reader unfamiliar with these contextual factors will either misinterpret or have difficulty in interpreting the examples . . .

> (Kachru 1992: 45)

Braj Kachru makes a similar statement about a Harikatha passage in Raja Rao's *Kanthapura* when he says that it is not the narrative technique or collocational relationships 'but the historical and cultural presuppositions [that] are different than what has been traditionally the "expected" historical and cultural milieu for English literature' (Kachru 1989: 160). It is not only the non-Indian reader who will have to reorient him/herself to read this text, even the North Indian reader will have to do so. The linguistic skills of the writer are used to locate the novel: location is carried out in the language itself. The historical and cultural milieu in which the text is thus positioned will have to be read and understood for the reader to be able to interpret the text fully, as in any translation. Hence the need for Indian English writers including Rushdie to signal the Indian-ness, the otherness, of their texts in the language itself. The ways in which they accomplish this task will be studied in the next section of this chapter, taking for analysis one passage from each of two Indian English novels.

II

The language employed by Indian English writers, the strategies they use to convey Indian realities in the English language, can be illustrated and studied by choosing at random passages from two novels separated by nearly fifty years. The first is from Raja Rao's *Kanthapura*:

'Ah, well,' she said, 'if you want to know, I shall go straight to Narsamma herself and find it out'; and straight she went, her sari falling down her shaven head, and she walked fast, and when she came to Moorthy's house she planted herself straight before his mother and cried, 'Narsamma, I have come to ask you something. You know you said you did not want my daughter for your son. I am glad of it now and I say to myself, thank heavens I didn't tie my daughter to the neck of a pariah-mixer. Ah, well! I have horoscopes now from Bangalore and Mysore – with real B.A.s and M.A.s, and you will see a decent Assistant Commissioner take my daughter in marriage. But what I have come for is this: Tell me, Narsamma, it seems your son wants to marry Coffee-Planter Venkatnarayana's daughter. He will do nothing of the kind. God has not given me a tongue for nothing. And the first time your honoured guests come out after the marriage papers are drawn, here shall I be in this corner, and I shall tumble upon them, I a shaven widow, and I shall offer them a jolly good blessing-ceremony in the choicest of words. Do you hear that, Narsamma? Well, let him take care, Moorthy. And our community will not be corrupted by such dirt-gobbling curs. Pariah! pariah!' She spat at the door and walked away, to the consternation of Narsamma, and the whole village said Venkamma was not Waterfall Venkamma for nothing, and that Narsamma should not take it to heart. And when Narsamma saw her at the river the next day, Venkamma was as jolly as ever and she said she had a bad tongue and that one day she would ask Carpenter Kenchayya to saw it out, and Narsamma said, 'Oh, it does not matter, sister,' and they all talked together happily and they came back home, their baskets on their heads, content.

(Rao 1971: 56–7)

This passage is a good example to study as it consists of both narration and dialogue. First, let us look at cultural markers. Venkamma's 'shaven head' marks her out as a widow. In the rigidly demarcated caste structure of this village a 'pariah-mixer' is one who has broken the code of caste purity and maintenance by mixing with untouchables. The 'horoscopes' that Venkamma refers to are not weekly forecasts but charts of planetary positions drawn up at the time of birth, which have to be matched for a couple to be able to marry. The 'marriage papers' are part of the betrothal ceremony, and it is considered inauspicious even to see a widow at times of celebration and religious ceremony. 'Community' here refers to caste. 'Pariah' is more than the name of the outcaste community; like such names all over India it is a curse word. It must also be pointed out that 'sister' does not denote kinship but, like other kinship terms, is used in India as a term of politeness. At the mention of the women meeting at the river, Indian readers would visualize women bathing and washing clothes. It is the washed clothes that the women carry back in the baskets on their heads.

Next, the modifiers used in conjunction with the names of the characters cry out to be noticed. 'Coffee-Planter Venkatnarayana', 'Waterfall Venkamma' and 'Carpenter Kenchayya' are all nominal groups with an identifying function and are all deviant from standard English. Almost all characters in *Kanthapura* are identified thus: 'cardamom-field Ramachandra', 'corner-house Moorthy', 'pock-marked Sidda', etc. The modifier which fixes the identity of the character may derive from property owned or lived in, profession ('Postmaster Suryanarayana'), physical characteristics or habit, ('Nose-scratching Nanjamma'), hierarchical positions ('Patel Ranga Gowda'), location ('Kuppur Suryanarayana') or caste ('Pariah Rachanna'). In the complex gradation of this village society, occupation may also be caste-bound. So 'Carpenter Kenchayya' is identified not only by occupation but as lower caste. This mode of reference is particularly South Indian and is very common in Kannada and Tamil. It must be noted, however, that even South Indians would not employ it in English: this use is unique to Raja Rao's *Kanthapura*.

There are other culture-specific idioms which may be strange to English ears and eyes: grammatical deviations; loan-shifts as lexis-bound translations from the Indian language of the context; and semantic shifts arising from contextual deviation due to a different usage of English. (These are also calques.) We have already noticed a case of semantic shift when Narsamma addresses Venkamma as 'sister'. Kachru has this to say about kinship terms:

> In English *brother*, *sister*, or *brother-in-law* all belong to the lexical set of kinship terms. In ... [Indian English] extra semantic features are assigned and their range of functions in other lexical sets widened e.g. [+ affection], [+ regard], [+ abuse], [+ mode of address].

> (Kachru 1983: 46)

Thus, the use here of 'sister' as a mode of address for a woman not related to the speaker points to politeness and lack of hostility; Narsamma is signalling that she holds Venkamma in regard. It is thus a strategy used by the character to end an unpleasant episode, to accept an apology. Kinship terms can be used differently in Indian English: 'for instance, *mother* as a term of respect, *sister* of regard, and *father-in-law* in the sense of abuse' (ibid.: 117). The last is akin to *brother-in-law* which may be a term of endearment as well as abuse; both terms depending for their abusive connotation on a value system where to allege 'morally loose' behaviour by their womenfolk is a deadly insult to the men. A man can be called a 'father-in-law'/'brother-in-law' only if the speaker has slept with his daughter/sister and this dishonours the entire family. The strength of this abuse is of course culturally and geographically generated and located.

An example of collocational deviation in this extract is the expression Venkamma uses when she thanks the 'heavens I didn't tie my daughter to the neck of a pariah-mixer'. The British reader may not expect to find a woman *tied to the neck* of anyone. This is a common expression which conveys a sense of burden – much like a mill-stone – in many Indian languages and is especially used to refer to matrimonial relationship. The torrent of abuse that Venkamma promises as a 'blessing-ceremony' also derives from a non-British culture and linguistic system. (In the same novel you have references to 'hair-cutting ceremony' and 'rice-eating ceremony'.) Venkamma's 'bad tongue' is another calque where there is a cultural deviation rather than a formal one, it belongs to the same culture that has notions of the 'evil eye' and the 'bad gaze'. There is also cultural significance in the fact that she does not stand 'in front of' Rangamma but 'straight before' her. This is a literal translation from Kannada and is used to construct the Kannadaness of the text, the context and the narrator's speech.

Thus this passage illustrates Raja Rao's successful attempt to create a culturally dependent speech style and narrative structure. The grandmother-narrator's oral story-telling is reflected in this written passage with its long sentences and abrupt shifts to direct speech. As Raja Rao points out in the foreword, 'we [Indians] tell one interminable tale. Episode follows episode, and when our thoughts stop our breath stops, and we move on to another thought' (Rao 1971: 6). This is the style of story-telling he has followed in the novel; it reads almost like a transcript of a series of recordings rather than a piece of creative writing.

The second passage (again randomly chosen) is from Salman Rushdie's *Midnight's Children*:

> Padma's story (given in her own words, and read back to her for eye-rolling, high-wailing, mammary-thumping confirmation): 'It was my own foolish pride and vanity, Saleem baba, from which cause I did run from you, although the job here is good, and you so much needing a looker-after! But in a short time only I was dying to return.
>
> 'So then I thought, how to go back to this man, who will not love me and only does some foolish writery? (Forgive, Saleem baba, but I must tell it truly. And love, to us women, is the greatest thing of all.)
>
> 'So I have been to a holy man, who taught me what I must do. Then with my few pice I have taken a bus into the country to dig for herbs, with which your manhood could be awakened from its sleep ... imagine, mister, I have spoken magic with these words: "Herb thou hast been uprooted by Bulls!" Then I have ground herbs in water and milk and said, "Thou potent and lusty herb! Give my Mr Saleem thy power. Give heat like that of Fire of Indra. Like the male antelope, O herb, thou hast all the force that Is, thou hast powers of Indra, and the lusty force of beasts."'
>
> (Rushdie 1982: 192–3)

The narrator signals immediately that this is a transcript of a speech made by an illiterate woman with an aside that works like a prefatory note: '(given in her own words, and read back to her for eye-rolling, high-wailing, mammary-thumping confirmation)'. This note also alerts the reader (or since the reader will already know this, one could say it reinforces the fact) to Padma's character as well as her cultural otherness: 'eye-rolling, high-wailing, mammary-thumping'. The layered nature of otherness is underlined by the fact that the main narrator is the 'Saleem baba' referred to in the passage, himself an other to the speakers of British English. Indian English speakers can be classified according to their competence in different modes of English and assigned their place in the cline of bilingualism; Padma, for example, is shown to be a bilingual with very poor control of English. Further, Indian English speakers can be separated on the basis of region as well as ethnicity, so that one might have a person with a very low competence in English, with high interference from the mother tongue. The cline of Englishes in India ranges from *educated* Indian English to varieties such as *Babu English* and *Butler English*.

Having placed Padma low down in this cline, Rushdie introduces various kinds of grammatical and lexical deviation. Before looking at these we must examine the way Padma addresses the narrator. 'Saleem baba' indicates the class status of the two characters – 'baba' being used in this manner for the offspring of the upper class by their servants – but may also indicate a difference in gender and age, giving Padma a maternal, proprietorial position akin to an ayah's. In other words, while 'baba' places Saleem in a higher class than Padma it also diminishes his position, making a boy of him. On top of all this, 'baba' is also a term of affection, so it is not surprising that it is the one term in this passage left untranslated – for how could all this have been conveyed in English?

The deviations in English are striking in Padma's first sentence itself. The literally translated 'from which cause I did run from you' (from Hindustani/Urdu, which Rushdie knows) should jar on an English reader even if the excessive 'pride and vanity' does not. The last segment of this sentence – 'you are so much needing a looker-after' – with its 'so much' and 'looker-after' and its 'to be + verb + ing' construction provides further examples of deviation caused by literal translation. What Rushdie has attempted here is to locate the character in terms of region, class and gender through the construction of a specific English using the strategies and resources of a translator. Do people actually speak like this? Perhaps, but never so consistently. Most Indians, regardless of bilingual competence, would switch codes as well as mix them, speaking even whole sentences in a different language. It is impossible for someone with such a competence in English as low as Padma's to speak purely in English, however deviant it might be.

The point here is that although the passage may read like a transcript of the speech of an Indian with low competence in English (i.e. like some kind of Indian English), it is actually a carefully constructed translation. Padma's prayers, the quotes within quotes, include archaic vocabulary ('thou' and 'hast') to indicate that they are in an older language (perhaps Sanskrit); the contrast between this and Padma's English is highlighted by the intervening 'Then I have ground . . . '. The names of the divine beings cannot be translated, but Rushdie inserts the very Indian 'Mr Saleem'. (This use of the honorific with the first name is actually more common in

South India, but Rushdie's aim is not versimilitude.) Curiously
Rushdie uses 'holy man', a term which does not carry the same
connotation as 'sadhu'. But 'holy man' is the term that exists in
English and Rushdie's strategy is to translate everything possible.
He does not attempt to have Padma explain the mythical references,
translation being impossible, because she would be sure that Saleem
being Indian (even if a Muslim, and that tells a tale of Hindu major-
ityism) would know them. The other (North) Indian expression that
is left untranslated is the onomatopoeic exclamation 'hai-hai' which
like all such exclamations though understandable is so culture-
specific as to be untranslatable.

III

Indian English writers are thus not so much translating Indian-
language texts into English as using various strategies to make their
works read like translations. This leads to Meenakshi Mukherjee's
complaint about Bhabhani Bhattacharya that 'he does something
very strange and inexplicable': 'He uses expressions that are obviously not English, their deliberate quaintness being meant to suggest
that they are translated from Bengali. In reality, however, *they have
no counterparts in Bengali either*' (Mukherjee 1971: 179; emphasis added).
When Bhattacharya uses words and terms like 'childling', 'wifeling',
'picture-play', 'sun-up', etc., or writes whole sentences which look
and sound strange (one of the examples Meenakshi Mukherjee gives
is 'Villagefuls of folk were on the high road'), he is not translating
from Bengali. Nor is he writing Indian English. Mukherjee finds it
'difficult to understand what is gained by coining . . . strange adjec-
tives when legitimate English attributes could have served as well'
(ibid.: 180). But 'legitimate' English would not reinforce the otherness of the culture depicted. Many Indian English writers create the
language in which they write, and part of their intent is to make
things difficult for the monolingual (English) reader. Far from using
Indian words and expressions for local colour, to create an exotic
ethnographic text, they attempt to make the process of reading as
difficult as that of writing. Mulk Raj Anand declares that Raja Rao
and he had purposes other than to 'elaborate the illusion of realities in India in the Anglo-saxon language, for sale to the jaded
reading public, in a manner which may be easy . . . to swallow'
(Anand, 1979: 39). As Bhabha argues when discussing the appear-

ance of a Hindi letter in Adil Jussawalla's poem, 'Missing Person', not only does the untranslated letter signal the hybridity of the post-colonial context, it also explodes the notion of the purity of the colonizing culture: 'Now we can begin to see why the threat of (mis)translation ... among those displaced and diasporic peoples who picked through the refuse, is a constant reminder to the post-imperial West, of the hybridity of its mother tongue, and the heterogeneity of national space' (Bhabha 1990: 203). This is true not just of the untranslated letter but also of the transliterated word, as well as all linguistic deviations which derive from a different culture. In a different context, writing about Canadian literatures, Sherry Simon argues that Quebec literature exhibits cultural hybridity and self-doubt which are characteristic of much contemporary writing. She observes that

> These doubts increasingly take the form of the cohabitation within a single text of multiple languages and heterogenous codes. In this case, translation can no longer be a single and definitive enterprise of cultural transfer. Translation, it turns out, not only negotiates between languages, but comes to inhabit the space of language itself.
>
> (Simon 1992: 174)

This use of translation, which 'inhabits the space of language itself', allows Indian writers to create a space for themselves in between Anglo-American English and Indian culture. This is not unique in any way to Indian English literature or writers. As Samia Mehrez points out,

> these texts written by post-colonial bilingual subjects create a language 'in between' and therefore come to occupy a space 'in between'. In most cases, the challenge of such space 'in between' has been double: these texts seek to decolonize themselves from two oppressors at once, the western ex-colonizer who naively boasts of their existence and ultimately recuperates them and the 'traditional', national cultures which shortsightedly deny their importance and consequently marginalize them.
>
> (Mehrez 1992: 121)

As in the case of their anglophone post-colonial counterparts, English automatically gives Indian English writers an outsider perspective; but it is one that derives from their belonging to Indian culture – it permeates and changes the language and is expressed in and through this hybrid English. Thus the medium of expression is so much part of their creativity that they are not very successful when translated into Indian languages. They are situated in the interface of cultures. This is perhaps why, as A.K. Ramanujam reports, R.K. Narayan is 'not too well received' in Tamil or Kannada translation (see Naik 1982: 289). Creating an English that resists easy appropriation by the British or the West as a whole is thus a primary task, but it is complicated by the fact that English does give Indian English writers a Western audience and that the translation skills they put to use primarily address audiences across cultures (including across India). Hence, initially, the earlier Indian English writers employ footnotes and/or glossaries to explain certain terms. Anand records that he deliberately gave up this practice: 'while I used glossaries of Indian words with their translations, at the end of my novels, in the first few years, I have not offered these appendices for some years now' (Anand 1979: 36).

Recent Indian English writers who publish in India do not do so because they see their primary audience in India itself, and not because they feel easier with the language or because there is an acceptable and vibrant Indian English available to them. Rushdie may be right when he says that 'The children of independent India seem not to think of English as being irredeemably tainted by its colonial provenance. They use it as an Indian language, as one of the tools they have to hand' (Rushdie 1991: 64). But their contexts have not changed; English is not the language of the streets or even the most-spoken or preferred language in offices. There is a greater acceptance of code-switching and code-mixing and overall a less puritanical attitude to language, but all that this has achieved is a greater legitimacy for Indianisms in English. Indian writers will have to accept the challenge of writing about non-English speakers and non-English cultures, as well as about people who speak English but not all the time and never purely so. They will have to use strategies of translation, still be aware of having audiences across cultures. R.K. Narayan was once asked if his texts are ever translated into English. He could easily have replied that they are, in the original – partially at least.

Note

This chapter would not have been possible without initial suggestions from Harish Trivedi and later discussions with N. Kamala.

References

Anand, M.R. (1979) 'Pigeon Indian: some notes on Indian English writing', in M.K. Naik (ed.), *Aspects of Indian Writing in English: Essays in Honour of Professor K.R. Srinivasa Iyengar* (Madras: Macmillan).

Bhabha, H. (1990) 'Interrogating identity: the postcolonial prerogative', in D.T. Goldberg (ed.), *Anatomy of Racism* (Minneapolis: University of Minnesota Press).

Dyson, K.K. (1993) 'Forging a bilingual identity: a writer's testimony', in P. Burton, K.K. Dyson and S. Ardener (eds), *Bilingual Women: Anthropological Approaches to Second Language Use* (Oxford: Berg).

Kachru, B. (1983) *The Indianization of English: The English Language in India* (New Delhi: Oxford University Press).

——— (1989) *The Alchemy of English: The Spread, Functions and Models of Non-native Englishes* (New Delhi: Oxford University Press).

Kachru, Y. (1992) 'The Indian face of English', *Seminar* 391 (March).

Mehrez, S. (1992) 'Translation and the post-colonial experience: the franco-phone North African text', in L. Venuti (ed.), *Rethinking Translation: Discourse Subjectivity Ideology* (London: Routledge).

Mukherjee, M. (1971) *The Twice Born Fiction* (New Delhi: Heinemann).

Naik, M.K. (ed.) (1979) *Aspects of Indian Writing in English: Essays in Honour of Professor K.R. Srinivasa Iyengar* (Madras: Macmillan).

——— (1982) *A History of Indian English Literature* (New Delhi: Sahitya Akademi).

Narayan, R.K. (1979) 'English in India: some notes on Indian English writing', in M.K. Naik (ed.) 1979.

Rao, R. (1971 [1938]) *Kanthapura* (New Delhi: Orient).

Rushdie, S. (1982 [1981]) *Midnight's Children* (London: Picador).

——— (1991) *Imaginary Homelands* (New Delhi: Penguin and Granta).

Simon, S. (1992) 'The language of cultural difference: figures of alterity in Canadian translation', in Venuti (ed.) 1992.

Singh, K. (1986) 'Indish', *Seminar* 321 (May).

Tonkin, E. (1993) 'Engendering language difference', in P. Burton, K.K. Dyson and S. Ardener (eds), *Bilingual Women: Anthropological Approaches to Second Language Use* (Oxford: Berg).

Venuti, L. (1992) *Rethinking Translation: Discourse Subjectivity Ideology* (London: Routledge)

Chapter 3

Translating and interlingual creation in the contact zone

Border writing in Quebec

Sherry Simon

Writing and translation meet as practices of creation in what Mary Louise Pratt has so aptly called the 'contact zone' (Pratt 1992: 6). This is the place where cultures, previously separated, come together and establish ongoing relations. Historically, these zones have grown out of colonial domination and have been characterized by 'conditions of coercion, radical inequality and intractable conflict' (ibid.). Increasingly, however, we find that Western society as a whole has turned into an immense contact zone, where intercultural relations contribute to the internal life of all national cultures.

The idea of culture as an envelope which securely binds all the members of a national community within the same coherence of meaning today belongs to the realm of myth. The great migrations of post-colonialism have produced a new socio-demographic situation: all Western nations now have increasingly mixed populations. The ease and rapidity of global communication have created an international mass culture, which competes and interacts with local forms. Even those exotic cultures, which we once counted on to furnish simple counter-models to our own confusion, are as endangered as the fragile environment which once supported them. And so the idea of culture as a set of unchanging and coherent values, behaviours or attitudes, has given way to the idea of culture as negotiation, symbolic competition or 'performance' (Clifford 1988). Every culture speaks a language traversed by two kinds of codes, the complicit idioms of the vernacular and the vehicular codes of international communication.

Because, then, cultures are bonded spaces characterized by a plurality of codes and languages, it is not surprising that translation has come to figure prominently in contemporary literature. Whether used as an implicit mode of literary creation in post-colonial writing or as an explicit source of inspiration in various modes of 'border writing', translation and plurilingualism inhabit many contemporary texts. As a consequence, the place of the translator is no longer an exclusive site. It overlaps with that of the writer and, in fact, of the contemporary Western citizen.

WHEN DID QUEBEC BECOME POST-COLONIAL?

The situation of Quebec is difficult to map onto the post-colonial grid.[1] Politically, Quebec became post-colonial, along with the rest of Canada, in 1867 at the time of Confederation. In cultural terms, however, Quebec long considered itself to be a territory colonized by the power of English. During the 1960s, the work of the theorists of decolonization (including Albert Memmi and Jacques Berque) provided a strong framework for understanding Quebec as a cultural colony, impoverished and alienated (Schwartzwald 1985). The spectacular changes which have transformed this situation and given Quebec a new economic, political and cultural confidence gradually put an end to the usefulness of this paradigm, however. As a French-speaking political community, implicated in the cultural dynamics of North America and receiving immigrants from across the globe, Quebec can be said to participate fully in the contradictions and tensions of contemporary post-coloniality.

The culture of Quebec has always been that of a borderland, a site marked by continuous linguistic contact. From the initial encounter of the French colonists with the Native peoples and the creation of the mixed languages of the coureurs de bois, who lived among the native peoples and travelled North and West across America, to the British conquest – which, making accommodation with the Catholic church in New France, allowed for the perpetuation of the French language – and through the various constitutional arrangements which until now have allowed for the maintenance of a French-speaking society in North America within the political framework of the Canadian federation, the culture of Quebec has been in constant interaction with other languages, but most persistently with English.

This contact has historically been considered threatening to the survival of the French language: daily battle is waged against the nagging encroachment of English forms and expressions, and language laws make French obligatory in the workplace and in commercial transactions. But while these necessary efforts do repel the agents of linguistic contamination, some Quebec literature invites language interference and prefers to play on the drama of language contact. The most celebrated episode of literary transgression was the integration of 'joual' (or Montreal urban dialect, heavily laced with English and 'incorrect' French expressions) into the literature of the 1960s and 1970s. The literary and cultural effects of this movement have been much discussed as an expression of anti-colonialism, as the transformation of a degraded and alienated form of language into a self-affirming figure of national emergence (Simon (ed.) 1995). Still, to characterize Quebec literature as the result of interlingual creation might seem somewhat tendentious. After all, Quebec literature in French has most often been treated as the expression of a singular cultural identity, a conscious affirmation of difference in the context of Anglo Saxon hegemony in North America. This linguistic and cultural identity, however, can no longer be considered self-enclosed and self-generating. As critic Pierre Nepveu has written, Quebec fiction seeks to redefine the order of social identification, and construct architectures of complexity reflecting the pluralism of Quebec society (Nepveu 1988). Quebec cultural productions are indeed increasingly explicit in showing the interplay and exchange which are necessary to any process of creation. In other words, it is recognized that the life of culture is not to be found in *conservation*, but in the risky play of dialogue.

This chapter will discuss the work of Jacques Brault, Nicole Brossard and Daniel Gagnon to illustrate modes through which language contact and translation become generative of literary work. In particular I would like to show how cultural productions in Quebec today play on language relationships in ways which baffle and upset official images of symmetrical dialogue, and how interlanguages become the basis for a new cultural aesthetics. Brossard and Brault are two of the most important writers in contemporary Quebec, having achieved the widest recognition for a large body of work.[2] Jacques Brault uses the process of 'non-translation' to produce poetic texts which carry few marks of their initial provenance. Nicole Brossard's novel *Mauve Desert* describes and enacts the work of translation, giving voice to the translator and finally integrating this translation work into the body of the book itself. Daniel Gagnon's short, lyrical texts are idiosyncratic and difficult to categorize.[3] Gagnon writes on the frontier between languages, producing double versions of texts which are written in a hybrid idiom, 'my so bad english'. Working within different aesthetic projects, all three use interlinguistic exchange as theme or method and place translation at the heart of their creative work. Their work is self-consciously provocative, jarring traditional alignments, blurring boundaries of cultural identity, and writing against a cultural tradition which has been deeply suspicious of the work of translation.[4]

JACQUES BRAULT: THE TRANSLATOR'S SIGNATURE

Jacques Brault's *Poèmes des quatre côtés*, or 'Poems of/from the four sides', is a slim volume, entirely in French, composed of four sets of poems, interspersed with sections of prose and engravings. Each section carries the designation of one of the four points of the compass. In the prose texts, Brault proposes his thoughts on the process of 'non-translation'; in the poems he illustrates the process.

Brault's reflections on translation have several sources of inspiration. A reader of Maurice Blanchot, Henri Meschonnic and Jacques Roubaud, Brault is suspicious of the absolute separation between 'original' and 'derivative' poetic activity. He is attentive to the dynamics of loss involved in all writing. His first comments in *Poèmes des quatre côtés* evoke the physical situation of the poet-translator, uncertain of his desire, then swept up by the appeal of strange words and voices. Throughout the volume he emphasizes the creative aspects which are common to both writing and translation, making all imaginative work part of a dynamic relationship with otherness. But Brault insists as well on the cultural weight of translation. As a member of a French-speaking community in North America, he is intensely aware of the traditional mistrust of translation which prevails in Quebec – translation most often involving the massive importation of American cultural materials onto the Quebec market. He wishes to propose a different use of translation – one which will contribute to the cultural interests of Quebec.

When *Poèmes des quatre côtés* first appeared some critics assumed that the poems were 'imaginative recreations', others that they were indeed translations. But none could be sure. Why? Because Brault gives no explicit indication of the original sources of the poems. He simply explains, in one of the prose pieces, that he has been inspired by the works of four English-language poets, Gwendolyn McEwen, Margaret Atwood, John Haines and e.e. cummings, and that he has used their poems to create new ones. He indicates the names of the volumes from which he has selected the poems, but not the titles of the poems translated.

Such moves clearly make the critic's work difficult; the path to the sources, *ad fontes*, has been obscured. Brault's decision is hardly a whimsical gesture, however. It is consistent with the role which he gives translation in a context of unequal cultural relations. Brault's theory of 'non-translation' is explicitly located in the confrontation between the strength of English-language culture in North America and the fragility of Quebec's French-language cultural production. Non-translation is directly inspired by poet Gaston Miron's concept of the 'non-poem'. Miron laid claim to the 'non-poem', the glorification of alienation and linguistic poverty, in the same way that the novelists rehabilitated 'joual' for literary use, aiming at reversing a tradition of cultural self-deprecation and humiliation.

Brault's 'non-translation' responds to the appealing otherness of English-language culture by a double gesture of homage and reappropriation. The complexity of his relationship to the otherness of Anglo culture is to be contrasted with the traditional stances of Quebec writers, which consists in either euphorically shouting the praise of cultural bilingualism, or condemning any incursion outside of the fragile linguistic base provided by the home culture. Brault explains rather that translation is to be considered an exemplary process of confrontation between two cultural realities.

> Since I have been navigating in all sorts of foreign waters, which sweep along all sorts of historical, cultural, social and symbolic deposits, I feel more profoundly at home and I am cured of my land sickness. Because it was as much the fact of my being a Quebecer as my passion for poetry that obliged me to make a detour through estrangement on my way home. Ill at ease with my language, as one is uncomfortable with one's body, I finally realized that in practice the most vital relationship with oneself comes through the mediation of others. This is the core of non-translation. I felt aggressed by the English language? Well, I resolved to traverse this language until I came to my own (yet unknown) tongue, and that during this difficult and salutary passage I would lose myself in the other and the other would find itself in me.[5]

Here Brault defies any easy assumptions about the writer's 'at-home-ness' in language. Rather than setting out on a mission of cultural counter-conquest, Brault uses translation to establish a new relationship with himself. It is not a question of simply overturning cultural influences, of reversing the tide of influences, but of creating a new idiom through the encounter of languages and traditions.

Brault suggests in fact that Quebec poets, traditionally unreceptive to the idea of translation, would find advantage in the 'de-alienating odyssey' which such work can become. What is more, he suggests, translation is a good investment. It is only if you translate others, if you establish your presence on the world translation market, that others will even consider translating you. Much reticence towards translation, he explains, consists in a misconception of its goals grounded in an idealistic ideology of writing. There is no absolute truth to be conveyed in translation, just as there is no absolute meaning to be attained once and for all in the text.

Brault's non-translation is very close in inspiration – if not in practice – to the projects of 'transtextualization' which have been conceived in response to situations of unequal cultural exchange. The most articulate of these projects comes out of Brazilian modernism and is known as *antropofagia* or cultural cannibalism (Vieira 1994). Translations, often parodic, are part of the reworking of foreign influences. They aim to absorb and assimilate the literary influences which contribute to the oppression of dominated cultures.

But while Brault shares the sensibility of these writers towards the unequalness of cultural exchange, and shares their confidence in the powers of translation to help redress this inequality, he does not share their parodic intent. Having chosen the work of near-contemporaries, poets with whom he senses a similar poetic sensibility, Brault approaches translation with a respectful attentiveness. But here lies a paradox. When we do compare Brault's translated poems with the originals (the detective work having been done by the author of a thorough study on the subject[6]) it becomes evident that Brault has not deviated from conventional norms as much as his concept of 'non-traduction' might have suggested. The 'liberties' which Brault takes are entirely consistent with the aesthetic aims of poetic translation.

What defines the non-translation, then? And in what way does it carry a transgressive charge? Brault's act of defiance consists in cutting the poems off from their sources. Not only does Brault refuse to give precise indications as to the identity of the original texts (he gives only the titles of the volumes from which he has taken the poems), he also eliminates their titles. His translated poems integrate the poem's title into the body of the poem, effectively decapitating them, making them further unrecognizable as products of their authors' hands.

This double gesture is essentially what turns Brault's translations into non-translations. By cutting the works off from their sources, by signing his own name as 'author' of this book, Brault creates a new poetic order in his own image. This gesture, as Annie Brisset explains, is fully characteristic of emergent literatures, which use translation as a means of self-affirmation (Brisset 1996). The author's name is effaced; the name of the translator identifies the new functions of the work, giving it the legitimacy of naturalization. The primacy of the author, of origin, is undermined. Cut off from the poetic series to which they belong, the poems are forced into the shape of a literary project for which they were not originally destined. They will conform now to the topography of Brault's literary landscape.

Non-translation concerns, then, the meaning of the poet's signature. By substituting his own name for the list of authors whose work he rewrites, Brault is not simply signalling a triumphant act of appropriation. He is emphasizing the fragility of the relationship between name and work, between subjectivity and writing – fragility which he situates at the heart of all creativity. As a reader of Maurice Blanchot, Brault is aware of the silence at the centre of poetry, of the radical insignificance of the poet's name. 'I speak in order not to speak; my signature escapes me' (Brault 1975: 68). Brault uses his name to situate his translations within a new cultural order, that of the language of Quebec. The name refers to this collective origin, to the *relation* between languages and poetic universes, more than it does to the selfhood of the poet. 'I float in an interlanguage, vaporous words veil my eyes; a text, belonging neither to me nor to another, takes on the form of a chiasmus. I lose . . . and find . . . myself in it' (ibid.: 50).

TRANSLATING THE DESERT

With the work of Brault, Nicole Brossard's *Mauve Desert* is surely the most self-aware and fully achieved reflection on translation in contemporary Quebec fiction. What is most unusual about the novel is its shape. The text is divided into three parts, physically separated in the volume. The first is a dramatic story of murder and betrayal, entitled *Mauve Desert*; the second is a section called 'A Book to Translate' in which the translator discusses and fleshes out aspects of the initial story; and a third section entitled *Mauve, the Horizon* (given its own book cover, complete with title, name of author, translator and publishing house) is a rewriting of the first chapter, in French 'translation'. The same story is repeated in these first and third sections, both times in French, but the second version contains changes in rhythm, intensity and phrasing.

Mauve Desert, the first part of the book, tells a story of love and death against the backdrop of the Arizona desert. An adolescent, Melanie, speeds along the desert roads in her mother's Meteor. A man, whom we understand to represent science, power and violence, kills a woman whom he perceives as threatening to that power. The lines of the narrative are clean and brilliant, at the same time transparent and mysterious.

The second part is written by the translator, Maude Laures, who discovers *Mauve Desert* by accident in a bookstore and becomes impassioned with it. The chapter that she writes, 'A Book to Translate', is an outgrowth of that reading, and is a kind of preface to the translation which follows. In the imaginary dialogue which is part of that chapter, the author explains to the translator: 'I remember one day buying a geology book in which I found a letter. It was a love letter written by a woman and addressed to another woman. I used the letter as a bookmark. I would read it before reading and after reading [. . .] I imagined the face of the woman for whom it was meant. It was during that time that I started writing the book you want to translate' (Brossard 1990: 83). The translator fleshes out the skeleton of the narrative, imagining details which were barely suggested in the original, exploring hypotheses for unexplained enigmas. We see the translator here as an independent agent, adding new life to the narrative.

This does not mean that the translator takes liberties with the text. On the contrary, when the time comes for her to set about the meticulous task of 'reading backwards in her language' (ibid.), she proceeds with painstaking care. The result, as we see, is *practically* identical with the original. Despite – or perhaps because of – the long reveries which have allowed the translator to enter the imaginative world of the text, the translation looks surprisingly just like the original.

The triple structure of the book is striking. Translation becomes a mode of generation of the literary work, the means through which much of the book is generated; translation is also the thematic subject of the work, in that the considerations of the second section are attributed to the subjectivity of the translator and considered to accompany the translation process.

It is particularly appropriate that this foregrounding of the translation process be at the heart of a work by the best known of Quebec's feminist writers. Translation has been recognized as particularly important to feminist interchange in Canada and Quebec, and an important motor of creation and cultural exchange.[7] To be sensitive to the gendered aspects of language use is to understand the subjectivity expressed in any act of rewriting. Translation can never be a neutral act of repetition: mediation involves transmission but also displacement.

Like Italo Calvino's *If on a Winter's Night a Traveller*, from which Brossard draws her epigraph ('Reading is going toward something that is about to be, and no one yet knows what it will be . . .'), *Mauve Desert* is about the complex network of emotional investments which create the life of the book. Brossard and Calvino both underscore the active role which the translator plays in this process. But they differ strongly in the way they characterize this role. Calvino's translator is a surly, untrustworthy cosmopolitan polyglot – a character out of a Nabokov novel. He takes pleasure in sabotaging the work of the author, finding ever new ways of creating hitches in the chain of transmission of the literary work. Calvino uses the most stereotyped scenario of sexual relations to portray his vision of literary relationships: (male) Author, Translator and (female) Reader are caught up in a triangle of seduction and jealousy. Suffering from the impotence of his status – in comparison to that of the Author – the Translator must resort to the most unworthy tactics in order to attract the Reader's attention. Brossard redraws the lines of literary desire. The translator undertakes her slow, meticulous task for quite the opposite reasons than those which motivate Hermes Marana. No international intrigues here, no high commercial stakes, and no motives of vengeance: rather, the passionate life of the word.

How are we to understand the triple structure of Brossard's book? Like Calvino, Brossard clearly wishes to foreground the existence of the book as a made object, as the result of complex financial and emotional investments. Translation is not only a process of linguistic exchange; it is *work* which enables a new book to come into being. The three sections of the book mimic the stages of progression in the life of a book. This life begins with publication, and continues through fortuitous encounters with those who infuse it with meaning.

Why include, however, under the same covers a story that is told twice, in almost identical terms? We are reminded here of the well-known story by Borges, 'Pierre Menard, Author of Don Quixote'. Even if the texts produced by Cervantes and the much later author Pierre Menard are verbally identical, Borges explains, their meaning is quite different. Brossard serves us a similar lesson in *Mauve Desert*, showing how temporal succession and intralingual displacement generate new meanings. In creating a fictional equivalent for an interlingual translation, Brossard provides the reader with an opportunity to experience the kinds of shifts which occur when texts move from one language to another.

From the very minimal changes that do occur, however, we may infer that Brossard holds a rather optimistic view of translation. There is no suggestion here of the essential incommunicability of culturally specific meaning; no spectre of the aporia of linguistic transfer. This is particularly significant in the case of Nicole Brossard, whose work – though quite abundantly translated – has grown out of a language-centred feminism. During the 1970s and early 1980s, Brossard was one of the most active and articulate proponents of writing focused on the signifier, and in active conflict with conventional syntactic form. Nevertheless, unlike the work of her contemporary, France Théoret, for instance, Brossard's writing does not falter or show impotence; it has even been called 'classical' in the broad sweep of ever-present command.[8] Though aware of the conceptual constraints which limit writing and communication in a patriarchal universe, though obsessed with the figures of death which patrol yet its wide desert spaces, Brossard speaks in *Mauve Desert* of the life of the word. This life is not spontaneous, not attached to any authentic mode of being. It is laboriously composed, and then patiently transferred and rediscovered.

Through this process of transmission which has no beginning, the translator becomes a postmodern heroine. She constantly threatens to transgress the boundaries of her role, the geographical distance separating the hot clear air of the desert and the weak winter light of the north, the line of authority which allows the author to make decisions which the translator would like to contest. Brossard's translator refuses to participate in an economy of loss, in the pathos of dislocation, the loss of spontaneous contact with one's inner self, of emotional immediacy and wholeness, which is so often associated

with translation. Brossard's optimism brings novelty to a field dominated by clichés of betrayal and failure, and suggests that translation
can participate in new logics of exchange, contribute to the creation
of new solidarities.

DANIEL GAGNON: THE AESTHETICS OF INTERLANGUAGE

Daniel Gagnon is the author of a double work: *La Fille à marier* in
its translated French version, and *The Marriageable Daughter* in English.
The novel is made up of a series of fifty imaginary letters written
by Jeanne, the 12-year-old narrator, to her made-up penpal Phyllis
in Medicine Hat. Her letters tell of her impossible love for Nicolas,
who is dead, of various older men who abuse her, and of the despair
of being unable to communicate with any of the people around her.
Enthusiastically, apologetically, she reaches out to Phyllis, in long
streams of constantly changing metaphors, magical and idyllic at
first, more and more riddled with disease and decay towards the
last. The second section seems to end with a suicide attempt. And
at the end she seems to be on the verge of either death or capitu-
lation to the deathworld of drugs and psychiatric treatment.

La Fille à marier cannot be separated from *The Marriageable Daughter*,
a translation done by Gagnon himself and published in 1989. The
first text to be published was the French version; the English text
is presented as a translation of that book. But Gagnon himself has
said that in fact he wrote the English text first. And there are many
clues in the text which confirm this, associations of words and images
which manifestly make more sense in English than in French. Here's
one example where clearly the English came first:

> This letter to you in the Queen's English, the wailing of a
> newborn infant in wanderings, roaming haphazardly, stag-
> gering, vacillating, wavering in vacuity in Canadian emptiness,
> freezing in the Police ice from sea to sea, glorious and free, we
> stand on guard for thee beneath the shining skies, our home
> and native land, and the poor Indians, the lost Indian summer,
> O chère Phyllis, où es-tu, where are you?
>
> (Gagnon 1989: 12)

In the French this is:

Cette lettre dans une langue correcte, chant incohérent d'une nouveau-née régulièrement ballotée dans un sens et dans l'autre, errant au hasard, chancelante, vacillante, titubante dans la vacuité du vide canadien, se congelant dans la glace du pôle d'une mer à l'autre, glorieux et libres nous nous tenons au garde-à-vous sous les cieux illuminés de notre pays, et les pauvres Indiens, l'été indien perdu, ô dear Phyllis, where are you?

(Gagnon 1985: 8)

The 'Queen's English', 'from sea to sea', 'glorious and free' – these idioms are stronger and more coherent than the suggested French equivalents. However, there are also a few counter-examples where word associations in French clearly seem to precede the English translation: 'je suis sur le pas de la porte, pas de pas de valse, pour céder le pas aux bêtes immondes, leur permettre de passer' (ibid.: 16): 'I am standing in the doorway, no waltz steps, to give the filthy beasts precedence, allow them to pass' (Gagnon 1989: 10). The play on words around 'pas' in French is not reproduced in the English text. In addition, there is some extra material in the French version which does not exist in the English one.

In fact there is no way of declaring any one of these texts to be the original. If indeed the English did come first, as clues seem to indicate, it was written *through* and *with* French. Writing the text in English was already an operation of translation which the printed French version simply comes to confirm. In fact as Phyllis makes clear from the start: 'do you understand me well? excuse my so bad English, mister Smith mon professeur d'anglais gave me your precious name, if it will cure your pernicious anaemia, he said, and now I have my kindred soul' (ibid.: 9). ('O Phyllis, tu es ma chère soeur à Medicine Hat, en Alberta au Canada, ne l'es-tu pas? aren't you? do you understand me well? excuse mon si mauvais anglais, mister Smith my english professor m'a promis de corriger mes fantes, il m'a donné ton précieux nom et maintenant j'ai une âme soeur.') English is already a language deliberately infused with the alterity of an alien code. It is 'so bad English' which makes Jeanne ask her friend if 'a boy [did] ever touch you somewhere on your corpse Phyllis?' (Gagnon 1989: 10).

In the vocabulary of Brian Fitch's study of Samuel Beckett's bilingual text, we must conclude that there is no linguistic *prime instance*; both original and variants belong to the same *megatype* (Fitch 1988). Fitch shows that when read together, the French and English versions of Beckett's texts become commentaries one on the other. Beckett writes 'across languages': 'In whichever of the two languages Beckett happens to be writing at a given moment, there is always the presence of the other language with its wholly different expressive potential hovering at his shoulder, always at arm's reach and within earshot' (Fitch 1988: 156). This awareness can only accentuate the false security of the mother tongue. All language becomes denaturalized, distanced. The experience of the bilingual writer becomes a heightened awareness of the 'ambivalent status, for its user, of all language' (Fitch 1988: 160).

Daniel Gagnon's double text speaks to this modernist awareness of the alienation of linguistic codes. It expresses an uneasiness with language. But at the same time, there is a contradictory fascination with the automatic phrases of idiomatic language. There is indeed in both texts an extremely liberal, even profligate, use of idiom. It feels sometimes as if the author has been ransacking a dictionary of idiomatic expressions and then savouring the pleasure of trying them out: 'rivers wet their whistle, nothing ventured nothing gained, so they take the plunge, jump and pole vault with coated tongue, I skip meals' (Gagnon 1989: 13). This ludic and exuberant use of idiomatic expressions declares the affiliation of the text to specific linguistic traditions, and expresses what Marjory Sabin has identified as the essence of the English modernist tradition: the dialogue between linguistic affiliation and alienation, between the idioms of common speech and suspicion of the vernacular (Sabin 1987).

Gagnon's broken language carries, in addition, meanings which are specific to the socio-historic context of Canadian bilingualism. Jeanne conveys the fascination of a Sherbrooke schoolgirl for the West; this unknown territory offers the possibility of a secret language of escape, a personal language of revolt. But English is also the language of Jeanne's schoolteacher, whose presence in the narrative always carries a threat of violence. English figures both as the source and as the possible remedy for Jeanne's oppression.

Gagnon's double text uses linguistic plurality in ways which are richly suggestive of 'interlanguage' as defined by Régine Robin. This is 'an imaginary relationship which the writer maintains with his or her mother tongue and with the other languages which make up his or her linguistic universe: a relationship of love, fixation, hate, rejection, or ambivalence' (Robin 1990: 171). It is dominated by the strangeness of Freud's 'unheimlich': in a perpetual movement away from his/her 'own', 'proper' language, the writer introduces into the very body of the work a trace of what is different, what lies outside. The frontiers between here and there therefore become unstable – 'here' being, through a process of permanent and always incomplete translation, a permanently uncertain place.

POETICS OF TRANSLATION

The three texts considered in this chapter can be said to offer successive adumbrations of a poetics of translation. These texts bring to realization an aesthetics of cultural pluralism in which the literary object is fragmented, in a manner analogous to the contemporary social body. We should note, though, that the manner in which this fragmentation is enacted in the double work of Daniel Gagnon is quite different from Brault's somewhat more conventional 'non-translations' or Brossard's serene internal translation. The idiom of Gagnon's *Marriageable Daughter* is mixed and broken. It expresses weakness and incapacity, the inability to show mastery of a unified code of literary communication. Devoid of the local strength and linguistic coherence we often associate with successful works of literature, the text has many of the characteristics of a 'bad' translation. What generally passes for a bad translation, in fact, is a text which reminds its readers that it is suspended between languages, suggesting the translator's incapacity to escape the influence of the source language and embrace the fullness of the target language. Both in its French and English versions, Gagnon's book voluntarily adopts this uncomfortable intermediary position.

As a double text, traversed by linguistic plurality, *La Fille à marier / The Marriageable Daughter* takes on an emblematic status. It becomes suggestive of the language difficulties experienced by those who live between two cultures, in the many contact zones of the contemporary world. It takes aesthetic risks in foregrounding its own uncertainty, breaking literary convention by forfeiting the security of a unified idiom. The precariousness of the code in which Gagnon writes destabilizes the very idea of translation. We have been used to thinking of cultures and languages as autonomous singularities. One translates a text, written in one language, emerging out of one culture. But what if, as is here the case, the 'original' text is inhabited by more than one language? Can the transfer of these texts, as Derrida asks, *still be called translation* (Derrida 1985: 215)?

Inevitably, the mixing of codes – and of modes of literary generation – brings confusion and disorder. Whether it be to disturb the contours of literary property (Brault), the shape of the book (Brossard) or the identity of literary language (Gagnon), all these writers use translation to challenge categories of textual order. Their works show how 'language contact' can be put to imaginative use.

While all of these experiments involve the contact between French and English, obviously the most frequent form of language contact in the Quebec context, other productions, especially in theatre, could be evoked, which interact with a variety of languages which are given mythical powers (Chinese in Robert Lepage's *Dragon Trilogy*, German in many works by the dance/theatre group Carbone 14) or immigrant languages (such as Italian in the theatre of Marco Micone). And so translation and plurilingualism take on new dimensions and meanings in contemporary cultural production.

What the poetics of translation confirms for us is that our understanding of translation today as a reality and as an ideal has more to do with discontinuity, friction and multiplicity than it has to do with the creation of new commonalities. Culture no longer offers itself as a unifying force; language, nation, culture no longer line up as bounded and congruent realities. Language, in particular, has lost its ability to ground us in a shared universe of references. In recognizing that 'everyone is potentially, to a greater or lesser extent, a nonnative speaker' (Kramtsch 1997: 368) language professionals have started to sound like Joyce, Beckett and Nabokov, Rushdie, Derek Walcott or Jacques Derrida in claiming that we are never 'at home' in any language.[9] It has become a commonplace of critical discourse to speak of the hybrid aesthetics of contemporary post-colonial writing, its creolization and multiplicity. Texts, like cultures, like national territories, are more and more the sites of competing languages, diverse idioms, conflicting codes. This 'Otherness within' works to reconfigure a practice of translation defined in the West since the Renaissance as a transfer between linguistically unified texts. Increasingly, translation and writing become part of a single process of creation, as cultural interactions, border situations, move closer and closer to the centre of our cultures. Writing across languages, writing through translation, becomes a particularly strong form of expression at a time when national cultures have themselves become diverse, inhabited by plurality. Whether in the context of the tensions of bilingualism or the developing modes of global vehicular idioms, the mixing of codes points to an aesthetics of cultural pluralism whose meanings have yet to be fully explored.

Notes

1 It is significant that in a recent issue of the important journal *Essays on Canadian Writing* (56 (Fall 1995)) devoted to post-colonial theory, 'Testing the limits: post-colonial theories and Canadian literature', Quebec is hardly mentioned at all.

2 Brossard, born in 1943, has published more than fifteen books of poetry and seven novels. Five of her books have appeared in English translation: *Surfaces of Sense*, trans. Fiona Strachan, (Toronto: Coach House Press, 1989); *The Aerial Letter*, trans. Marlene Wildeman (Toronto: The Women's Press, 1988); *French Kiss*, trans. Patricia Claxton (Toronto: Coach House Press, 1986); *Lovhers*, trans. Barbara Godard (Montreal: Guernica Editions, 1986); *These Our Mothers*, trans. Barbara Godard, (Toronto: Coach House Press, 1983); *Daydream Mechanics*, trans. Larry Shouldice (Toronto: Coach House Press, 1980).

   Brault, born in 1933, has published several volumes of poetry (including *Moments fragiles*, 1984), a novel (*Agonie*, 1985) and several volumes of essays. *Agonie* was translated as *Death-Watch* by David Lobdell (Toronto: Anansi, 1987); Barry Callaghan has translated *Moments fragiles* as *Fragile Moments* (Toronto: Exile Editions, 1987). Gertrude Sanderson translated Brault's *L'en dessous l'admirable* as *Within the Mystery* (Montreal: Guernica Editions, 1986).

3 Gagnon is the author of *La Fille à marier* (Montreal: Editions Leméac, 1985) and *The Marriageable Daughter* (Toronto: Coach House Press, 1989). He has also published *Le Péril amoureaux* (Montreal: VLB Editeurs, 1986), *Mon Mari le docteur* (Montreal: Editions Leméac, 1986); *La Fée calcinée* (Montreal: VLB Editeurs, 1987); *O ma source!* (Montreal: Guérin Littérature, 1988) and *Venite a cantare* (Montreal: Editions Leméac, 1990).

4 A longer development (in French) of all the themes suggested in this chapter can be found in Simon (1994).

5 Brault 1989. The translation is mine.

6 Irène Sotiropoulou-Papaleonidas, *Jacques Brault. Théories/pratique de la traduction. Nouvelle approche de la problématique de la traduction poétique* (Quebec: Editions Didion 1980).

7 See 'Feminist poetics', in *Mapping Literature: The Art and Politics of Translation*, ed. D. Homel and S. Simon (Montreal: Véhicule Press, 1988). See also Susanne de Lotbinière-Harwood, *Re-belle et infidèle / The Body Bilingual* (Toronto: The Women's Press, 1991) and the section on feminist translation in the journal *TTR* (*Traduction, Terminologie, Rédaction*), special issue devoted to the translation of theory, 4 (2) (1991).

8 Louise Dupré, *Stratégies du vertige* (Montreal: Editions du Remue-ménage, 1990).

9 See Jacques Derrida, *Le monolinguisme de l'autre* (Paris: Galilée, 1996), p. 112, for a critique of 'the so-called mother tongue':

La langue dite maternelle n'est jamais purement naturelle, ni propre ni habitable. *Habiter*, voilà une valeur assez *déroutante* et équivoque: on n'habite jamais ce qu'on est habitué à appeler habiter. Il n'y a pas d'habitat possible sans la différence de cet exil et de cette nostalgie. Certes. C'est trop connu. Mais il ne s'ensuit pas que tous les exils soient équivalents. A partir, oui, *à partir* de cette rive ou de cette dérivation commune, tous les expatriements restent singuliers.

References

Brault, J. (1975) *Poèmes des quatre côtés* (Saint-Lambert: Editions du Noroît).

—— (1975) 'Entretien' with Alexis Lefrançois, *Liberté* 100 (17) (Jul.–Aug.).

—— (1977) 'Quelques remarques sur la traduction de la poésie', *Ellipse* 21: 10–35.

—— (1984) *Agonie* (Montreal: Boréal).

—— (1989) *La Poussière du chemin* (Montreal: Boréal).

Brisset, A. (1996) *Translation and Sociocriticism* (Toronto: University of Toronto Press).

Brossard, N. (1987) *Le Désert mauve* (Montreal: L'Hexagone).

—— (1990) *Mauve Desert*, trans. Susanne de Lotbinière-Harwood (Toronto: Coach House Press).

Clifford, J. (1988) *The Predicament of Culture* (Cambridge, Mass.: Harvard University Press).

Derrida, J. (1985) 'Tours de Babel', in J. Graham (ed.), *Difference in Translation* (Ithaca, NY: Cornell University Press).

Fitch, B. (1988) *Beckett and Babel* (Toronto: University of Toronto Press).

Gagnon, D. (1985) *La Fille à marier* (Montreal: Editions Leméac).

—— (1989) *The Marriageable Daughter* (Toronto: Coach House Press).

Kramtsch, C. (1997) 'The second-language student', *PMLA*, 112 (3).

Nepveu, P. (1988) *L'Ecologie du réel. Mort et naissance de la littérature québécoise* (Montreal: Boréal).

Pratt, M.L. (1992) *Imperial Eyes: Travel Writing and Transculturation* (London and New York: Routledge).

Robin, R. (1990) *Le Roman mémoriel* (Longueuil: Editions du Préambule).

Sabin, M. (1987) *The Dialect of the Tribe: Speech and Community in Modern Fiction* (New York: Oxford University Press).

Schwartzwald, R. (1985) *Institution littéraire, modernité et question nationale au Québec de 1940 à 1976*, Doctoral thesis, Laval University.

Simon, S. (1994) *Le Trafic des langues. Traduction et culture dans la littérature québécoise* (Montreal: Boréal).

—— (ed.) (1995) *Culture in Transit: Translating the Literature of Quebec* (Montreal: Véhicule Press).

Vieira, E.R.P. (1994) 'A postmodern translation esthetic in Brazil', in *Translation Studies: An Interdiscipline* (Amsterdam: John Benjamin).

Chapter 4

Composing the other

André Lefevere

There is now general agreement among those who think and write about translation, that the activity called 'translating', which involves mediation between at least two code systems, should neither be equated nor confused with the wider cluster of problems associated with 'translation', or 'translation studies'. A text formulated in code 1, usually equated with 'the source language', is reformulated in code 2, usually equated with 'the target language', and during that reformulation certain rules are observed. These rules were long thought to be eternal and unchanging, centring mainly on fidelity or any number of its synonyms; in recent years most scholars writing in the field of translation studies have come to accept that such rules are mainly imposed by those people of flesh and blood who commission the translation, which is then made by other people of flesh and blood (not boxes and arrows) in concrete situations, with a given aim in mind. In other words, the rules to be observed during the process of decoding and reformulation depend on the actual situation, on the function of the translation, and on who wants it made and for whom. Fidelity will, for instance, still be paramount in the translation of medical texts, but not in the translation of advertisements, in which case it may well be counterproductive.

In what follows I would like to challenge further – as I have done before, on occasion – the supposedly primary or fundamental role played by linguistic codes in the operation known as 'translating'. It is my contention that people who translate texts do not, first and foremost, think on the linguistic level, the level of the translation of individual words and phrases. Rather, they think first in terms of what I would like to call two grids. I do not want to speculate on the primacy of one grid over the other; rather, I would suggest that we think of them as intertwined. One is what I would like to call a 'conceptual grid', the other a 'textual grid'. Both grids are the result of the socialization process. An educated member of any culture in the West, for instance (as we might describe someone who has more or less successfully survived the socialization process), will know that certain texts are supposed to contain certain markers designed to elicit certain reactions on the reader's part, and that the success of communication depends on both the writer and the reader of the text agreeing to play their assigned parts in connection with those markers. The writer is supposed to put them in, the reader is supposed to recognize them. Texts that start with 'Once upon a time', for instance, will elicit quite different expectations in the reader than texts that start with 'Leave Barcelona 8:15 a.m.; Arrive Amsterdam 11.30 a.m'. In the first case readers are not supposed to worry about the referential nature of the text in question. In the second case they would be justifiably upset if they were to be met at the Barcelona airport by a wizard in flowing robes telling them he has unfortunately not been successful, yet, in conjuring up a flight for them, but that he will keep working on it, and would they be so kind as to take a seat and be patient. I might be accused of a sleight of hand at this point: am I not ignoring the utter complexities of many postmodern texts, which contain many more markers than the 'Once upon a time' type? By no means; indeed, postmodern texts furnish probably the strongest proof for my contention: one can only understand and appreciate fragments and collages when one is familiar with the wholes those fragments are taken from, and with the way either the fragments, or the wholes, or both, are played off against each other. There are more and more markers, but they are still supposed to work. One might even take a step further and say they only work among those who are more or less professional readers of texts, since these alone are likely to recognize and appreciate most of the markers in the text.

Similarly, an educated member of any culture in the West will know, after having gone to school and / or university, and after graduating from television, what kind of subject matter can be treated without too many problems, and what kind of subject matter is likely to be more controversial. Murder, for instance, is a safe subject to be treated in any art form in the USA at present. Abortion is not.

Problems in translating are caused at least as much by discrepancies in conceptual and textual grids as by discrepancies in languages. This fact, which may be obscured to some extent in the process of translating between languages that belong to Western cultures (and most thinking and writing on translation, having been done in the West, relies on this kind of translating), becomes blatantly obvious when we are faced with the problem of translating texts from Western to non-Western cultures, and vice versa. A very trivial example that belongs in the domain of the conceptual grid is Kellogg's recent failed attempt to market Corn Flakes for the benefit of the emerging middle class in India. In spite of a big advertising campaign, the product only took off when it was no longer marketed as 'Corn Flakes' but as 'Basmati Flakes'. In terms of the textual grid, the most obvious example of totally unsuccessful translation is that of the Arabic qasidas into any Western language, as I have shown in my *Translation, Rewriting, and the Manipulation of Literary Fame* (Lefevere 1992).

If we want to seriously entertain the hypothesis raised above, we shall have to accept two consequences. One is that both the writer of the original and the translator are faced with the two grids just mentioned, and that both have to come to terms with those grids. Here, much more than on the linguistic level, lies an argument in favour of the creativity of translators: like writers of originals, they too have to find ways of manipulating the grids in such a way that communication becomes not only possible, but interesting and attractive. The second consequence, and this is the one that will concern us for the rest of this chapter, is that the grids, in their interplay, may well determine how reality is constructed for the reader, not just of the translation, but also of the original. This is of extreme importance in the analysis of early texts written by Western cultures about non-Western cultures. My contention is that Western cultures constructed (and construct) non-Western cultures in terms of the two grids whose 'existence' I have postulated earlier. In short, Western cultures 'translated' (and 'translate') non-Western cultures into Western categories to be able to come to an understanding of them and, therefore, to come to terms with them. This brings us, of course, straight to the most important problem in all translating and in all attempts at cross-cultural understanding: can culture A ever really understand culture B on that culture's (i.e. B's) own terms? Or do the grids always define the ways in which cultures will be able to understand each other? Are the grids, to put it in terms that may well be too strong, the prerequisite for all understanding or not?

My answer is that they need not be, but that a great deal of work has to be done if they are not to be. The most pressing task ahead, as I see it, is the gradual elimination, in translating between cultures, of the category of *analogy*, as pernicious as it is, initially, necessary. When we no longer translate Chinese T'ang poetry 'as if' it were Imagist blank verse, which it manifestly is not, we shall be able to begin to understand T'ang poetry on its own terms. This means, however, that we shall have to tell the readers of our translations what T'ang poetry is really like, by means of introductions, the detailed analysis of selected texts, and such. We shall, therefore, have to learn to skip the leap we often call 'of the imagination' but which could be much more aptly called 'of imperialism'. The question is whether Western cultures are ready for this. Nor should the blame be laid on Western cultures only: Chinese translating of Western texts in the nineteenth century only stopped using analogy as the central and self-evident category when the power structure of the Empire, and with it the exclusive use of classical Chinese among literati, came crashing down.

It is obvious from the above that a huge investment in re-education/re-socialization is needed if we are ever to arrive at the goal of understanding other cultures 'on their own terms', and that this investment is not going to be made all that willingly by the present socialization process. It is equally obvious that this investment will exceed by far the compass of the number of pages allotted to this chapter. Rather than lose myself in vague exhortations and pious platitudes I shall therefore try to demonstrate 'my' grids in action, not in terms of translating on the linguistic level, but in terms of translating on the level of both the conceptual and the textual grids. I shall try to show, in sum, how three different Dutch texts dealing with what the Dutch called 'India' ('their' India, as opposed to the one that 'belonged' to the British), and which is now called Indonesia, construct, or rather 'compose', that 'India' for the Dutch reader.

The three texts are, in chronological order, first, *Batavia*, by Jan de Marre, published in Amsterdam in 1740. The text type in this case is the epic, and the conceptual grid is decidedly and self-evidently not only pro-Dutch, but also very much in favour of the Dutch East Indies Company, the 'Vereenigde Oostindische Compagnie', or 'VOC', as it was and is known in Dutch, and which is, often affectionately, called 'Maatschappij' (almost something like 'the firm') in the text, not least because that way it rhymes effortlessly with 'koopvaardij', or 'commerce', being the activity that provided the writer with the leisure to compose his epic in the first

Title	Location
791.436 15+277	
801.2 +433	
301.22 A823	

place. The second text is *Agon, Sultan van [of] Bantam*, by Onno Zwier van Haren, published in Leeuwarden (Frisia) in 1769. Here the text type is neo-classical drama, complete with five acts and the closest Dutch can come to alexandrines. The conceptual grid is more or less the reverse of de Marre's: the whole plot is told from the point of view of the 'natives', not the Dutch, who are identified with what de Marre would lovingly call the 'Maatschappij'. The third text is *Lotgevallen en vroegere zeereizen van Jacob Haafner* [Jacob Haafner's Adventures and Early Travels by Sea], edited and published by his son, C.M. Haafner, in Amsterdam in 1820. Here the text type is the first-person narrative of discovery, and the conceptual grid is also anti-Dutch, more virulently so than in *Agon*, not least, I suggest, because Haafner does not have to observe any kind of neo-classical decorum, nor does his diction have to be lofty and his characters heroic and virtuous. If, as he did, you want to expose the vices, the folly, and the corruption of Dutch colonization in the East Indies, the first-person narrative of discovery may well, indeed, be the text type that will serve you best.

Let us start with Jan de Marre's *Batavia*, an example which, as is often the case in the writings of those who propose a new hypothesis, 'proves' that hypothesis almost to perfection, and which should therefore be approached with some caution by the reader. In his 'Toewying', or 'Dedication', de Marre begs the reader's pardon in the following terms: 'Should you discover something ['aught' would be a more contemporary translation] in my Singster's nature / That is wild to your decorous ears / Remember that she was born on a keel.' (n.p.). It transpires that de Marre was a merchant trader, who wanted to write a description of 'India'. This description, which he calls a 'eulogy', was, he tells us in his Preface, 'composed in my artlessness, since before that time I had read little poetry, and even less dedicated myself to that pastime' (p. 2). As a result, his eulogy initially 'then consisted of few pages' (p. 2). Yet it came 'under the eye of famous poets, who thought they found something in same' (p. 3). As a result, de Marre resolved 'to decorate the work with inventions, the soul of poetry, and to augment it with a story of wars, of the founding, the commerce, and the navigation of the city' (p. 3). To do so as best he could, he sought 'the judgment of famous people, and masters in the art of poetry' (p. 4). He is probably referring to members of the then thriving 'dichtgenootschappen' or 'writers' societies', the successors to the late medieval and Renaissance 'rederijkerskamers', the Dutch equivalent of the 'master

singers', which dominated literary production in the Dutch Republic
in the eighteenth century and exerted an influence so conservative
that it may rightly be called stifling. De Marre succeeded so well in
'seeking their advice, following the example of the most decorous
poets' (p. 4) that he feels obliged to offer the reader two cryptic
apologies: 'But it will appear even stranger that I praise the City of
Commerce to such an extent, as if nothing could be compared to
it, because incoming news bears witness of its unhealthy air, its dry
and stinking canals, the decay of its buildings, and its depopulation
as the result of much dying' (p. 5). This description, incidentally,
reads very much like Haafner's: 'This city, with its lethal and poiso-
nous emissions – built in a foolish way, after the custom dominant
in Holland, with canals that, dried out by the heat of the sun, have
become puddles of mud, yield a terrible stench every day, and
produce devastating fevers' (p. 105). De Marre adds in his defence:
'that accidents do not obliterate the essence of things, and I walked
the city in its splendour' (p. 5). In other words, if reality does not
fit the textual grid, change reality until it fits the grid. Similarly, de
Marre 'took the liberty, where needed, to write the names of Indian
places as they are pronounced according to custom, and are best
known, so as not to cause any ambiguity, and because they all,
according to the nature of the Indian language, did not flow well
in verse' (p. 8). De Marre's second apology concerns the use of
notes, which are needed 'to expand on some things that would not
have flown well in verse, or would have made same too boring'
(p. 6). In other words, if reality refuses to fit the textual grid, supplement that textual grid by another, though in moderation. A very
revealing example is the description of 'Onrust' [Unrest] on p. 223.
First the text:

> There lies our Onrust, that with so many delights
> Spreads the morning's shadows on the level of the waters.
> Behold how glorious it shines in power,
> As it guards our shore with a hundred Argus eyes,
> Forestalls the cunning of an evil neighbour,
> Or in war's frenzy, thundering from its wall,
> Protects the land's carpentry wharf, the keels inviolate.

Then the note: ' "Onrust", a small island and fortress, two miles to
the West of Batavia, where the Maatschappij has its big carpentry
wharf and many warehouses'.

The East Indies Company (henceforth the 'Maatschappij') is the central character in the epic. In the best tradition, she is mentioned in the second line of Book I, so that there can be no doubt as to the subject matter of the epic, and then invoked again a few lines later, on p. 2 of the text: 'Oh Maatschappij, in spite of the enemy's jealous eyes / Seated so firmly on the pinnacle of happiness'. Half-way through the epic, the Maatschappij returns as the muse: 'Oh Maatschappij! who has heard us so graciously! / Let me lift my tones in a new mood / To depict your city true to life in my painting' (p. 155). Since de Marre's text is an epic, mythological references are not lacking (the god Bacchus is mentioned on p. 4), nor are references to ancient history (on pp. 4–5 early voyagers to the East or their patrons are listed: Ninus, Semiramis, Sesostris, Hieram, Alexander the Great and Ptolemy Philadelphus), or classical allusions (on p. 126 Van den Broeck, one of the 'heroes' of the Maatschappij, is likened to the Roman general Regulus, who was also captured and tortured by the enemy, but remained steadfast and refused to betray his countrymen. Similarly, on p. 239, the 'Batavier', or inhabitant of Batavia, who goes for an afternoon outing in the country, is metamorphosed into Lysias: 'Love here plays its part, the tall tamarind trees / And dark shadows please Lysias, / Where he makes his beauty lie down on the shore of the lake').

De Marre makes frequent use of the most obvious epic tool to change a topic, or a scene, or both: visions and dreams abound in the six books of his *Batavia*. First, on p. 17, the 'Koopvaardij' [Commerce] appears to a gathering of Dutch merchants, to prophesy a glorious future and to announce the imminent birth of the Maatschappij (p. 20), to which the Koopvaardij 'completely unexpectedly' (*sic*, p. 23) gives birth three pages later. Needless to say, to continue the allegory, the Koopvaardij sends out the Maatschappij to the East on p. 28. Similarly, the whole of Book III is one long vision, in which Jan Pieterszoon Koen, arguably the most important of the early governors general dispatched to India by the Maatschappij, tells its history in the East to the author, who is taking his siesta, exhausted after a morning walk through Batavia. Within that vision a Malay priest has another vision and prophesies the coming of Islam (pp. 110–12). To round off the historical dimension, a fair part of Book VI (pp. 278–305) is devoted to the history of the Maatschappij's unlucky counterpart, the 'West Indische Compagnie (WIC)', who never even approached its/her 'sister's' wealth and glory after an unsuccessful attempt at establishing itself in Brazil. Allegory also reappears with Fight and Discord, who incite the Indian rulers to attack the Maatschappij (p. 108). Envy and Discord, on the other hand, are made responsible for the débâcle of the West Indische Maatschappij in Brazil.

Other stock epic elements in *Batavia* are the obligatory praises of tea (p. 56), coffee (pp. 57–9) and even opium (pp. 71–2): 'But when, o salutary juice, through your so miraculous power / Sickness flees; when you soften the starkest pain'. Not surprisingly, de Marre has also peppered his epic with the requisite Homeric similes, although most of them appear to be concentrated in Book III. There is the simile of the lion (twice: pp. 96 and 120), of the peasant (twice: pp. 114 and 278), of the sailor (twice: pp. 118 and 134), of the sea itself (p. 124), lightning (p. 130), the doe (p. 134), the evil-doer (p. 140) and the tiger (p. 148). Stock epic features also appear in the 'allocutions', mostly addressed to the enemies of the Maatschappij and designed to make them give up their wicked ways (pp. 148 and 206) and, perhaps most obviously, in the 'epitheta ornantia' such as 'the East rich in spices' (as on p. 143), the 'countries rich in cloves' (also as on p. 143), 'the all-restoring East' (as on p. 270). The sea is often either 'the never resting salt' (as on 267) or 'the busy salt' (as on p. 209), and the Western parts of Dutch India are referred to as 'the pepper-bearing West' (as on p. 216). Next to the epitheta, de Marre also makes use of epic clichés: the sea is, of course, always 'ploughed' (as on p. 165), and those ships are attacked in battle by 'the fury of iron thunderballs' (as on p. 271). In this case it is worth also citing the original Dutch, 'het woên der ijzren donderkloten', because of the shift in semantic connotation the word 'kloot' has acquired between de Marre's time and ours. That shift has restricted the word to a merely sexual connotation (as in the English 'balls'), which it did not have for de Marre. For those able to read *Batavia* in Dutch, this dates the text more than could ever be rendered in any English translation.

De Marre's use of the epic arsenal is most enlightening when he runs his variations on epic 'topoi'. Obviously, his own epic will outlast time (pp. 156–9), he makes the obligatory nod to 'Maro en Homeer' (p. 229), sings the praises of the happy peasant, who is not weighed down by the cares of state (p. 309–10), and tells Batavia's potential rivals, such as 'Dantzich' (p. 163) and Lemnos (p. 171), where Vulcan/Hephaistos had his smithy in the mythology of antiquity, to 'be silent'.

De Marre's *Batavia* becomes most interesting for our present purposes when its author gets carried away by a stock topos, and pursues it to the extent where it begins to conflict with the general tenor of his epic. This happens on p. 176, among other pages, when the 'vanitas' topos leads to the following diatribe: 'What do you gain, oh fool, after struggling through these miseries? / Nothing ['naught'] but a body labouring under the yoke of illnesses, / A soul as wild as the wet you have ploughed; / A handful of gold, a status everybody will disdain'. This is the side of the Maatschappij we find most obviously documented in Haafner, and to some extent also in van Haren. It is obvious that an epic constructed around the Maatschappij, and in which the Maatschappij functions as the muse, could hardly go much further in its criticism than in the passage just quoted and still maintain a claim to logic and unity. Again, the text type makes impossible for one writer what it allows the other two.

Before we leave the epic as text type behind, it is worth mentioning de Marre's obligatory descriptions of a storm (p. 90), a 'burning mountain' or volcano (p. 100), a naval battle (p. 116) and a shipwreck (p. 174). The storm is most interesting for our purposes, especially if we contrast de Marre's description with that of Haafner. In de Marre's storm the 'vloteling', most likely a neologism denoting a 'denizen of the fleet', remains conscious of epic decorum throughout: 'In such a misery floats the 'vloteling', whose eyes / Trembling, look up to the arches of the skies / Moved themselves, and stare at the fury of the clouds until the light / Laughs on him, and appears with a happier face' (p. 90). Haafner's sailors behave more in keeping with the adventure story, and therefore also with what we may assume to have been closer to reality. His description ends as follows: 'This terrible storm had lasted for eight days and cost us eleven members of our crew, both because of the falling of the masts, the breaking down of the pumps, and the heavy seas that had thrown a few men, as well as our cattle, overboard; the most part of the crew that was left over, which had not had a moment of rest all this time, now suddenly became ill because of tiredness and the suffering they had undergone' (p. 65).

But let us now turn to the conceptual grid, the composition of the reality of Dutch India as influenced by the textual grid. On p. 46, de Marre gives the plot of van Haren's *Agon*, but from the Dutch, not the Bantam side:

Now your heroic host sets forth for Bantam's proud walls,
Where the old ruler, strengthened by secret evil-doers,

Discord-sowing flatterers, and traitors to his son,
Tries to come again in the possession of his abandoned throne.
What's this? You strengthen the son with well-manned keels,
Chase away the mutineer who wants to destroy all of Bantam,
Make safe, through the courage of heroes, at the same time,
Your commerce, people, and throne, the prince
    and the kingdom.

In his play, van Haren tells the same story from the point of view of Agon, the old sultan of Bantam, who is about to abdicate in favour of his two sons, Abdul and Hassan. It becomes obvious that Abdul, who does not want to see the kingdom divided, but wants to become its sole inheritor, is in league with the Maatschappij against his brother and his father. The latter two fight the fleet the Maatschappij has sent against them with great heroism, but fail to overcome it, not least because Abdul intervenes with his troops on the side of the Maatschappij, against his father and his brother. As the play ends, Abdul will be king, but Bantam's freedom will be lost.

The theme of intrigue and treason, for or against the Maatschappij, for or against the rulers, is prominent in both de Marre and van Haren, and has obviously shaped the Dutch perception of the 'natives' by the time Haafner's son publishes his father's early adventures. The dangers to the Maatschappij's rule are stereotyped in *Batavia* (p. 33) as follows:

These are not Iberians, who mean you harm;
No, these are your friends, who intrigue for your ruin:
I hear the cry of anguish that rustles through Java's forests:
I see evil Christians, with the sword in their fists,
Marching up to your inheritance: I see the cunning
    Bantam flattering
To lead you into the snare, under the guise of help.

The Maatschappij is, therefore, constantly the target of attacks by both Christians – the Iberians, who stand for the Spaniards and the Portuguese (also called the Lusitanians), and later the English – and by pagans, among whom the Bantamese appear to occupy the most prominent position. It is interesting to note, in this respect, that de Marre sees the Dutch colonial adventures in Holland, to some extent, as the logical conclusion of the Dutch War of Independence

against Spain, an interesting parallel to the post-World War II situation, when most of the Dutch thought that the liberation of Holland
from Nazi occupation would find its logical conclusion in the re-
occupation of Indonesia by Dutch troops.

It is no coincidence that the allegorical figure most in evidence
in *Batavia* is Discord. The Dutch use it to divide the Indonesian
rulers, and the British and the Portuguese use it against the Dutch.
The rule of thumb seems to be that if it is 'our' discord, meaning
discord that leads to a favourable outcome for the Dutch, it is all
right; if it is 'their' discord, on the other hand, it is reprehensible.
De Marre can, therefore, describe the Portuguese in terms immediately reminiscent of the Dutch, without being in the least conscious
of the fact that his description might easily be turned against him.
This is how he describes the operations of the Portuguese in
India (p. 8):

> O glorious Indus! how you did [didst thou] curse the hour
> In which a people sick for gold first discovered your shores,
> And, in the guise of help, brought about your destruction,
> Divided your kings, to achieve, by evil cunning,
> Victory in their mutual discord.

Van Haren's Agon, on the other hand, sees through the cycle. He
tells his adopted daughter Fathema: 'This might of Holland, now
so to be feared by us / I have known before in the hand of the
Portuguese' (p. 235b). He goes on to say that Portugal 'quickly saw
the East diminish its power / As soon as riches had brought luxury
and rest' (p. 235b), and laments that his fellow rulers do not see the
opportunity this affords them: 'But the East, more intent to avenge
itself on them / Than to break through Europe's discord Europe's
might, / Instead of becoming free, as before / Just bought a new
Lord for more blood' (p. 236a). He predicts the fall of the Dutch
in a never-ending cycle, but one that will not bring any advantage
to the peoples of Asia themselves: 'Batavia already sees its walls
weakening, / Because of a bastardized offspring, that will also fall
quickly / When another Nordic brood comes from the West again'
(p. 236b). The allusion is to the British, and both the British and
the Portuguese are the ghostly 'others' all through *Batavia*. The
Portuguese are the example not to follow; the British are the future
to be feared. Interestingly, Agon, the prototype of the wise ruler in
the neo-classical drama of Europe, also understands that the Asians

cannot do to the Europeans what the Europeans do to them. When his younger son Hassan suggests (p. 243b):

> We have the French here, the British, and the Danes,
> Who outwardly always seemed to act in your interest,
> Although all Christians are as hot to plunder.
> People say they are attached to law and superstition;
> Maybe if we gave them a place here
> To live free according to their law and rituals,
> Or offered trade to one people only . . .

Agon answers (p. 243b):

> None of them can withstand Holland here,
> And help from their hands, even if they freed us,
> Would bring us into their power and would not cost less.
> Their friendship is always the price of the highest bid,
> And money only is the Europeans' God.

Whereas the Maatschappij is rightly afraid of the British, it knows how to deal with the 'native' rulers: its troops 'Hurl lightning on the shore and tear, for its punishment / Strong Joepandan off its foundations, / And found, on the rubble of those toppled walls / A fortress that will brave their spite, nay, the centuries' (p. 45). Here is the same event, seen through Fathemah's eyes in *Agon*: 'Macassar's throne in the dust through Holland's proud power, / And the rice field of the East smothered in its own blood!/Samboepo itself in flames' (p. 237b). Fathemah goes on to say that her mother lost her life when 'Samboepo', which corresponds to de Marre's 'Joepandan', fell. The text type of the neo-classical tragedy allows for multiple points of view to be heard, whereas in the epic the reader is always limited to the epic poet's voice. Consequently, van Haren is able to paint a picture of the Dutch in their India which contains many more nuances and talks about the 'natives' in much more positive ways than de Marre's. Haafner, too, has something to say about Macassar, the country whose capital city is Samboepo. He states (p. 123) that the

> natives' resentment is fired by the dethroning of their lawful princes, on the flimsiest pretexts, and the filling of the throne with Bouginian chiefs. They send such dethroned princes to

Batavia, where the High Council, simply on an accusation, or
even a statement by the governor, condemns them to languish
away the rest of their lives at the Cape, on Robben Island, or
else, in exile. In the meantime the governor of Macassar finds
his due by means of the recommendation he gives this one or
that for the vacant throne, for which he has his hands richly
filled and also stipulates special privileges for himself.

But if the Portuguese are no longer a threat, though the British
remain so, the greatest threat is that of 'going native', of 'luxury
and rest' that, presumably, threaten the moral fibre of the Dutch,
as they have, supposedly, threatened that of so many other nations.
De Marre describes it as follows (p. 204):

> Where no native cloth fits the people's limbs any more,
> But inheritance and goods are spent on foreign state,
> Where it sorely destroys itself through all that dalliance,
> And, without scruple, scorns the customs of its fathers,
> Whose frugality founded the state, which shortly
> Will see itself thrown into perdition through so much luxury.

Haafner (p. 114) waxes more graphic, since the confines of his text
type allow him to do so:

> especially dissipation with loose women, of which there are
> many in the Kampon-Java or Javanese Kassies, deprive many
> Europeans of their lives. And those who are fortunate enough
> to recover from the illnesses endemic to the country, or from
> the results of their dissipation, lead a languid life at best. You
> see the greater part of the Europeans, pale as ghosts, with fat,
> swollen bellies and thin legs, slink away with an expression of
> annoyance and sadness on their faces, in spite of their often
> unnamable riches.

Van Haren's Agon, the mouthpiece of the enlightened 'native' ruler,
sees 'going native' as the eventual answer to all his problems
(p. 235b):

> Your well-being, that of my sons, and of their kingdoms
> Requires that we should retreat a short time
>   before time and fate,

Until the Batavian, divided in his own bosom,
Made effeminate by the hot climate, and drunk by luxury,
Sees the urges of the East float among the Dutch,
And Europe's vices intertwined with ours.
Then our vengeance nears.

If 'going native' is the worst that can happen to the Maatschappij,
at least from de Marre's point of view, it follows that the 'natives'
will be painted in the worst possible light in *Batavia*. All 'natives' are
'A people, for which the fields weep at its laziness, / Given to murder
in their wrath, full of dissimulation, / Cowardly in their disaster,
reckless in good times' (p. 40), but, in keeping with the dangers of
'going native', the mestizos, who are, of course, living proof of this,
are the worst, and the foreigner is given explicit warnings against
them (pp. 68–9):

The courageous mestizo walks along these streets,
And beckons, and looks around with eyes full of
    seductive dalliance,
To see if a wanderer would be moved by this glory
To throw himself away, foolishly, on this made-up venom.
But beware, foreigner! it would be lethal for you:
The evil Venus who may now please your soul,
Shall send you all too bitterly into a marsh of calamities,
And you, who in a short while will be the world's
    laughing stock,
Will soon see the folly of this cursed pleasure.

Yet even if these warnings may help to keep the Dutch out of dissi-
pation, the lifestyle of the Dutch in Batavia would definitely be
frowned upon in Amsterdam (p. 110):

The morning alone is intended for the transaction of their business; after eating they hold the siesta or afternoon sleep, and
they spend the evening enjoying themselves. As soon as they
come home from doing their business, they throw off their coats
and take off their wigs, since nobody except sailors and soldiers
wears his own hair, because of the heat and the sultriness, but
they all have their heads shaved, which is definitely quite a bit
cooler. And so in undress, only in a vest and trousers of black
satin, and their heads covered with a cotton nightcap, you see

them walking in the afternoon along the streets or in front of
their houses; even when they go to pay a visit they will hardly
put on a hat.

This description is certainly a far cry from what de Marre claims
the good citizens of Batavia are like (p. 308):

> When the city's dwellings give off a big shadow,
> The dew drips like pearls on avenues of tamarind trees,
> Under which the people cools its desire for generous
>   friendship,
> Washes the dust of the roads from its hot liver,
> Prepares the evening meal in the pavilion above the water,
> Marries the sound of the shrill fiddle to happy laughter,
> And, never fearing the gaze of evil tongues,
> Contented, looks at the face of the morning sun to come.

Haafner further maintains that it is Dutch rule that has made the
'natives' into what the Dutch – at least in *Batavia* – perceive them
to be (p. 107):

> As long as these acts of violence and mistreatment that cry to
> heaven are not reined in, you must not hope that the wretched
> creatures who labour under your iron sceptre will fear death or
> the torments with which you render it more heavy; rather they
> look on it as the end of their suffering, and rightly so, and,
> thinking of their imminent liberation, they undergo the most
> cruel pains with an incredible steadfastness, without allowing a
> sigh to escape or even to show pain in any feature of their faces.

Perhaps the most telling opposition between *Batavia* and Haafner's
Lotgevallen is to be found in the description of the Malay custom of
'amok'. Here, first, is de Marre (pp. 71–2):

> When you [opium] help the mutineer's vengeful heart
>   to fury,
> Incite the evil-doer to a horrible evil deed,
> Where he runs out of his senses, and murders along
>   market and street,
> Or shouts Amok! Amok! in blood-curdling tones;
> Then you are full of danger for those who live in the town.

Now for Haafner (p. 107):

> One should not imagine, as so many travellers and white inhab-
> itants pretend, that these creatures who have been plagued so
> much shout amok for every little thing and give themselves up
> to certain death – Oh no! Only after the most steadfast and
> often the most humiliating torments does he take the decision
> to die, but not unavenged, like the meek Hindu, who bends his
> neck sighing, but without resistance, under the murderous axe;
> he, on the other hand, grips the snaked kris in his fist, and
> captured by the intoxicating power of bang, or opium, he first
> kills his torturer and runs then, his long jet-black hair waving
> wildly around his head, through the streets rich with people.

Finally, van Haren's Agon describes the Dutch as 'natives' from the
Indonesian point of view (p. 233b):

> The Northern European, who leaves the Amstel's shore,
> Keeps his cool soul in this scorched climate;
> His soul, not captured, as ours is, by hot passion,
> Seeks slowly and serenely its essential interests:
> Its cruelty, avarice, its anger itself is cold

and laments that his oldest son, Abdul, has 'gone European',
blaming the fact on one of the Maatschappij's officials who 'Has
taught this young man Europe's customs, / Maybe filled his heart
with its dissipations' (p. 243a).

It is also van Haren's Agon who, in the dialogue of the neo-classical
tragedy that makes it possible to speak of such lofty subjects as history
(which also belong in the epic, but less so, at least at the time, in the
autobiographical tale of adventure), provides the counterpoint to
Book III of de Marre's epic, in which Jan Pieterszoon Koen, it will
be remembered, recounts the glorious history of the Maatschappij.
Agon tells one of the Maatschappij's ambassadors, who has just given
a heavily condensed version of de Marre's third book: 'One could
also, Sir, name on your list / With all your boasting, Formosa,
Moçambique, Macau, / And show how there, in more fights than
one / No victory was affixed to your flag' (p. 249b).

Both Van Haren and Haafner, not surprisingly, state the real
cause of the Maatschappij's superiority in the East. In *Agon* Ibrahim,
the priest, states: 'Europe's knowledge in war is far superior to ours'

(p. 251b); whereas Haafner says in his own voice, or at least in that of his autobiographical persona: 'It is only to their irresistible superior fire power that the Europeans owe their settlements in this and most Indian countries; in courage, power and skill they rank far below the natives' (p. 110).

Van Haren's Agon also reveals the real bottom line of the Maatschappij's operations: 'Expenditures have been made, they also have to be paid. / Their mercantile spirit already counts the gains / Of our slavery, or at least of our money' (p. 243b). Since the mercantile spirit is the mainstay of the Maatschappij, its other main enemy, next to the 'dissolute natives', is corruption or, to put it differently, that its officials begin to increase their own wealth at the expense of the Maatschappij. As long as they increase their personal wealth otherwise than at the Maatschappij's expense, it is content to leave them alone. But the fear of corruption is so great that it is expressed at least five times in *Batavia*, on pp. 152 (by none other than the legendary Jan Pieterszoon Koen), 165, 182–3, 192 and 246. The fear of corruption is so great because it links up with the other fear, that of the 'natives', as stated in the form of an 'epic allocution' on pp. 182–3:

> But you, who shamelessly go against the laws,
> And live far too bitter with the natives of the land,
> Hold them in bondage, and want to flay the skin off
>   their bodies,
> To increase your riches through their poverty,
> You yourselves are the cause of the rebellion of
>   the common folk,
> You give birth to this mutiny, and to the city's fall with it.
> Can your conscience still bear such a gnawing
> When you want to risk everything because of your greed,
> And dare to involve yourself, the city, and so many souls,
> Yes the state and the Maatschappij in this evil with such
>   bad intent?

Finally, the fear of corruption also links up with the fear of the Portuguese, or rather, with the fear of the bad example the Portuguese had set and the Dutch are now about to follow, against the better advice of their leaders: 'Through such an evil did the Lusitanian see his fall, / Where he cruelly oppressed the peoples of the land, / When right and justice were everywhere moved aside in favour of greed' (p. 183). As was to be expected, Haafner is more matter of fact about this corruption. He states that the members of the High Council of the Dutch Indies 'have mostly achieved this rank by means of the lowest corruption and by the money they have extorted from the poor Indians in their former, subordinate positions' (p. 117). He also describes in detail the custom of the yearly visit the governor of Amboina pays to all locations on the island. During that visit, the governor appoints 'native' officials, or 'orangcayas', everywhere, who are responsible for the yearly tribute. Haafner goes on to say (p. 121):

> If one such Indian chief, who has not applied for this hateful position, nor desires it, might refuse to fulfil the governor's wishes, his fate is terrible – a certain governor of Amboina once had one of these unfortunate men, and for that reason, tied before the mouth of a cannon and he had the cannon fired subsequently – It is true that nobody hinders the orangcayas from making up their loss by oppressing their black subjects, but they are too much of stupid pagans still to want to oppress the people of their own country and their subjects and to reduce them to hunger and destitution.

No wonder Haafner looks forward to the end of the rule of the Maatschappij, which he imagines near: 'the most recent war with the British has already given it a terrible blow, and without the French, even though they have their own special interests at heart, we would no longer possess as much as one thumb's breadth of soil in the East Indies' (p. 127). That was published in 1820. In 1769, on the other hand, Agon dies at the end of van Haren's play, and the audience is told that his youngest son, Hassan, has also died in battle. Abdul, the eldest son, does what all rulers had to do eventually: reach some kind of accommodation with the Maatschappij: 'In the wary East nobody is free any more, / And everybody intent on soft rule. / Batavia's fortress has made everything give way / And it is no longer a shame to retreat before Holland' (p. 239b) – a sad judgement on rulers who are reduced to this state of affairs because, in the words Agon speaks at his abdication: 'The Batavian who seeks to subjugate the whole of the East, / Free in Holland, will not allow freedom here' (p. 242a), even though de Marre writes that the 'Batavian fleet' found 'the means to deliver the spicy Moluccas / Yes, the whole East from tyranny' (p. 14). But that was the tyranny of the Portuguese.

I trust the point I wanted to make has been made by now. In conclusion I would like to add a few observations as well as a few disclaimers. It is obviously not my intention to claim that it is the epic that made de Marre into a colonialist, any more than that it is the story of personal adventure that made Haafner into an anti-colonialist. They had obviously both taken up those conceptual positions before they began to write what they wrote. It is my contention, though, that de Marre's decision, at a time when genres were viewed in a strictly hierarchical order, to write an epic about the Maatschappij reflects his admiration for that Maatschappij. He must have felt that only the epic could do it justice. And once he casts the Maatschappij as the heroine of his epic, she can do no wrong; she will go under, if at all, because of her own failings, as described and warned against in the epic. In the meantime, though, all her actions are to be praised and supported. It follows that if the Maatschappij is to be the pure heroine of the epic, all those who dare stand against her have to be the villains of that same epic even if they are, as is so often the case, merely acting in self-defence.

By opting for neo-classical tragedy (then rated second, or first *ex aequo* in the hierarchy of genres), van Haren was able to open a philosophical debate about the role of the Dutch and the Maatschappij in the East Indies. The genre gave him the opportunity to use different mouthpieces for different philosophical and political positions. Obviously his conceptual grid was not unthinkingly and adoringly pro-Maatschappij and pro-Dutch. He knew what he was talking about, even though he had never been to the East Indies, and he had his own axe to grind. He had been one of the leading statesmen of the Dutch Republic, who must have been privy to decisions made on the highest level, affecting the Maatschappij and the country as a whole, and he was brought low by an accusation of incest with two of his daughters. That accusation, never proved or disproved, banished him from public life and made him take up a second career as a writer. It remains – to anticipate criticism that is not entirely without ground – to analyse to what extent the operation of the two grids I have postulated can be more easily detected and dissected in a historical period in which literature was still first and foremost a craft, one that statesmen could learn in disgrace and merchants in retirement, and not an activity inspired by the muse, laudanum, or both, to be engaged in only by those 'called' to it, preferably with their eyes in some fine frenzy rolling.

Finally, the genre Haafner chooses to relate his *Adventures* gives him ample scope to reveal the feet of clay on which the Maatschappij walks in the East Indies. Because he is not bound to lofty tone and diction, he is able to furnish moving descriptions and incisive comments that reveal, perhaps more than anything else, the folly of the colonial endeavour, Dutch or otherwise. We have discussed three writers who composed the same reality, constrained by three different conceptual and textual grids. I hope the part played by those grids has become abundantly clear.

References

Haafner, J. 'Lotgevallen en vroegere zeereizen van Jacob Haafner', ed. C.M. Haafner (Amsterdam, 1820). Repr. in *De Werken van Jacob Haafner*, vol. 1, ed. J.A. de Moor and P.G.E.I.J. van der Velde (Zutphen: De Walburg Pers, 1992) pp. 41–160.

Haren, O.Z. van. 'Agon, Sultan van Bantam', *Leven en werken van W. en O.Z. van Haren*, ed. J. van Vloten (Deventer: A ter Gunne, 1874) pp. 232–55.

Lefevere, A. *Translation, Rewriting, and the Manipulation of Literary Fame* (London and New York: Routledge, 1992).

Marre, J. de. *Batavia* (Amsterdam: Adriaan Wor en de Erve G. onder de Linden, 1740).

Chapter 5

Liberating Calibans

Readings of *Antropofagia* and Haroldo de Campos' poetics of transcreation

Else Ribeiro Pires Vieira

> Creative translation . . . this parricidal dis-memory
> (Haroldo de Campos 1981a: 209)

> Translation as transfusion. Of blood. Ironically, we could talk of vampirization, thinking now of the translator's nourishment.
> (Haroldo de Campos 1981a: 208)

As with any rich offering, satisfaction can be accompanied by surfeit or excess. Such may be the case for the world's digestion of the Brazilian-derived metaphor of anthropophagy.[1] From its avant-garde emergence in the 1920s, within the context of several manifestos presenting alternatives to a still persistent mental colonialism after 100 years of political independence for Brazil, *Antropofagia* has developed into a very specific national experimentalism, a poetics of translation, an ideological operation as well as a critical discourse theorizing the relation between Brazil and external influences, increasingly moving away from essentialist confrontations towards a bilateral appropriation of sources and the contamination of colonial/hegemonic univocality. Disrupting dichotomous views of source and target, *Antropofagia* and its application to translation entails a double dialectical dimension with political ingredients; it unsettles the primacy of origin, recast both as donor and receiver of forms, and advances the role of the receiver as a giver in its own right, further pluralizing (in)fidelity. Yet, in the last few years, throughout the world, outside the setting of its own local cuisine, *Antropofagia* has become a too quickly swallowed body of thought, a word devoured literally and not digested as a complex metaphor undergoing metamorphoses in different contexts and critical perspectives. *Antropofagia*, which, in Haroldo de Campos' view, is a sign of the polyphonic identity of Brazil, rings not a note of furious aggression but rather one of irreverently amorous devouring. Deriving from a non-Eurocentric way of conceiving spiritual force as inseparable from matter, related to the local natives' animism, it ultimately entails a tribute to the other's strength that one wishes to have combined with one's own for greater vitality. While undercutting the plenitude of any origin as the only source of strength, it makes an incision and a conjoining to unite the blood and marrow of the one with the other.

Proceeding with culinary care, this essay follows de Campos' poetics of transcreation from the 1960s to the present, with specific reference to the digestive metaphor in Brazil. We shall discuss the critical discourse on *Antropofagia*, created by de Campos himself and seen to operate in various segments of Brazilian culture which, in different ways, have appropriated and exploited the digestive metaphor. As I contextualize the anthropophagous play of permanence through discontinuity and difference, both in critical discourse and in translation metalanguage, two different moments of enunciation of subaltern subjectivities (*à la* Spivak) will be considered: first in the 1920s with Oswald de Andrade and again from the 1960s to the early 1980s. Referring to the tension between the national identity of a peripheral post-colonial culture and incoming contributions from hegemonic ones, I argue with Johnson that cannibalism, initially an irreverent verbal weapon and a form of resistance in the *Manifesto Antropófago* (Anthropophagous Manifesto) of the 1920s, re-emerges in the 1960s and 1970s as both a metaphor and a philosophy of culture (Johnson 1987: 42). The political dimension of *Antropofagia* will be seen to have been broached by de Campos, among others, in his view of nationalism 'as a dialogical movement of difference . . . the rupture instead of the linear course; historiography as the seismic graph of fragmentation, rather than the tautological homologation of the homogeneous' (de Campos 1981b English version 1986: 45).[2]

Translation as 'verse making', 'reinvention', a 'project of recreation' (in the 1960s), 'translumination' and 'transparadisation' (stemming from his translation of Dante), as 'transtextualization', as 'transcreation', as 'transluciferation' (stemming from his translation of Goethe's *Faust*), as 'transhelenization' (as from his translation of the *Iliad* of Homer), as 'poetic reorchestration' (from his rendering of the Hebrew Bible into Brazilian Portuguese), as 'reimagination' (from his transcreation of classical Chinese poetry into Portuguese) are but some of the neologisms coined by Haroldo de Campos that offer a vanguardist poetics of translation as textual revitalization while pointing to the Anthropophagic dimension of feeding on the very text he is translating to derive his metalanguage. 'Re' and 'trans' are recurrent prefixes that locate translation at a remove from mono-logical truth in the direction of a transformative recreation of inherited tradition. Translation is further theorized as 'uma desmemória parricida' / 'a parricidal dis-memory' (de Campos 1981a: 209). Arguing with Foucault that 'knowledge is not made for understanding; it is made for cutting' (Foucault 1986: 88), my own anthropophagic hyphenation of 'dis-memory', as I rendered 'desmemória' into English, highlights the dual positionality of de Campos' vanguardist theory of translation in relation to tradition: a hyphen that both separates and unites inasmuch as 'dis-memory' speaks of a translation project which unleashes the epistemological challenge of discontinuity but reunites threads into a new fabric; a translation project which murders the father, means in his absence yet reveres him by creating a continued existence for him in a different corporeality. Also in the space of 'trans' is the notion of 'translation as transfusion of blood' (de Campos 1981a: 208) – a more conspicuously anthropophagic metaphor that moves translation beyond the dichotomy source/target and sites original and translation in a third dimension, where each is both a donor and a receiver – a dual trajectory that, again, points to the specificity of the digestive metaphor in Brazilian culture we shall briefly discuss.

'TUPI OR NOT TUPI, THAT IS THE QUESTION'

Tupi, to be. In the famous line from Oswald de Andrade's *Manifesto Antropófago* of the 1920s, both 'Tupi' and 'to be' read the same, except for a minor phonological change: in 'to be' the bilabial consonant is aspirated and voiced whereas in 'Tupi' it is non-aspirated and voiceless. Such a voicelessness pronounces difference and inscribes a colonial perspective into the Shakespearean intertext and, for that matter, to the Western canon. Since the Tupis were a tribe inhabiting Brazil at the time of the discovery, the colonial dilemma is not one informed by Christian scruples as to what may come after death, but has to do with the duality, plurality of the origin and, accordingly, of the cultural identity of Brazil, both European and Tupi, both civilized and native, both Christian and magic; a culture that grew out of the juxtaposition of not two but many civilizations and which carries to this day the paradox of origin. Tupi, to be: the attempt in the 1920s to discontinue mental colonialism through the desanctifying devouring of the Western legacy.

A further reading of the play operating within 'Tupi or not Tupi' arises not from a minor phonological but from a major theological echo. For the ontological question of the sixteenth-century ecclesiastical debates as to whether the Indian had a soul, and the concomitant Aristotelian-derived debate regarding the permissibility of his or her enslavement, effectively asked whether the colonist or his legislators could or should, either morally or economically, allow the Tupi to be. To be, Tupi – through language, permission for the voicelessness of the Tupi to sound out, allowing difference to disrupt homogeneity.

The devouring of Shakespeare and the revitalization of Hamlet's dilemma in the *Manifesto* points to the assimilative perspective of cannibalism both as a programme and as a praxis: foreign input, far from being denied, is absorbed and transformed, which brings cannibalism and the dialogical principle close together. However, it stands to reason that Oswald de Andrade's dialogism has political imports for Brazil, because the denial of univocality means assertion of the Brazilian polyphonic and pluricultural space and, ultimately, liberation from mental colonialism.

Cannibalism is a metaphor actually drawn from the natives' ritual whereby feeding from someone or drinking someone's blood, as they did to their totemic 'tapir', was a means of absorbing the other's strength, a pointer to the very project of the Anthropophagy group: not to deny foreign influences or nourishment, but to absorb and transform them by the addition of autochthonous input. Initially using the metaphor as an irreverent verbal weapon, the *Manifesto Antropófago* stresses the repressive nature of colonialism; Brazil had been traumatized by colonial repression and conditioning, the paradigm of which is the suppression of the original anthropophagical ritual by the Jesuits, so 'the cure is to use that which was originally repressed – cannibalism – as a weapon against historically repressive society' (Nunes in Johnson 1987: 51).

The awareness of Europe's debt to the New World pervades the *Antropofagia* in Oswald de Andrade's *Manifesto*. In the overt attempt at freeing Brazilian culture from mental colonialism, the *Manifesto* redirects the flow of Eurocentric historiography. The New World, by means of the permanent 'Caraíba' revolution, becomes the source of revolutions and changes; the Old World is pronounced indebted to the New World because without it 'Europe would not even have its poor declaration of the rights of man'. Again, through a reading of history from a reverse angle, the Christian missionaries who are traditionally said to have gone to Brazil to save the population are recast in the *Manifesto* as runaways from a civilization Brazilians are now, in turn, dissecting. The reversal of history culminates in the date of composition of the *Manifesto*. Contradicting both the Christian calendar and orthodox historiography that sets the year 1500 as the discovery *and* origin of Brazil, Oswald de Andrade's *Manifesto* is dated in the 374th year of the ritual devouring of a Portuguese bishop which, metaphorically, marks the synthesis of the European and autochthonous elements, signposting the emergence of Brazilian culture.

ANTROPOFAGIA REVISITED

Having briefly demonstrated how the digestive metaphor was initially used in Oswald de Andrade's *Manifesto* of the 1920s irreverently to present a non-Eurocentric historiography, I now move from what Spivak calls 'strategic essentialism' to a brief survey of the more recent revitalization of the digestive metaphor in the 1960s and 1970s. A web of narratives and social reports will be shown to theorize metaphorically the tension between world culture and the identity of a peripheral national literature within the complex interplay of neo-colonialism and transnationalization in the Third World, a term that came to be applied to post-colonial countries and which brought a heightened awareness of hierarchy and underdevelopment. Segments of Brazilian cultural production, including literature, cinema, popular music and the discourse of criticism might be seen as having incorporated such new sensitivities, at times returning to the view of a non-contaminated culture, at others asserting identity via the appropriation and recycling of the world's cultural objects.

In this context, Johnson's study of the re-emergence and re-evaluation of *Antropofagia*, from which I select three examples, is illuminating in that it includes several forms of rewriting. In 1967, Oswald de Andrade's play *O Rei da Vela*, a virulent critique of capitalism, economic dependency and authoritarianism, was staged and recreated, among other things, as a radical critique of the economic and political model imposed by the regime following the 1964

Revolution. Two years later, Joaquim Pedro de Andrade adapted *Macunaíma, a* novel of the 1920s associated with *Antropofagia*, into a film, where the image of cannibalism is used to criticize Brazil's savage capitalism and the country's relations of dependency on advanced industrial powers. The novel *Galvez, Imperador do Acre* (The Emperor of the Amazon) by Márcio Souza (1976) keeps the anthropophagic attitude and creates an allegory of economic and cultural imperialism. The symbol of the castrating function of colonialism is to be seen in the character of Sir Henry Lust, a British scientist who collects Indians' genital organs (Johnson 1987: 54–5).

The two generations of *Cinema Novo* (Brazilian New Cinema) also reintroduce the discussion on cultural identity and dependence using the digestive metaphor or variations upon it in their examination of the question of Brazil and external influences. As remarked by Hollanda and Gonçalves in their study of the *Cinema Novo*, its first generation, associated with the name of Glauber Rocha, attempted to make decolonized films by deconstructing the dominant American and European models and by defending the thesis named *A Estética da Fome* (The Aesthetics of Hunger). Hunger, Glauber Rocha claims, is the distinctive trait of the social experience of underdeveloped and peripheral countries – so the *Cinema Novo* represented 'Latin hunger' and its cultural manifestation, violence. Underdevelopment is thus the very stuff of *Cinema Novo* (Hollanda and Gonçalves 1989: 44–5).

The second generation of *Cinema Novo*, whose main exponent is Arnaldo Jabor, reflects differently on the relationship between Brazil and what is foreign. Says Jabor:

> From 1965 to 1980 the country changed a lot. Brazil . . . became a country of technological surplus, of contradictions generated by the invasion of the multinationals, a hungry and empty country surrounded by superfluities and pockets of development like São Paulo. We are still hungry, but the situation has changed. I think that the aesthetics of today is that of 'I want to eat'. The aesthetics of . . . the wish to appropriate the [colonizer's] equipment . . . but not one of lament.
>
> (Jabor in Hollanda and Gonçalves 1989: 87)

A parallel development to that of the two generations of *Cinema Novo* is to be seen in Brazilian popular music. In the mid-1960s, when a CIA and multinational-capital-backed dictatorship was established in Brazil, protest singers like Nara Leão held the view that art should be committed and express a political opinion mostly against authoritarianism. Nara Leão's 'mais que nunca é preciso cantar' ('more than ever it is necessary to sing') reveals the tone of mobilization used to elicit an emotional rather than a critical response from the public (Hollanda and Gonçalves 1989: 22–4). Singers also relied heavily on rural music as an expression of a genuine, non-contaminated national culture (Wisnik 1987: 122). Later, *Tropicalismo* (Tropicalism), a segment of Brazilian popular music associated with Caetano Veloso, among others, moves away from the protest song and from the idea of a non-contaminated national culture, theorizing differently the relationship between Brazil and external influences. Arnaldo Jabor stresses that 'The importance of *Tropicalismo* was to say that Brazil is also the calf's foot-jelly, the general jam, the great multinational confusion that was planted here ... *Tropicalismo* made Brazil aware that reality is more complex than the empire versus the colony' (Jabor in Hollanda and Gonçalves 1989: 88). Rather than stressing a non-contaminated national culture, *Tropicalismo* appropriates the cultural forms generated in the international circuit of mass communication. Thus, Brazilian culture emerges as a focus of tensions between the rustic and the industrialized, the acoustic and the electric, the national and the foreign; as such, history emerges as the locus of a complex and unlevelled simultaneity, to use Wisnik's terms (Wisnik 1987: 122). *Tropicalismo*, the critic Santiago adds, takes up the anthropophagic move while decentring the geography of Brazilian culture from the land of the palm trees to London, and displacing the Portuguese–Brazilian linguistic axis to a sort of Esperanto – for example, 'My country has got palm-trees where the Big-Ben chimes' (Santiago 1978: 124). Still according to Santiago, this linguistic salad, evidence of cosmopolitanism, means that the linguistic sign has no nationality and that in this period of the opening up of cultural frontiers all languages are valid (ibid.: 131–2).

The anthropophagous metaphor continues, then, to contaminate Brazilian critical discourse. Santiago further stresses the political implications of the traditional study of sources and influences in Brazil and Latin America which casts the artist in a position of tributary to the flow of another culture. This conventional critical discourse, Santiago goes on, does not differ in the least from neo-colonialist discourse: both talk of insolvent economies. The sources, he specifically claims, become the unreachable star that, without allowing itself to be contaminated, shines for Latin American artists when they depend on its light for their work. The star illumines the movement of the artists' hands, but at the same time subjects them to its superior magnetism; critical discourse based on influences sets the star as the only value. To find the ladder to the star and to contract with them the debt which would minimize the unbearable distance between moral artist and immortal star is, for Santiago, the conventional role of the Latin American artist; a new critical discourse stresses difference, not debt and imitation, as the only critical value. And he concludes that, while submission may be *a* form of behaviour, transgression becomes *the* form of expression (ibid.: 20–7).

HAROLDO DE CAMPOS ON ANTHROPOPHAGY

In this climate of re-evaluation and rereading of the digestive metaphor, Haroldo de Campos himself emerges, from the 1960s, as the creator of a discourse around *Antropofagia* with the publication of *Oswald de Andrade – Trechos escolhidos* (Oswald de Andrade – Selected Passages) (1967) and, in the 1970s, of *Morfologia do Macunaíma* (Morphology of Macunaíma) (1973), writing that moves away from economic dependence as a referent towards a view of *Antropofagia* as a critical, poetic and ideological operation. This section, specifically regarding his critical discourse and his views of translation as criticism associable with *Antropofagia*, focuses on 'Da Tradução como Criação e como Crítica' ('On Translation as Creation and Criticism') (first published in 1963).[3]

In the early 1960s de Campos had started meditating on the possibility of an experimental and avant-garde literature in an underdeveloped culture as a discussion not dissociable from the tension in Latin America between the world's cultural legacy and local specificities (de Campos 1986: 42). The timing, of course, was not accidental. For it was precisely at this juncture that the term 'Third World' was spawned with increasing regularity but decreasing recognition of crucial differentialities. As Cold War tensions climaxed, binary conceptions dominated more than ever, paradoxically highlighting the *space* between West and East but homogenizing the many cultures not incorporable into such easy schemata so that 'Third World' became reified as *one*. Plurality, as a political and cultural possibility, virtually receded in Latin America, for instance, after the

Cuba missile crisis of 1962. And the impact of such reductivities was also felt culturally and artistically.

Tracing the meanders of this path, it is in Octavio Paz that de Campos initially finds an illuminating contention, namely, that the notion of underdevelopment is an offshoot of the culturally reductionist idea of economic progress not readily associable with artistic experience. He thus advances the need to consider the national element in a dialogical relationship with the universal (ibid.: 43–4). Hence his reading of Oswald de Andrade's *Anthropophagy* as follows:

> the thought of critical devouring of the universal cultural heritage, formulated not from the insipid, resigned perspective of the 'noble savage' . . . but from the point of view of the 'bad savage', devourer of whites – the cannibal. The latter view does not involve a submission (an indoctrination), but a transculturation, or, better, a 'transvalorization': a critical view of History as a negative function (in Nietzsche's sense of the term), capable of appropriation and of expropriation, de-hierachization, deconstruction. Any past which is an 'other' for us deserves to be negated. We could say that it deserves to be eaten, devoured. With this clarification and specification: the cannibal was a polemicist (from the Greek polemos, meaning struggle or combat) but he was also an 'anthologist': he devoured only the enemies he considered strong, to take from them the marrow and protein to fortify and renew his own natural energies.
>
> (ibid.: 44)

Opposing the view of an ontological nationalism, which seeks to locate the origin of a national *logos*, considered as a point, he advances a counterpoint, a modal, differential nationalism as a dialogical movement of difference: 'the dis-character, instead of the character, the rupture instead of the linear course; historiography as the seismic graph of fragmentation', involving the novel notion of tradition as a counter to the prestigious canon (ibid.: 45). It is worth noting his 'culinary care' in pointing out a bilateral flow in the digestive metaphor while tracing the manifestation of what he calls modal nationalism to the nineteenth-century Brazilian novelist Machado de Assis: 'The great and unclassifiable Machado, swallower of Sterne and of innumerable others (he gives us the metaphor of the head as a ruminator's stomach, where . . . all suggestions, after being broken down and mixed, are prepared for a new remastication, a complicated chemistry in which it is no longer possible to distinguish the assimilating organism) from these assimilated material '(ibid.: 45).

Refusing the essentialist metaphor of a gradual, harmonious natural evolution associated with the ontological view of nationalism and questioning logocentric questions of origin, de Campos sees literature emerging in colonial Brazil as 'the non-origin', as an obstacle, as 'the non-infancy'. The etymology of *infans* as one who does not speak reverberates in his argument: born adults, Brazilians had to speak the elaborate international rhetorical code of the Baroque, articulated as difference (ibid.: 47). 'A partogenesis without an ontological egg' is his playful contradiction of the legend of the egg of Columbus (ibid.). It is in the Brazilian Baroque, when the 'rule of anthropophagy' develops, deconstructing the logocentrism inherited from the West (ibid.: 49), that he pinpoints the first practitioner of *Anthropophagous* translation, Gregório de Matos, in whose translation of Góngora, he argues, one finds a distinctive sign of alterity in the gaps of a universal code (ibid.: 48). But he claims in the essay 'Translation as Creation and Criticism' (1992: 38) that the first actual theorist of translation, and more specifically of creative translation, is the pre-Romantic Manuel Odorico Mendes. In his translation of the *Odyssey*, Odorico Mendes synthesized 12,106 lines into 9,302, maybe to accommodate in pentameters Homer's hexameters, or to avoid the monotony of transposing the sound effects typical of a language with declensions to an analytical one. He further made up compound words in Portuguese to translate Homer's metaphors; 'anthropophagically', he interpolated lines from other poets such as Camões into Homer (1992: 38–9).

Haroldo de Campos points out that the anti-normative tradition in Brazilian contemporary poetry informs the Concretist movement, which challenges the universal code and appropriates and reclaims the patrimony of a peripheral literature, criticizing and 'chewing over' a poetics (de Campos 1986: 51). With the attempt of São Paulo's Concretist poets of the 1950s (principally the de Campos brothers and Décio Pignatari) to theorize and create a Brazilian poetics, there emerged a continuous translation activity of re/transcreation also linked to Ezra Pound and his view of translation as criticism; while translating the *Cantos* themselves, they nourished on and applied Pound's own criteria for creative translation (1992: 42). A series of translations followed – of e.e. cummings, the German avant-garde, Japanese *haikus*, Dante, Joyce – whose 'fragile and apparently unreachable beauty' had its entrails dissected and revitalized into the body of a foreign language and poetics (1992: 43). The translation of creative texts, de Campos argues, is always recreation or parallel creation, the opposite of a literal translation, but always reciprocal; an operation in which it is not only the meaning that is translated but the sign itself in all its corporeality (sound properties, visual imagetics, all that makes up the iconicity of the aesthetic sign) (1992: 35). With Pound, translation is seen as criticism, insofar as it attempts theoretically to anticipate creation, it chooses, it eliminates repetitions, it organizes knowledge in such a way that the next generation may find only the still living part. Pound's well-known 'Make it new' is thus recast by de Campos as the revitalization of the past via translation (1992: 36).

Having contextualized the discourse on *Antropofagia* associated with Haroldo de Campos himself, as well as his subscription to Pound's view of translation as criticism and recreation, it remains to be seen how he combines these two sources of nourishment to advance his poetics of transcreation and more specifically his view of translation as transtextualization. In the trajectory, Goethe, one who 'carnivalizes Hell and carnalizes Heaven' (de Campos 1997: 29), and Benjamin will be seen to be further presences he anthropophagically absorbs and transforms.

ON 'TRANSPARADISATIONS' AND 'TRANSLUCIFERATIONS'

Heavenly and daemonic. Transculturating the sacred and the diabolic. Irreverent and reverent. Moving beyond essentialist binarisms, Haroldo de Campos *aportuguesa* the Hebrew language and *hebraiza* the Portuguese language. These bilateral movements in his translation of the Hebrew Bible point to the double dialectics that informs *Antropofagia* inasmuch as they highlight the ontological nationalism he had advanced, one that homologizes and, at the same time, inscribes difference in tradition. The Hebrew Bible, he explains, presents a proverbial and aphorismatic style where the solemn and the colloquial intermingle in a markedly poetic form. Subscribing to Benjamin's view that fidelity relates to the signifying form beyond the transmission of a communicative content, he further stresses the resources he used specifically from Brazilian Portuguese. Focusing on the fact that the literary emergence of Brazilian Portuguese occurred during the Baroque, he argues that the transposed language counteracted the constraints of a European and long-standing rationalist tradition, despite all the efforts of the purists; the language was shaken by the subversion of speech, of orality in its several registers, not to mention several lexical inventions; it is a plastic idiom that opens its sounds and its syntax to the fertilizing impact of the foreign language. In order to render the original's interplay of the oracular and the familiar/colloquial whereby the voice of God partakes with that of man, he transtextualizes the Hebrew text into the corresponding existing tradition of the Brazilian writer Guimarães Rosa, as in *Grande Sertão: Veredas* (The Devil to Pay in the Backlands,) or João Cabral de Melo Neto, *Autos* (Plays), who have, in their turn, fed on the popular oral tradition together with innovation and revitalization of the arcane in popular speech (1981b: 31–5).

Transilluminations of Dante's *Paradise* and transorchestrations of the Hebrew Bible coexist with a movement towards a counter-sublime, the daemonization of translation apparent in the 'bad savage's' nourishment from Goethe in the act of translating him. The interweaving of literatures, the coexistence of several discourses, a re-evaluation of the axiology of mimesis, a break with the hierarchy between original and translation, and so on, are elements that are explicitly brought into a synthesis in de Campos' paratext to his translation of *Faustus* (Faust) in 1979 (published in 1981). The title of the work, unlike conventionally translated books, is not *Faustus* but *Deus e o Diabo no Fausto de Goethe* (God and the Devil in Goethe's Faust), which asserts the cannibalistic/dialogical principle from the start, because, for the Brazilian contemporary reader, the nourishment from Glauber Rocha's film *Deus e o Diabo na Terra do Sol* (God and the Devil in the Land of the Sun) is all too obvious. The intertext in the very title suggests that the receiving culture will interweave and transform the original one, which is confirmed later, as we shall see, throughout the exposition of de Campos' translational project. Anyway, from the very title we can say that translation is no longer a one-way flow from the source to the target culture, but a two-way transcultural enterprise. The cover iconography further asserts the autonomy of the translator/recreator while problematizing the question of authorship in translation; the visibility of de Campos' signature on the cover contrasts with Goethe's less conspicuous signature which only appears on the third page. It is also worth highlighting that, at the end of the book, the section 'Works by the Author' actually lists de Campos' work, which suggests the articulation of a space conventionally deemed marginal or even irrelevant as compared to the original author's centrality – that is, stresses the translator's own production.

Moving from the cover iconography to the main bulk of the para-text, in the first section called 'A Escritura Mefistofélica' ('The Mephistophelian *Écriture*'), de Campos presents his concept of 'plagia-tropy', developed as early as 1966. His claim is that Goethe's *Faustus*, the first one, relies a good deal on parody in the etymological mean-ing of 'parallel canto' and, as such, marks a rereading of the Faustian tradition – the intertexts being various, ranging from the Bible to Shakespeare. Goethe is quoted verbatim in his defence of the accusa-tion of plagiarism on the grounds that one can only produce great works by appropriating others' treasures, as also is Pound with the view that great poets pile up all the things they can claim, borrow or steal from their forerunners and contemporaries and light their own light at the top of the mountain (de Campos 1981a: 74).

Plagiotropy, for de Campos, who stresses the etymology of 'plagios' as 'oblique', 'transverse', means the translation of tradition. Semi-otically speaking, it is an unlimited semiosis as found in Pierce and Eco, and has to do with the etymological meaning of parody as 'parallel canto' to designate the non-linear transformation of texts throughout history (ibid.: 75–6). This etymological reactivation of 'parody', as has been shown, was elaborated by de Campos in 1973 in his *Morfologia do Macunaíma* and introduced even earlier in his intro-duction to *Oswald de Andrade: Trechos Escolhidos* in 1966. At that time, he argues, he was not familiar with Bakhtin's work on Dostoevsky, which only became available in the West through Kristeva in 1967. Anyway, Bakhtin's dialogism and polyphony as well as Kristeva's reformulation of them in 'intertextuality' approximate de Campos' own etymological reading of parody, as he demonstrates in an extended note on parody and plagiotropy (ibid.: 73–4). What is theorized becomes a cannibalist practice. If plagiotropy in Goethe is evident, like the echo of Hamlet in the song of the gravediggers, de Campos nourishes on Goethe's poetic practice to derive his own translational praxis. The Shakespearean intertext is not translated by the insertion of existing translations of Shakespeare, but by appro-priating the Brazilian literary tradition. It is João Cabral de Melo Neto, specifically in *Morte e Vida Severina* (Death and Life of Severino), who provides the diction for the intertext in the translation (ibid.: 191–2). Translation, as he defines it, is a *persona* through whom tradition speaks. 'Translator, transformer', if one follows the example of the Brazilian poet Sousândrade (1833–1902), the patriarch of creative translation who would insert in his homeric translations lines from Camões and others (ibid.: 191).

In the section 'A Escritura Mefistofélica', de Campos also presents a long and detailed interpretation of *Faust*, and the emphasis is quite political, even though he does not make it explicit. Instead of presenting the consolidated body of criticism, as in conventional translators' prefaces, he follows Bakhtin's hint and analyses *Faust* from the point of view of carnivalization. Carnivalization means, as in Bakhtin's analysis of Roman Carnival, 'familiarization, a break with hierarchies (the temporary upholding of the hierarchical differences, the proximity of the superior and the subaltern), the atmosphere of liberty . . . the general ambiguity of relations . . . the desecrating impudence of gestures' (ibid.: 78). Yet he extends Bakhtin's perception, for prior to the explicit scene of masks in the Imperial Palace, the elements of carnival are present in Mephistopheles' language which 'in its corroding negativity, ridicules everything, desecrates everything, beliefs and conventions' (ibid.: 79). In the second section, 'Bufoneria Transcendental: O Riso das Estrelas' ('Transcendental Buffoonery: The Stars' Laughter'), he takes up the non-explicit political tone of his analysis of *Faust*. This time he relies on Adorno and Benjamin, more specifically on the latter's concept of allegory and the principle of synchrony that reconstitutes the tradition of the oppressed, in contradistinction to the official historiography of the winners (1981a: 127). Yet, de Campos claims, Benjamin's theorization of allegoric discourse comes close to Bakhtin's polyphony (de Campos 1981a: 132) as well as to carnivalization, in that all of them break with the paradigm of purity, of the absolute. There is no more place for tranquillizing interpretations: 'We are in an era that has already been called postmodern but that could be better defined as post-utopian. The non-place of u-topia . . . . To a poly-topia of power corresponds, in each case . . . a tropology of monological discourse, of the monolithic creed: of the only word and of the final word' (ibid.: 176–7). And he concludes his section on the analyses of *Faust* by emphasizing that the Bakhtinian *logos* is an important tool of analysis insofar as it opposed the utopia of monological truth to the dialogical truth of utopia, whereby utopia loses its claim to totality and manifests itself in its ambivalence and ambiguity (ibid.: 177).

Cannibalism, understood as a break with monological truth as well as a form of nourishment, is to inform the third main section of the paratext, in fact a *postscriptum*, wherein de Campos actually theorizes translation. What the two first sections have in common

with the third is that they present reverse or non-conventional readings of Goethe and of translation. For the reverse reading of
translation, he relies both on *Antropofagia* and on Walter Benjamin's
'The Task of the Translator'.

His theorization presented in the third part of the paratext is
called 'Transluciferação Mefistofáustica' ('Mephistofaustic Transluciferation'), a transformation of Faust's Lucifer, a title that
connects both to cannibalism and to the work of Benjamin.
'Transluciferação Mefistofáustica', he explains, is what translation
sets out to do: as a 'parricidal dis-memory' it 'intends to erase the
origin, to obliterate the original' (ibid.: 209); yet, recalling my initial
remarks on the use of the hyphen that separates and unites, the
very thrust of translating implies a gesture of acknowledgement. It
is further apparent that the metaphors for his title are drawn from
the very title he is translating. The use of the text one is translating
as a source of nourishment for one's theorization gives a further
cannibalistic dimension to de Campos' work, a point that de Souza
has made, while also calling attention to the number of expressions
used throughout the text to exemplify the satanic feature of the
translator's task: 'luciferian translation', 'a satanic enterprise' (de
Souza 1986: 183).

The irony of the metaphor is that de Campos had been describing
Benjamin's 'angelical' theory of translation, emphasizing its effect
of liberating the translator from servitude. But while subscribing to
Benjamin's theory, in itself liberating, he also subverts and departs
from it. If Benjamin casts the translator's task in an angelical light,
that of liberating the pure language, de Campos highlights the
satanic import of it, for 'every translation that refuses submissively
to serve a content, which refuses the tyranny of a pre-ordered *Logos*,
breaks with the metaphysical closure of presence (as Derrida would
say)', is 'a satanic enterprise' (de Campos 1981a: 180). The transformation of an angelic into a satanic theory can also be understood
by recalling de Campos' remarks on the 'critical devouring of the
universal critical heritage, formulated not from the insipid, resigned
perspective of the "noble savage" . . . but from the point of view of
the "bad savage", devourer of whites – the cannibal' (de Campos
1986: 44). There is a further point in which he departs from
Benjamin's angelical theory: teleogy for Benjamin is related to the
recovery of the pre-Babelic harmony of the pure language; teleology
for de Campos has to do with the turbulence of asserting the difference. Anyway, if translation is a form, and that is where he

subscribes to Benjamin's liberating views on translation, there is nothing more alien to it than submission, for translation implies fidelity not so much to the original, but to another form. The pragmatics of translation, he claims, is to translate a form, the *Art des Meinens*, 'rewriting it . . . in the translator's language in order to get to the transcreated poem as an isomorphic re-project of the originating poem' (de Campos 1981a: 181).

The question of mimesis in translation is also taken up. Translation does not copy or reproduce, but 'virtualizes the notion of mimesis not as a theory of copy . . . but as the production of difference in sameness' (ibid.: 183). 'Transcreation', de Campos claims, is a radical translation praxis. To transcreate is not to try to reproduce the original's form understood as a sound pattern, but to appropriate the translator's contemporaries' best poetry, to use the local existing tradition (ibid.: 185). As such, one could infer that for him, to transcreate means also nourishment from local sources, nourishment that, at the same time, limits the universality of the original and inscribes the difference. Translation is a reading of the universal tradition, he claims, but, at the same time, of the local literary production, because if the translator does not have a stock of the best poetry of his time, he cannot reshape synchronically and diachronically the best poetry of the past (ibid.: 185). De Campos' own examples of appropriation of the local tradition are many. We have already mentioned his appropriation of João Cabral de Melo Neto's diction in *Morte e Vida Severina* to translate the Burial Chorus. Another example he provides is the use of Sousândrade to translate the German compound words that are alien to Portuguese and are conventionally given analytical translations. At the same time, the use of neologisms after Sousândrade brings de Campos close to Panwitz (a debt he acknowledges) when he Germanizes the Portuguese language to broaden its creativity potential (ibid.: 194, 202).

Translation, as such, in his terms, is a 'parallel canto', a dialogue not only with the original's voice, but with other textual voices, or, as he encapsulates it, 'Translation: transtextualization' (ibid.: 191, 200). Translation as transtextualization or transcreation demythicizes the ideology of fidelity. If translation transtextualizes, it is no longer a one-way flow, and de Campos concludes his text with two anthropophagic metaphors. One is 'transluciferation', which closes the text and provides its title; the other brings us back to the anthropophagic double dialectics of receiving and giving highlighted in this chapter's epigraph: 'Translation as transfusion. Of Blood' (ibid.: 208).

Translation that unsettles the single reference, the logocentric tyranny of the original, translation that has the devilish dimension of usurpation (de Campos 1997: 33–59); translation that disturbs linear flows and power hierarchies – daemonic dimensions that coexist with the *a priori* gesture of tribute to the other inherent in translating and the giving of one's own vitality to the other. Transcreation – the poetics that disrupts the primacy of the one model – a rupture and a recourse to the one and the other. Translation can be servitude, translation can also be freedom – for me, that very liberating transhistoricization of T.S. Eliot's *The Four Quartets* which might sign off but can never close this meditation.

By way of conclusion, however, I must stress that any discussion of *Antropofagia,* in the post-theoretical era, would be incomplete without my drawing attention to the major critique of it, namely that of Roberto Schwarz. Long-standing ideological binaries are entailed. As soon as the base–superstructure relationship is deemed to be threatened by Anthropophagy's locating translation 'at a remove from monological truth', then corrective responses are both inevitable and predictable. For readers of English, the easiest access to the counter-position may be found in 'Marco Histórico' ('A Historic Landmark'), of 1985, in *Misplaced Ideas* (Schwarz 1992: 187–96). The translator is John Gledson and his own, materialist, gloss is as self-explanatorily polarizing as it is eloquent: 'One can feel his [Schwarz's] anger at those who try to argue . . . that things are better because they are worse: because Brazilians have always imitated, but now are told that there is no reason to think that imitators are inferior to the things they copy, they are always in the vanguard' (ibid.: xix).

At the very least, Schwarz might be said to be downplaying the Paz–de Campos challenge to reductivism regarding the role of economics in artistic and cultural expression which I have already discussed. Most recently, Bernard McGuirk, in his *Latin American Literature: Symptoms, Risks and Strategies of Post-Structuralist Criticism* (1997), further interrogates Schwarz regarding the latter's claim that 'the key trick played by the concretists, always concerned to organize Brazilian and world literature so that it culminates in them, is a tendency which sets up a confusion between theory and self-advertisement' (Schwarz 1992: 191–5). McGuirk asks: 'Are we to be locked again into the long familiar tensions of a Nietzsche–Marx binary?' (McGuirk 1997: 8–9). His own proposal is pertinent not only to his primary purpose of 'locating inequality' in critical appropriations of Latin American literatures and cultures but also to the very questions of translation raised by Haroldo de Campos:

> How, then, is the encounter with the other to be represented?
> . . . Just as I have made the claim for overlapping (or, to re-use a by now familiar Brazilian metaphor, mutually feeding) critical discourses, I would argue, too, that the Levinasian focus I have chosen is but one mode whereby cultures and societies might be theorized differently. Rather than the utopian horizontal of materialism, or the religious verticality of transcendentalism, a *trans-jectory* of movement both *across* frontiers and through the *up*lifts of self in other, other in self, becomes operative. Through such *trans*lation the writing self is to be located in writing others – multi-epigraphically, mosaically.
>
> (ibid.: 16–17)

Readers everywhere will expect no definitive answers regarding such polemics, but it is my contention that the specifically Brazilian experience demonstrably exemplifies the necessity of the discursive dislocatability of all translations.

Notes

1   For the present essay, I acknowledge the recent invaluable assistance of Haroldo de Campos himself. Space constraints do not allow me to do justice to his work – a lifetime dedicated to literature, criticism, translation as an art, in a total of forty books. For an extended study of his brother Augusto de Campos' specific relation to *Antropofagia* and increasing move towards visual translation see Vieira 1997.
2   Haroldo de Campos' *Da Razão Antropofágica: Diálogo e Diferença na Cultura Brasileira* was produced in 1980 and first published in Portuguese in Lisbon in 1981, then reprinted in Brazil in the fourth revised and enlarged edition of the collection of essays *Metalinguagem e Outras Metas* (1992), pp. 231–56. References and quotations throughout this text will be made from the 1986 English version, 'The Rule of Anthropophagy: Europe under the Sign of Devoration.
3   References here will be to the version reprinted in the fourth revised and enlarged 1992 edition of *Metalinguagem e Outras Metas*, pp. 31–48.

References

de Andrade, O. (1968) 'Manifesto Antropófago', in A. Candido and J.A. Castello, *Presença da Literatura Brasileira*, vol. 3 (São Paulo: Difusão Européia do Livro), pp. 68–74.

de Campos, H. (1963) 'Da Tradução como criação e como crítica', *Tempo Brasileiro* 4–5, (June–Sept.). Repr. in de Campos (1992), pp. 31–48.

—— (1967) *Oswald de Andrade: Trechos Escolhidos* (Rio de Janeiro: Agir).

—— (1973) *Morfologia de Macunaíma* (São Paulo: Perspectiva).

—— (1981a) *Deus e o Diabo no Fausto de Goethe* (São Paulo: Perspectiva).

—— (1981b) 'Da Razão Antropofágica: Diálogo e Presença na Cultura Brasileira', *Colóquio/Letras* 62 (Jul.) (Lisbon: Fundação Calouste Gulbekian). Repr. in de Campos (1992), pp. 231–55.

—— (1986) 'The rule of anthropophagy: Europe under the sign of Devoration', trans. M.T. Wolff, *Latin American Literary Review* 14.27 (Jan.–June): 42–60.

—— (1991) *Qohélet = O-que-sabe: Eclesiastes: poema sapiencial*, trans. H. de Campos with the collaboration of J. Guinsburg (São Paulo: Perspectiva).

—— (1992) 'Translation as creation and criticism', *Metalinguagem e Outras Metas: Ensaios de Teoria e Crítica Literária*, 4th rev. and enlarged edn (São Paulo: Perspectiva).

—— (1997) *O Arco-Íris Branco: Ensaios de Literatura e Cultura* (Rio de Janeiro: Imago Editora).

de Souza, E.M. (1986) 'A Crítica Literária e a Tradução', in: *I Seminário Latino-Americano de Literatura Comparada* (Porto Alegre: Universidade Federal do Rio Grande do Sul), pp. 181–6.

Foucault, M. (1986) 'Nietzsche, genealogy, history', in *The Foucault Reader*, ed. P. Rabinow (Harmondsworth: Penguin).

Hollanda, H.B. de and Gonçalves, M.A. (1989) *Cultura e Participação nos Anos 60*, 7th edn (São Paulo: Brasiliense).

Johnson, R. (1987) 'Tupy or not tupy: cannibalism and nationalism in contemporary Brazilian literature', in J. King (ed.), *Modern Latin American Fiction: A Survey* (London and Boston: Faber & Faber), pp. 41–59.

McGuirk, B. (1997) *Latin American Literature: Symptoms, Risks and Strategies of Post-structuralist Criticism* (London and New York: Routledge).

Santiago, S. (1978) *Uma Literatura nos Trópicos: Ensaios de Dependência Cultural* (São Paulo: Perspectiva).

Schwarz, R. (1987) 'Nacional por Subtração', in *Tradição Contradição* (Rio de Janeiro: Jorge Zahar Editor/Funarte).

—— (1992) *Misplaced Ideas: Essays on Brazilian Culture*, trans. and ed. J. Gledson (London and New York: Verso).

Vieira, E.R.P. (1992) 'Por uma Teoria Pós-Moderna da Tradução', unpub. PhD thesis, Belo Horizonte, Universidade Federal de Minas Gerais.

—— (1997) 'New registers in translation for Latin America', in K. Malmkjaer and P. Bush (eds), *Literary Translation and Higher Education* (Amsterdam: John Benjamins).

Wisnik, J.M. (1987) 'Algumas Questões de Música e Política no Brasil', in A. Bosi (ed.), *Cultura brasileira: temas e situações* (São Paulo: Ática), pp. 114–23.

Chapter 6

A.K. Ramanujan's theory and practice of translation

Vinay Dharwadker

A.K. Ramanujan occupies a unique position among Indian and post-colonial theorists and practitioners of translation. His independent work focuses on the underrepresented language-combination of English, Kannada and Tamil, and his work in collaboration with other scholars enlarges the combination to include Indian languages like Telugu, Malayalam and Marathi that continue to be marginalized in world literature. Over almost forty years – between the mid-1950s and the early 1990s – he translated texts in several genres from most of the important periods of Indian literary history, covering classical poetry and *bhakti* poetry in Tamil, Vīraśaiva *vacanas* in Kannada, *bhakti* and court literature in Telugu, folktales and women's oral narratives recorded in the nineteenth and twentieth centuries, and poetry and prose fiction written in the post-independence decades.[1] He usually chose originals of exceptional aesthetic, historical or cultural significance, and produced a large number of versions that are marked by literary excellence in themselves. His output as a translator is distinguished not only by its quantity, quality and variety, but also by the body of prefaces, textual and interpretive notes and scholarly commentary that frame it, reflecting on particular materials and cultures as well as the general process of translation.[2]

Ramanujan's contributions to the art of translation, his influence as a model translator of Indian texts, and his impact on the understanding of India among scholars and general readers alike are too extensive and complex to be judged primarily or solely on the basis of a practical criticism of particular translations. In this chapter I shall therefore examine his work in a wider theoretical and methodological perspective, focusing on his general conception of translation and on the articulation of a comprehensive and coherent theory of translation in his practice. Such a perspective enables us to understand his pragmatic goals as a translator in relation to his strategies for attaining them, and to clarify his wide-ranging concerns regarding the conditions, outcomes and limitations of translation. It also allows us to evaluate his intentions and accomplishments with precision, to analyse his connections with other theorists and practitioners of translation in detail, and especially to link his activities as a translator to his larger enterprise as a writer and intellectual, which I have described elsewhere as the invention of a distinctive variety of post-colonial cosmopolitanism.[3]

RAMANUJAN'S CONCEPTION OF TRANSLATION

In his published work Ramanujan reflected on translation most often in the context of poetry, and conceived of it as a multi-dimensional process in which the translator has to deal with his or her material, means, resources and objectives at several levels simultaneously. At each level of effort, the translator has to pursue the impossible simultaneous norms of literary excellence in the translation and fidelity to various ideals, even while accepting a number of practical compromises in the face of conflicting demands and allegiances. For Ramanujan, the translator's task is defined by this peculiar set of freedoms and constraints, several of which are particularly important. The translator is expected to render textual meanings and qualities 'literally', to successfully transpose the syntax, design, structure or form of the original from one language to another, and to achieve a communicative intersection between the two sets of languages and discourses. At the same time, the translation has to attempt to strike a balance between the interests of the original author and those of the translator (or between faithful representation and faithless appropriation), to fulfil the multiple expectations of its imagined readers, and to construct parallels between the two cultures and the two histories or traditions that it brings together.

At the most elementary yet challenging level of effort, a translator attempts and is obliged to carry over a text from its original language into a second one as 'literally' and 'accurately' as possible. Ramanujan approached the problem of rendering the so-called literal meanings and qualities of a source-text by trying 'to attend closely to the language of the originals . . . detail by detail' (*SS*, 13).

His desire to make his final versions as accurate and reliable as possible usually led him to a close reading of the original, a systematic analysis for himself of its devices and effects, and a time-consuming procedure of drafting, correcting and polishing the translation. As he says disarmingly of his labour-intensive input into *Poems of Love and War*, 'I began this book of translations fifteen years ago and thought several times that I had finished it . . . . I worked on the last drafts in a third-floor office of the Department of English at Carleton College where I sat unsociably day after day agonizing over Tamil particles and English prepositions' (*LW*, xv–xvi).

Ramanujan was acutely conscious that even the most scrupulous translator's care and craftsmanship cannot solve the problems of attempting what John Dryden, in 1680, had called *metaphrase*, the method of 'turning an author word by word, and line by line, from one language into another'.[4] According to Ramanujan, two principal difficulties prevent a translator from producing a perfect metaphrase, especially of a poem: (a) the words in the text 'are always figurative' (*HD*, xvi),[5] and therefore cannot be rendered literally; and (b) a truly literal version can never capture the poetry of the original, for 'only poems can translate poems' (*LW*, 296), and a poem is always made at several levels, of which the so-called literal level is only one (*HD*, xvi). He believed that, given these obstacles, metaphrase is an unachievable ideal, and that 'Translations too, being poems, are "never finished, only abandoned" ' (*LW*, xv), so that the translator's task 'more often than not . . . like Marvell's love, is "begotten by despair upon impossibility" ' (*LW*, 297).

While struggling with 'the minute particulars of individual poems, the words' at the level of metaphrase (*LW*, 297), the translator also has to try and render into the second language the syntax, structure or design of the original text. Syntax, which Ramanujan treats as a synecdoche for structure, represents the site of textual organization where individual constitutive elements (such as words, images, symbols and figures) combine with each other to produce a larger unit, an ensemble of effects or a whole. In dealing with the original text's construction as a composite entity, Ramanujan sought to carry over not only its metaphrasable (or at least paraphrasable) meaning but also, equally importantly, its formal principles, its modulations of voice and tone, and its combination of effects on the reader. Thus, at the level of syntax, he attempted to translate a text 'phrase by phrase as each phrase articulates the total poem' (*IL*, 11).

More broadly, in his effort to render the original poem's structure as faithfully as possible, Ramanujan concentrated on several principles of poetic organization. For instance, he identified and tried to convey in his translation the specific order of elements in the source-text, so that he 'paid special attention to the images and their placement' (*IL*, 11). He also frequently played with the visual form or shape of his versions on the page, for this was 'a way of indicating the design of the original poems' (*IL*, 12). He further sought to emphasize the relations among the various parts of a poem, which made possible the arrangement of poetic elements as well as the visual form itself. So when he '[broke] up the lines and arranged them in little blocks and paragraphs, or arranged them step-wise', he used the spacing on the page 'to suggest . . . the distance or the closeness of elements in the original syntax' (*IL*, 11). Moreover, in his overall strategy of translation at the level of combination, he sought to make 'explicit typographical approximations to what [he] thought was the inner form of the poem' (*IL*, 11). That is, in moving from the level of literal signification to that of structural significance, Ramanujan attempted to translate not just the words, lines, sentences, images and explicit themes, but also the shaping principle of the source-text, its elusive 'poetic' core.

Ramanujan developed his conceptions of 'outer' and 'inner' poetic form from two culturally incommensurate sources. On the one hand, he owed the distinction in part to Noam Chomsky's analysis of surface and deep structure in discourse, and to Roman Jakobson's rather different structuralist analysis of the grammar of poetry, especially the latter's distinction between 'verse instance' and 'verse design'.[6] To a remarkable extent Ramanujan's differentiation between outer and inner form, which he formulated in the late 1960s or early 1970s, parallels the distinction between 'phenotext' and 'genotext' which Julia Kristeva developed around the same time from the same structural-linguistic sources, but which she deployed in a post-structuralist psychoanalytical theory of signifying practices.[7] On the other hand, Ramanujan owed his distinction to the classical Tamil distinction between two genres of poetic discourse, the *akam*, 'interior, heart, household', and the *puṟam*, 'exterior, public' (*LW*, 233, 262–9). For much of his career, Ramanujan treated the interior and the exterior as aspects, divisions or characteristics not only of textual and poetic organization, but also of social organization and cultural formation as such, specifically in the domains that

Rabindranath Tagore, working in a different Indian tradition early in this century, had independently designated in his novel *Ghare-bhāire* as 'the home' and 'the world'.[8] Ramanujan also applied the distinction between outer and inner form to his own practice as a scholar and poet when, in a rare and therefore frequently quoted comment, he said that

> English and my disciplines (linguistics, anthropology) give me my 'outer' forms – linguistic, metrical, logical and other such ways of shaping experience; and my first thirty years in India, my frequent visits and fieldtrips, my personal and professional preoccupations with Kannada, Tamil, the classics, and folklore give me my substance, my 'inner' forms, images and symbols. They are continuous with each other, and I no longer can tell what comes from where.[9]

Seeking to transpose the phenotext as well as the genotext of a poem from its original language into a second one, usually a language belonging to a different family altogether, the translator in Ramanujan had to deal with all the differences that separate one tongue from another.

Ramanujan believed that, in any given language, the production of discourse (*parole* in Saussure's sense) results from 'the infinite use of finite means' (*FI*, 323), and that the particular means provided by the *langue* or system underlying the actual usage are determinate and characteristic of that language (*langage*).[10] English and Kannada, for example, use two rather different finite sets of means – sounds, scripts, alphabets, lexicons, grammars, syntactic rules, stylistic conventions, formal and generic principles and so forth – to generate their respective infinite bodies of discourse, including poetry. Consequently, a modern English translation of a premodern Dravidian-language poem, no matter how skilful, can never be 'transparent' the way Walter Benjamin, for instance, idealistically and formalistically thought it could be.[11] Ramanujan felt that the systemic differences between two languages ensure that Benjamin's norm of a 'literal rendering of the syntax' of one is impossible in the other, and that a compensatory focus on individual words in such a situation (at the expense of structure or design) conflicts with the translator's obligations to render the poem's inner and outer forms faithfully. As he put it, in the case of tenth-century *bhakti* poetry:

When two languages are as startlingly different from each other as modern English and medieval Tamil, one despairs. For instance, the 'left-branching' syntax of Tamil is most often a reverse mirror image of the possible English. Medieval Tamil is written with no punctuation and no spaces between words; it has neither articles nor prepositions, and the words are 'agglutinative,' layered with suffixes. Moreover, the syntax is a dense embedding of clause within clause. I translate unit by syntactic unit and try to recreate the way the parts articulate the poem in the original. My English thus seems to occupy more visual space on the page than the adjective-packed, participle-crowded Tamil original. The 'sound-look,' the syntax, the presence or absence of punctuation, and the sequential design [of the translations] are part of the effort to bring the Tamil poems faithfully to an English reader.

(*HD*, xvii)

A text's resistance to translatability, however, arises from the differences between language-systems as well as, among other things, from the conflict between author and translator. In Ramanujan's view, the relationship between translator and author is subject to two pairs of contradictory desires, with the pairs contradicting each other in turn. One coupling consists of the translator's desire to make a poem out of the translation, and the negation of this desire by the reader's conventionalized demand for metaphrase or absolute literal fidelity to the original (without regard to its 'poetry'). The other coupling, which conflicts with the first, consists of the translator's desire to make out of the poetry of the original a poem of his or her own, and the negation of this desire by the obligation, conventionally enforced by readers, faithfully to make out of the intertextual encounter someone else's poem.

Despite the tension between faithful representation and supposedly parasitic appropriation, Ramanujan was unambiguous about the literary status of the translations he wanted to produce. As he explained quite early in his career, in the specific context of classical Tamil lyric poetry, 'The originals would not speak freely through the translations to present-day readers if the renderings were not in modern English, and if they were not poems themselves in some sense. By the same token, the translations had to be close, as close as my sense of English and Tamil would allow' (*IL*, 11). At the same time, fully recognizing the complexities of the conflict within the translator between self-effacement and self-articulation, or between transmission and expression, Ramanujan argued that

> a translator is 'an artist on oath.' He has a double allegiance, indeed, several double allegiances. All too familiar with the rigors and pleasures of reading a text and those of making another, caught between the need to express himself and the need to represent another, moving between the two halves of one brain, he has to use both to get close to 'the originals.' He has to let poetry win without allowing scholarship to lose. Then his very compromises may begin to express a certain fidelity, and may suggest what he cannot convey.
>
> (*LW*, 296–7)

But the dilemma is due to more than a split in the translator's self or a schism in his or her brain: it arises also from an *aporia* – a choice involving competing options that cannot be made on rational grounds alone – between loyalty and betrayal, commitment and freedom, reflection and refraction or, in one of Ramanujan's own late metaphors, mirrors and windows ('WM', 187–216). For, as Ramanujan confesses, 'A translation has to be true to the translator no less than to the originals. He cannot jump off his own shadow. Translation is choice, interpretation, an assertion of taste, a betrayal of what answers to one's needs, one's envies' (*SS*, 12–13). In following his own inclinations, prejudices and self-perceived strengths and shortcomings, the translator, no matter how skilled technically, risks being 'eccentric or irrelevant to the needs of others in the two traditions' (*SS*, 13), the one he translates from and the one he translates into. If the translator fails to achieve a balance between representation and appropriation, then he (or she) undercuts the utility of the translation as a representation of something otherwise inaccessible, as well as the value of such a representation beyond its 'utility'.

What potentially saves the translator from the seemingly inescapable subjectivity of his or her relationship with the author of the original is the dynamics of a binding series of 'several double allegiances' (*LW*, 296). For Ramanujan, these divided loyalties generate yet more levels at which translation performs, or has to fulfil, its polyphonic functions. The translator again risks being labelled a traitor, as in the old Italian formula *traditore, traduttore* ('the translator is a traitor'), but he or she can succeed by working through three sets of conflicting allegiances: to the reader, to the culture of the original text, and to the text's historical context or tradition.

No matter what else the translator does, he or she has to be true to the reader of the translation. A translator works in a relatively well-defined and predictable rhetorical situation, since his or her work is addressed to a reader who makes multiple demands on the translator and the translation. This reader, both 'real' and 'imagined', expects the translator to be faithful to the source-text, at the level of metaphrase and at that of outer and inner form. This reader also expects the translator to produce a version that is at once true to the original poem and a poem in its own right. The reader further expects the poem, as translated, to be a reliable representation of the original text, its language, its poetics and tradition, its historical and cultural contexts and so on. That is, in order to fulfil the reader's expectations, a translator has to submit to three concomitant, conflicting norms: textual fidelity, aesthetic satisfaction and pedagogic utility. While the translator can satisfy the demands of verbal faithfulness and poetic pleasure when he or she negotiates the difficulties of metaphrase, the search for inner and outer forms, and the intrusions of poetic desire and subjectivity that create a tension between representation and appropriation, he or she can fulfil the norm of pedagogic utility only by stepping beyond the immediate constraints of textual transmission, and invoking his or her allegiances to a phenomenon that stands outside the text and beyond its reader in translation.

The phenomenon in question is the culture in which the original poem is embedded before translation. The translator cannot carry across that culture as a whole: in fact, the translation of an individual text or a selection of texts is already a part of the effort to translate that culture. Ramanujan's strategy in the face of this version of the hermeneutic circle was to create an opening or aperture with the help of the reader.[12] He argued, therefore, that even as a translator carries over a particular text from one culture into another, he has to translate the reader from the second culture into the first one. This complementary process of imaginative transposition or intertextual acculturation can be initiated and possibly accomplished by framing the poetic translations with prefaces, introductions, afterwords, notes, glossaries and indices. As Ramanujan says in the Translator's Note to *Samskara*, 'A translator hopes not only to translate a text, but hopes (against all odds) *to translate a non-native reader into a native one*. The Notes and Afterword [in this book] are part of that effort' (*S*, viii; emphasis added). Or, as he puts it in *The Interior Landscape*,

> The translations and the afterword (which some readers may prefer to read first) are two parts of one effort. The effort is to try and make a non-Tamil reader experience in English something of what a native experiences when he reads classical Tamil poems. Anyone translating a poem into a foreign language is, at the same time, trying to *translate* a foreign reader into a native one.
>
> (*IL*, 11; emphasis in original)

Even as he attempts to initiate the foreign reader's movement towards the native culture of the translated text, however, Ramanujan invokes a different allegiance. This is the translator's fidelity to the original poem's historical situation and tradition – the framework, material and process of transmission over time and across generations, within a culture and even between different cultures – which make possible the survival of texts, ideas and practices in the first place. In giving the reader a sense of the translated poem's native tradition (in the translation itself as also in the scholarly discourse around it), the translator, together with his or her reader, enters an immense network of intertextual relations, transactions and confluences spanning both time and space. Ramanujan gives us a metonymic glimpse of such a network when, referring to his versions of classical Tamil poems, he remarks:

> Dancers and composers have translated my translations further into their own arts. Over the years, the poems have appeared not only in a variety of anthologies but in wedding services. The ancient poets composed in Tamil for their Tamil corner of the world of antiquity; but, as nothing human is alien, they have reached ages unborn and 'accents yet unknown.' I am grateful, and astonished, to be one of the links, undreamed of by them or by me.
>
> (*LW*, xviii)

But the traditions that become the sites of such multiple transpositions are not ready-made or already available. Echoing T.S. Eliot's argument that a tradition has to be acquired with great labour,[13] Ramanujan acknowledges that 'Even one's own tradition is not one's

birthright; it has to be earned, repossessed. The old bards earned
it by apprenticing themselves to the masters. One chooses and translates a part of one's past to make it present to oneself and maybe
to others. One comes face to face with it sometimes in faraway
places, as I did' (*LW*, xvii). At the most general level of effort, then,
the translator is engaged in carrying over not only texts but also
readers, cultures, traditions and himself or herself in radically meta-
morphic ways. Translation – which, in its most elementary form,
appears to be a matter of metaphrasing, say, a single 'adjective-
packed, participle-crowded Tamil poem of four lines' (*IL*, 12) – thus
no longer hinges upon a product, or even a bundle of relations. It
evolves instead into an open-ended, multi-track process, in which
translator, author, poem and reader move back and forth between
two different sets of languages, cultures, historical situations and
traditions. In a fluid process of this sort, which we attempt to freeze
under the label of 'intertextuality', the translations that succeed best
are those capable of making the most imaginative connections
between widely separated people, places and times. The poems and
stories Ramanujan himself chose to translate over four decades had
the power to make precisely such connections, and they continue
to energize his readers' heterotopic worlds.

A THEORETICAL CRITIQUE OF RAMANUJAN'S PRACTICE

Ramanujan's differences with other theorists of translation, particularly the post-structuralists, reached a friction-point the year
before he died, when Tejaswini Niranjana attacked him in the last
chapter of her book, *Siting Translation*.[14] The attack was surprising
because, as his long-time colleagues Susanne and Lloyd Rudolph
observed in an obituary published in India in July 1993, Ramanujan
characteristically 'picked friendships, not fights'.[15] Already in indif-
ferent health when Niranjana's book reached him, he refused to
retaliate in print with counter-arguments and counter-allegations,
trusting his readers as well as hers to judge the issues reasonably
and fairly. Despite – but also because of – Ramanujan's public
silence on the subject, it is important to examine Niranjana's attack
in detail for what it reveals about a style of scholarship and political argumentation that has become widespread in contemporary
criticism.

Niranjana formulates her critique on two basic levels, though she blurs them when convenient. At the first level, she deals with inspectable particulars and finds fault with Ramanujan's translation of a single short poem by Allamaprabhu, a twelfth-century Vīraśaiva *vacanakāra* in Kannada, which stands at the very end of *Speaking of Śiva* (*SS*, 168). She criticizes Ramanujan for his rendering and interpretation of specific words, images, concepts and structures, arguing that in the original they are not what he, in the translation, misrepresents them to be. To substantiate her assessments, Niranjana reproduces a Kannada text in English transliteration, comments extensively on its individual constitutive elements, and offers her own translation of Allama's *vacana* as a superior alternative to Ramanujan's. At the second level of critique, however, Niranjana refuses to engage with the specifics of Ramanujan' s work and abandons any pretence at documentation and demonstration. In effect, she attributes to Ramanujan a 'politics of translation' that is at once colonialist, orientalist, Christian, missionary, Utilitarian, modernist, nationalist and nativist, evidently intending these not just as individual terms of deprecation but as entire categories of abuse. Given the seriousness of some of Niranjana's charges – for example, that Ramanujan's representation of *bhakti* somehow 'essentializes Hinduism' and 'condones communal violence' – it is necessary to question her method of arriving at such provocative generalizations.

Niranjana manipulates the evidence skilfully. As the 'original' text of Allamaprabhu's *vacana* she reproduces a modernized Kannada version she finds in the Nandimath edition of the first volume of the *Śūnyasampādane* published in 1965. But for his selection and arrangement of Allama's poems in *Speaking of Śiva*, Ramanujan had used Basavaraju's 1960 edition of *Allamana Vacana Candrike*, a work different from, though related to, the *Śūnyasampādane*. Ramanujan mentioned the Nandimath edition of the first volume of the *Śūnyasampādane*, itself part of a larger editorial project at Karnataka University, Dharwar, under 'Further Readings' (*SS*, 12, 57), but when he actually quoted or summarized from the *Śūnyasampādane*, he used the Bhoosnurmath edition of the second volume of 1968. As Ramanujan's introductory note on Allamaprabhu's life and work explicitly states, he uses the Basavaraju *Candrike* and the Bhoosnurmath volume of the *Śūnyasampādane* for his material, and not the Nandimath volume (*SS*, 146, 148).[16]

Niranjana conceals these elementary textual facts from her readers. The suppressed difference between Ramanujan's and

Niranjana's respective source-texts becomes crucial when she compares his English translation to, and evaluates it against, the Kannada 'original' she has chosen for it. She does not consider it necessary to tell her readers whether the text of Allama's poem is exactly the same in the Nandimath *Śūnyasampādane* volume and the Basavaraju *Candrike*, or whether the two sources vary, as such editions and variants of *bhakti* texts so often do in all the major Indian languages. Instead, she fudges the question of textual variation in the 'original' Kannada, both in the main body of her discussion and in footnotes that do not provide the needed documentation. On the basis of her comparison of Ramanujan's translation and a Kannada source he did *not* translate, Niranjana asserts confidently that he makes errors in reading the original, thus suggesting that he was incompetent with premodern Kannada. To justify her own unproblematic access to the language, however, she states that 'Medieval Kannada is comprehensible to a speaker of modern Kannada' (*ST*, 180, f.n. 38) – a claim that ought to have applied more aptly to Ramanujan since, unlike her, he was a writer with four published books in that language, a practising linguist with a doctoral dissertation on it, and a widely published translator of its premodern and modern literatures. She then goes on to suggest that Ramanujan deliberately introduced ideological distortions in his rendering of the *vacana*, in order to incorporate in it his own hidden, reprehensible political agendas.

Obviously, if Ramanujan made a real mistake (for instance, in reading *hora* [*sic*] or *hera* ['outside'] for *here* ['back']), and systematically skewed the structure and semantics of the Allama *vacana* in question, then Niranjana ought to have been able to clinch her case simply by juxtaposing Ramanujan's version and the text he actually translated, and by methodically documenting each transparent error and wilful distortion. While I am sure that Ramanujan, like everyone else, was quite capable of making mistakes and even of twisting a text to fit his own biases, he never claimed to be free of shortcomings or prejudices. In fact, as I have already noted, he reminded his readers that a translator cannot jump off his own shadow, and that a translation is 'a betrayal of what answers to one's needs, one's envies' (*SS*, 12–13). In contrast, Niranjana visibly plays fast and loose with facts, as if her readers as well as Ramanujan's would never know, or even need to know, the difference: in a casual footnote on this particular 'mistake' she tells us that 'One of the Kannada versions available has *herasāri* for *heresāri*;

this could be one source of the confusion' (*ST*, 183, f.n. 48), but then refuses to document that crucial textual variant.

Niranjana's attack is also problematic because it is based overtly on a theory of translation which, from the perspective I have out-lined in the preceding section, is highly contestable. Even if her prac-tical analysis of the 'original' Kannada text and of Ramanujan's version were to be valid, it is grounded in Benjamin' s debatable argu-ments about translatability and the so-called law of translation in 'The Task of the Translator', and in their appropriation in Derrida's 'Des Tours de Babel'.[17] Benjamin's theory allows Niranjana to assert that Ramanujan fails 'to comprehend the economy of translation *in this poem*' because he does not 'understand "the specific significance *inherent in the original* which manifests itself in its translatability" ' (*ST*, 180; emphases added).[18] It also enables her to 'privilege the word over the sentence, marking thereby what Derrida calls in "Des Tours de Babel" a "displacement" from the syntagmatic to the paradig-matic level' (*ST*, 185). As I have suggested earlier, Ramanujan's the-ory and practice emphasize the need to treat language, poetry and translation as processes which involve multiple levels that cannot be collapsed onto each other, and in which words cannot have priority over sentences, and sentences cannot have priority over larger dis-cursive structures, because we do not use or find words outside sen-tences or sentences outside discourse. Niranjana does not consider such a viewpoint seriously anywhere in *Siting Translation* and, in effect, completely disregards Ramanujan's own principles of translation, while attributing a universal, neo-colonial authority to Benjamin's and Derrida's views, which are centred on modern European phi-losophy and much older Judaic traditions.

The problematic nature of Niranjana's theoretical assertions becomes evident when we place Ramanujan's conception of trans-lation beside Benjamin's and Derrida's conceptions. Ramanujan accepted some of Benjamin's ideas but rejected others, especially the latter's view that the reader was of no importance in the process of translation, and that translatability somehow is an intrinsic prop-erty housed inside the original text. Benjamin, a Marxist and Frankfurt School critic but also, contradictorily enough, a practising modernist and formalist with a strong interest in Jewish mysticism, was the source of one of Ramanujan's most important and long-lasting principles as a writer and scholar: the idea that the ideal critical essay would consist entirely of quotations.[19] Ramanujan's major essays in roughly the second half of his career, from the late

1970s to the early 1990s, including such late examples as 'Where Mirrors are Windows' and 'Three Hundred *Rāmāyaṇas*', are all structured explicitly as Benjaminian 'anthologies of quotations'.[20] Some of Ramanujan's statements on translation also seem to agree with several observations in Benjamin's 'The Task of the Translator'. In fact, Ramanujan appears to echo Benjamin's notions that 'a translation issues from the original – not so much from its life as from its afterlife', and that 'in its afterlife – which could not be called that if it were not a transformation and a renewal of something living – the original undergoes change' ('TT', 71, 73). At the same time, however, there are obvious theoretical differences between Ramanujan and Benjamin on several other points. Thus, while Benjamin argues that 'In the appreciation of a work of art or an art form, consideration of the receiver never proves fruitful', Ramanujan, himself an exemplary self-conscious reader–response critic in many respects, holds that the translator has to pay a great deal of attention to, and spend energy translating, the intended or imagined reader of the translation. So also where Benjamin asserts that 'the original . . . contains the law governing the translation: its translatability', Ramanujan appears closer to the position that, outside the closed circuit of modern European languages, the translatability of a text is determined, not by some code or property housed inside the text, but by a complex of contingent factors and chance encounters outside it: the pair of languages actually involved in the intertextual transfer, the translator's peculiar bilingual sensibility and skill, the interests of the potential readers of the rendering, and so on ('TT', 69, 70). A crucial area of disagreement between Ramanujan and Benjamin surfaces in the latter's claim that

> A real translation is transparent; it does not cover the original, does not block its light, but allows the pure language, as though reinforced by its own medium, to shine upon the original all the more fully. This may be achieved, above all, by a literal rendering of the syntax which proves words rather than sentences to be the primary element of the translator. For if the sentence is the wall before the language of the original, literalness is the arcade.
>
> ('TT', 79)

This may be true for translation from one European language into another (Benjamin worked mainly between modern French and modern German) but, as I have already indicated above, it is impracticable when dealing with, say, classical Tamil (or old Kannada) and contemporary English. In fact, both the ideal of transparency and the possibility of a literal rendering of the syntax are imaginable only within the Judaeo-Christian myth of Babel that Benjamin resurrects in his essay, and the ghost of an original *Ur-Sprache* that he mystically intuits within it. As a descriptive and comparative linguist, Ramanujan did not believe that there was such a lost transcendental, universal language underlying the differences between the Germanic, Romance, Indo-Aryan and Dravidian languages.[21]

Ramanujan also diverges from Jacques Derrida's arguments, articularly of the kind Niranjana mentions in the quotation above, where the French philosopher attempts to reverse Roman Jakobson's famous statement that 'The poetic function projects the principle of equivalence from the axis of selection [the paradigmatic axis] onto the axis of combination [the syntagmatic axis]'.[22] From Ramanujan's perspective, Derrida and his deconstructionist followers (including his translator and interpreter Gayatri Spivak) push the discussion of translation to a contextualist, theoretical and ideological extreme from which there is no conceivable return to poems, poetry or actual poetic translations. The kind of deconstructive argument that seems most inconsistent with Ramanujan's theory and practice occurs in 'Des Tours de Babel', where Derrida attacks Jakobson's distinction between intralingual, interlingual and intersemiotic transposition ('DT', 225–6). Ironically enough, for Derrida – the aboriginal champion of difference in a century that can be divided easily, as Judith Butler observes, between philosophers of identity and philosophers of difference – there is and can be no difference between these three types of translation.[23] Differentiation is impossible because, according to Derrida, Jakobson 'obviously presupposes that one can know in the final analysis how to determine rigorously the unity and identity of a language, the decidable form of its limits' ('DT', 225). In other words, since Derrida cannot distinguish in a philosophically satisfactory manner between, say, the boundaries of Kannada and the boundaries of English, any act of translating a text from Kannada into English is exactly like any act of rewording an English text in English itself, which is indistinguishable from any act of rephrasing a Kannada text in Kannada.

Ramanujan's technical training in linguistics almost certainly would have led him to argue that such a position is necessarily skewed and contestable. He knew that each of the ten or twelve Indo-European and Dravidian languages he had studied formally is historically and structurally a mongrel tongue; that any claim about its 'purity' is contrafactual and, therefore, merely an ideological or political construct; that each language and its body of historically articulated discourses is a vast palimpsestic network of rewritten signs, which interacts constantly with other similarly constituted proximate or distant networks in its cultural environment; that the mongrelization of languages occurs because their 'interiors' and 'exteriors' are separated by porous, elastic membranes and not by rigid walls; and that, despite such a permeability of boundaries, each language heuristically retains its 'identity' in relation to other languages, a unique 'inner form' that resists intrusions, outsiders and colonial conquests. Unlike Homi Bhabha, for instance, who is concerned with demonstrating that all identities are ineluctably ambivalent and hybrid in the end, Ramanujan accepted the hybridity of languages and cultures as a starting point and tried to show, instead, how different degrees and kinds of hybridization shape particular languages, and how, despite the universal fact of mongrelization, no two mongrels are actually alike.[24]

Again, the divergence between Ramanujan's conception of translation and Derrida's argument in 'Des Tours de Babel' becomes evident when we notice that what Derrida claims Jakobson 'presupposes' is not a presupposition at all, but is worked out explicitly and fully in a large number of essays, such as those collected posthumously in Jakobson's *Language in Literature*.[25] Moreover, I would argue, Derrida's terms 'obviously' and 'in the final analysis' in the sentence quoted above are highly questionable from a structuralist standpoint, because what Jakobson presupposes is not obviously what Derrida wants to make him seem to presuppose in order to turn him into a straw man for easy target practice on this occasion. Besides, what Derrida considers an adequately rigorous demonstration of 'the unity and identity of a language, the decidable form of its limits' would not be rigorous enough for Jakobson, Ramanujan and most professional historical, comparative and descriptive linguists. It is precisely the deconstructionists' undeconstructed (or unreconstructed) notion of 'rigorous' procedures that is a problem, not a source of solutions. If, for a few moments, we look at the practice of translation through Ramanujan's eyes, then Derrida's cannibalizing conception of philosophical rigour seems at once immensely reductive of the plurality of human understandings of such complex phenomena as language and poetry, and presumptuous and misplaced in its monologic will-to-knowledge outside the limited disciplinary capabilities of philosophy. If philosophers are unable to construct a philosophically satisfactory explanation of how or why languages manage to differ so much from each other that 'native speakers' of one are unable to 'master' another tongue even after a lifelong effort, then the fact that each language has definite limits, in effect, reveals only the limits and failures of philosophical reasoning.[26]

In contrast to Ramanujan's way of thinking, post-structuralist thought is so context-centred (despite, in the case of deconstruction, its self-professed textualism) that it divorces theory from practice, makes practice on the basis of such theorizing impossible (or, for Ramanujan at least, inconceivable), and makes theory hostile to 'mere' practice. In most types of post-structuralist theory, context invades, disrupts and mangles whatever actual practice it finds, and theory itself usurps the place conventionally given over to practice. The theorist's suspicion of the 'theoretically naive' practitioner, possibly still grounded in the former's unacknowledgeable envy of the latter, is of course very old: as Wordsworth put it, alluding to Plato, the true opposite of poetry is not prose but philosophy.[27] But in conversations about post-structuralism Ramanujan chose to say simply, 'I don't know what to do with it'. The statement is disarmingly simple, but it carries a peculiar weight in Ramanujan's thought.

RAMANUJAN'S POLITICS OF TRANSLATION

Niranjana's insinuations about Ramanujan's politics of translation appear, among other places, around her accusation that he reproduces 'the privileging of . . . "direct" experience' that is characteristic of 'European Protestantism' (*ST*, 181) in order to 'produce a post-Romantic translation of Allama's *vacana* that presents it as a "quest for the unmediated vision" ' (*ST*, 182). The innuendoes also surface in her suggestion that she is someone who will 'initiate here a practice of translation that is speculative, provisional, and interventionist' (*ST*, 173), and because of whom 'a retranslation of the *vacanas* can show, for example, that *bhakti*, or Vīraśaivism, was neither monolithic nor homogeneous' (*ST*, 176). Her unambiguous implications are that the Vīraśaiva *vacanakāras* themselves, in their Kannada texts, do not valorize a direct experience or an unmediated vision of their chosen god; that Ramanujan's practice as a translator was neither exploratory nor open-ended, and passively or perfidiously collaborated with colonial, orientalist and other dominant representations of India; and that he sought to represent *bhakti* and Vīraśaivism as uniform, single-valued phenomena.

What Niranjana elides is the fact that Ramanujan consistently uses 'experience' to translate two complex, frequently used quasi-technical terms in Vīraśaiva discourse in premodern Kannada, *anubhava* and *anubhāva*. The former word (from which the latter is derived) is Sanskrit in origin, is at least 2,500 years old, and passed morphologically unaltered into most of the Indo-Aryan and Dravidian languages around the beginning of this millennium. In the last two centuries of constant effort at English translation, no one has yet discovered or invented an equivalent for *anubhava* other than 'experience', since the multiple meanings of the two coincide to a remarkable degree. Niranjana does not remind her readers that Ramanujan explains his sense of the Vīraśaiva concepts of *anubhava* and *anubhāva* at length in the Introduction to *Speaking of Śiva*, in the section entitled 'The "Unmediated Vision"', where he self-consciously places quotation marks around his various renderings:

> [For the Vīraśaiva saints] all true experience of god is *kṛpa*, grace that cannot be called, recalled, or commanded. The vacanas distinguish *anubhava* 'experience', and *anubhāva* 'the Experience'. The latter is a search for the 'unmediated vision' the unconditioned act, the unpredictable experience. Living in history, time and cliché, one lives in a world of the pre-established, through the received (*śruti*) and the remembered (*smṛti*). But the Experience when it comes, comes like a storm to all such husks and labels . . . .
>
> A mystical opportunist can only wait for it, be prepared to catch It as It passes. The grace of the Lord is nothing he can invoke or wheedle by prayer, rule, ritual, magical word or sacrificial offering. In *anubhāva* he needs nothing, he is Nothing; for to be someone, or something, is to be differentiated and separate from God. When he is one with him, he is the Nothing without names. Yet we must not forget that this fierce rebellion against petrification was a rebellion only against contemporary Hindu practice; the rebellion was a call to return to experience. Like European Protestants, the Vīraśaivas returned to what they

felt was the original inspiration of the ancient traditions no different from true and present experience.

(*SS*, 31–3)

Predictably enough, when Niranjana brushes aside Ramanujan's commentary for being complicit with Eurocentric Christian-missionary and Utilitarian discourses on India, and offers instead her own representations of Vīraśaivism and Allamaprabhu, she cannot escape the vocabulary of 'experience' which, in her case, does not even claim to translate the Sanskrit-Kannada terms *anubhava* and *anubhāva*: 'The fragment we read belongs to Allama's "spiritual autobiography." It is part of a dialogue with a saint-to-be in which Allama tries to convey a sense of the "ultimate" experience, the experience of the "void," or *śūnya*' (*ST*, 178); 'The traces left by Allama's experience are always already there in the conception of this kind of experience in the *bhakti* or devotional tradition' (*ST*, 179). Apparently Ramanujan's account of precisely this phenomenon using the word 'experience' is inadmissible because it is supposedly part of 'a project deconstructed so skilfully in Paul de Man's "The Rhetoric of Temporality" ' (*ST*, 182), whereas Niranjan's own interpretation, almost suspiciously intertextual with Ramanujan's, is somehow exempt from the same, otherwise universally applicable criticism.

Niranjana also conceals the fact that Ramanujan adapts the concepts of 'quest' from European romance narratives and of the 'pilgrim's progress' from Puritan allegories in order to translate as efficiently as possible the concept in Vīraśaivism of a *ṣaṭsthala siddhānta*, a doctrine of six phases, stages, or stations, which constitutes 'one of the many "contexts" of these texts' (*SS*, 169). As a matter of fact, he discusses the six-phase system in a dense, informative appendix of six pages at the end of the book – which Niranjana ought to have noticed, since it begins on the page facing Ramanujan's translation of Allama's poem under discussion – where he says:

> The vacanas and later Vīraśaiva texts in Kannada and Sanskrit speak of the mystical process as a succession of stages, a ladder of ascent, a metamorphosis from egg to larva to pupa to the final freedom of winged being. Often the devotee in his [or her] impatience asks to be cut loose from these stages of metamorphosis . . . .

Six phases or steps (*sthala, sōpāna*) are recognized. The devotee at each stage has certain characteristics; each stage has a specific relationship between the *aṅga* or the soul and the *liṅga* or the Lord . . . . Creation comes into being by the lord' s engagement (*pravṛtti*); liberation for the aṅga is attained through disengagement (*nivṛtti*). The description of the first is a cosmology, not very different from the Sāṅkhya philosophy. The description of the disengagement is in the form of the six phases.

(*SS*, 169)

By the same token, Niranjana should acknowledge that Ramanujan's references to parallels between Vīraśaivism (or *bhakti*) and European Protestantism are part of his effort to provisionally translate the non-Indian reader from a Western-Christian culture towards the culture of the thirteenth-century Vīraśaiva saints. Ramanujan's comments in the Introduction seem to me to be obviously not intended to appropriate *bhakti* into Protestantism or Puritanism, but only to orient the unfamiliar Western reader to cross-cultural similarities that are remarkable for being present at all:

bhakti religions like Vīraśaivism are Indian analogues to European protestant movements. Here we suggest a few parallels: protest against mediators like priest, ritual, temples, social hierarchy, in the name of direct, individual, original experience; a religious movement of and for the underdog, including saints of all castes and trades (like Bunyan, the tinker), speaking the sub-standard dialect of the region, producing often the first authentic regional expressions and translations of inaccessible Sanskritic texts (like the translations of the Bible in Europe); a religion of arbitrary grace, with a doctrine of the mystically chosen elect, replacing a social hierarchy-by-birth with a mystical hierarchy-by-experience; doctrines of work as worship leading to a puritan ethic; monotheism and evangelism, a mixture of intolerance and humanism, harsh and tender.

(*SS*, 53–4)

In pointing out such parallels, towards the end of more than thirty pages of discussion of the distinctive features of Vīraśaivism and *bhakti* in the Introduction to *Speaking of Śiva*, Ramanujan made several crucial points at once. The analogies enable uninitiated common readers as well as professional historians and comparatists of religion to make sense of the complex relationship between *bhakti* and brahmanism or classical Hinduism; to see that, contrary to early and late colonial and orientalist arguments, 'India' and 'Hinduism' were neither static nor uniform, and instead contained their own principles of 'internal' change, renewal and diversification; to understand that, contrary to Christian-missionary arguments, *bhakti* movements like Vīraśaivism were neither derivations nor failures, but 'original' (without precedent) and 'vital' (alive, mutable); and especially to discover that the *bhakti* 'counter-cultures' within Hinduism historically preceded Protestant movements in Europe by a few hundred years, without the possibility of a Christian or European influence. Moreover, in choosing on this occasion to render and interpret Vīraśaiva discourse against the grain of classical Hinduism and the so-called Great and Little Traditions of South Asia (*SS*, 34), in placing that discussion in a broad comparative perspective, and in subtly distancing himself from the dogmatism, harshness and intolerance of the movement, Ramanujan also managed simultaneously to dismantle late nineteenth- and early twentieth-century Indian revivalist appropriations of *bhakti*. If this is what Ramanujan's translations and commentary set out to do and succeeded in doing twenty years before Niranjana attacked him, then he can hardly be the composite colonialist, orientalist, Christian-missionary, Utilitarian, nationalist and nativist 'collaborator' that she tries to make him out to be.

Finally, Niranjana's charges that Ramanujan represents *bhakti* in general and Vīraśaivism in particular as monolithic or homogeneous phenomena, and that he 'essentializes Hinduism' and somehow thereby 'condones communal violence' in contemporary India, derive from the same inconsistency of scholarly and argumentative procedures that I have pointed out so far. Niranjana articulates her own totalizing critique on the basis of a single translated poem in *Speaking of Śiva* and on an arbitrarily isolated group of Ramanujan's comments, without taking into account even the rest of his work in that book as a whole. Her strategy literal-mindedly imitates Derrida's standard procedure of claiming to ruin the entire edifice of Western metaphysics by supposedly demonstrating how one small part of it falls apart under his deconstructive gaze. What Niranjana does not realize is that Derrida's Heideggerian method can work only on the assumption that something like 'Western metaphysics' is such an integrated 'system' that any one part of it, however small, marginal or eccentric, necessarily and completely reproduces all the essential properties of the whole. This methodological axiom, however, cannot be transferred from the domain of academic philosophical writing to that of literary textuality at large without immense difficulty. Derrida is able to make the transfer only by making the curiously reductive, homogenizing, essentializing and Eurocentric avant-garde claim that all writing is equally *écriture*, 'writing in general' – which Michel Foucault was right, though ineffective, in criticizing as a transcendentalist move.[28] I would argue that no literature, not even 'Western literature', is merely or wholly a discursively displaced, condensed or reconfigured articulation of a 'metaphysics' that has been completed and systematized somewhere outside it and that somehow survives recoverably intact within it. That is, to use an Enlightenment trope, 'literature' is not just a 'handmaiden' of 'philosophy'; to modulate Wordsworth's Romantic formulation, poetry is not merely an extension of philosophy but opposes it actively; or, to vary Ramanujan's structuralist figure, while a phallogocentric metaphysics may well insert some of its elements into the elusive 'inner forms' of literature, it does not completely determine or dictate in advance what those forms will be. It is precisely at the untranscendable disjunction between 'philosophy' and 'literature' that literature manifests its distinctive and other power to textualize what has not been textualized elsewhere or before, just as it is exactly in the immanence of this discord that philosophical discourse lacks the strength to 'exhaust' literary writing.

To put it differently, if we are to criticize Ramanujan's practice, then we are obliged to examine the full range of his work. Over nearly forty years he transcribed, translated and commented on more than 3,000 individual poems and narratives as well as scores of larger works composed originally in half a dozen rather different languages. Since the great bulk of what he read and rendered had not been treated comparatively on this scale or in this manner earlier, neither could he know in advance then, nor can his readers know in advance now or in the future, what this immense, polyphonic heap of texts says, means or does. No reading of any one piece can prepare us fully for what we will discover in other pieces in other places in the pile, even adjacent ones. The assortment is a partial selection cutting across so many languages, regions, social formations, cultural position and histories that it cannot constitute a 'whole' in any familiar sense of the term. Many pieces turn out to share a limited number of characteristics with many other pieces, so that the heap can be arranged using multiple paradigmatic criteria into numerous smaller constellations, and some of the constellations can be placed provisionally into still larger groupings, but no defining set of common characteristics appears in every single piece in the pile. As a consequence, when we wish to judge whether Ramanujan represented Vīraśaivism, *bhakti* or Hinduism as monolithic, homogeneous or essentializable phenomena, we need to go beyond a single poem or a single series of comments, and examine all the material he produced on these subjects.

When we do so, we find immediately before us a large quantity of quotable and inspectable evidence that contradicts Niranajan's undocumented claims. Thus, in the Introduction to *Speaking of Śiva* itself we find Ramanujan reminding his readers in detail that *bhakti* is divisible into at least four varieties (*nirguṇa* and *saguṇa*, Vaiṣṇava and Śaiva); and, both in the commentary and in the very organization of the book, arguing that Vīraśaivism is not uniform, since even the four poets represented there – Basavaṇṇa, Dāsimayya, Mahādeviyakkā, Allamaprabhu – despite their common commitments are unmistakably distinctive. In *Hymns for the Drowning*, Ramanujan deals with an earlier and very different *bhakti* movement, concentrating on a single Tamil *āḻvār*, on the Śrivaiṣṇava Tamil *āḻvār* tradition as a whole, on an explication of 'the many-sided shift [that] occurred in Hindu culture and sensibility between the sixth and ninth centur[ies]' (*HD*, 103), and on a demonstration of the radically hybrid constitution of *bhakti*, far from any essentialist or essentializable Hinduism:

> Early bhakti movements [in Tamil and other languages], whether devoted to Śiva or to Viṣṇu, used whatever they found at hand, and changed whatever they used. Vedic and Upaniṣadic notions, Buddhist and Jaina concepts, conventions of Tamil and Sanskrit poetry, early Tamil conceptions of love, service, women, and kings, mythology or folk religion and folksong, the play of contrasts between Sanskrit and the mother tongues: all these elements were reworked and transformed in bhakti.
>
> (*HD*, 104)

In fact, in 'Where mirrors are windows', Ramanujan argued that he 'would prefer the plural, "Indian literatures," and would wonder if something would remain the same if it is written in several languages, knowing as I do that even in the same language, "a change of style is a change of subject," as Wallace Stevens would say' ('WM', 188). He criticized the dichotomy between the Great and Little Traditions in the anthropology of South Asia, to which he himself had subscribed 'for many years, though somewhat uneasily', rejecting it because 'At its best, it is a form of monism; at its worst, it is a form of cultural imperialism, an upstairs/downstairs view of India' ('WM', 189). He went on to suggest that 'cultural traditions in India are indissolubly plural and often conflicting but are organized through at least two principles, (*a*) context-sentivity and (*b*) reflexivity of various sorts, both of which constantly generate new forms out of the old ones' ('WM', 189). And he was particularly unambiguous when he stated that, in considering 'What we call Brahminism . . . and tribal traditions and folklore' ('WM', 189), we should include 'Bhakti, Tantra, and other countertraditions, as well as Buddhism, Jainism, and, for later times, Islam and Christianity . . . in this web of intertextuality' ('WM', 190). If Ramanujan repeatedly dislodges like this the discourses of authenticity, purity and separatism that drive the manipulative party-politics of communalism in contemporary India, then where and how precisely does he 'essentialize' Hinduism or 'condone communal violence'?

Notes

1 In this chapter I have transliterated Indian-language words, including some proper nouns, using standard diacritical notation. For Kannada, see the notation system in A.K. Ramanujan, *Speaking of Śiva* (London: Penguin Books, 1973), pp. 14–15; for Tamil, see A.K. Ramanujan, trans., *The Interior Landscape: Love Poems from a Classical Tamil Anthology* (Bloomington: Indiana University Press, 1967), pp. 12–14; for Sanskrit and Tamil, see G. Flood, *An Introduction to Hinduism* (Cambridge: Cambridge University Press, 1996), pp. xiii–xiv.

2 An overview of the career of A.K. Ramanujan (1929–1993) appears in my 'A.K. Ramanujan: Author, translator, scholar', *World Literature Today* 68 (2) (Spring 1994), 279–80. Quotations from seven of Ramanujan's works are cited in the text hereafter, with the abbreviations listed below.

IL A.K. Ramanujan, trans., *The Interior Landscape: Love Poems from a Classical Tamil Anthology* (Bloomington: Indiana University Press, 1967).

SS A.K. Ramanujan, trans., *Speaking of Śiva* (London: Penguin Books, 1973).

S A.K. Ramanujan, trans., *Samskara: A Rite for a Dead Man*, by U.R. Anantha Murthy (Delhi: Oxford University Press, 1976; corrected edn, 1978; new paperback edn, New York: Oxford University Press, 1989).

HD   A.K. Ramanujan, trans., *Hymns for the Drowning: Poems for Viṣṇu by Nammāḻvār* (Princeton: Princeton University Press, 1981).

LW   A.K. Ramanujan, ed. and trans., *Poems of Love and War: From the Eight Anthologies and the Ten Long Poems of Classical Tamil* (New York: Columbia University Press, 1985).

FI   A.K. Ramanujan, ed., *Folktales from India: A Selection of Oral Tales from Twenty-two Languages* (New York: Pantheon Books, 1991).

'WM'   A.K. Ramanujan, 'Where mirrors are windows: toward an anthology of reflections', *History of Religions* 28 (3) (1989), 187–216.

Ramanujan's important posthumous publications, not quoted here, include: V. Dharwadker and A.K. Ramanujan, eds, *The Oxford Anthology of Modern Indian Poetry* (Delhi: Oxford University Press, 1994); A.K. Ramanujan, V.N. Rao and D. Shulman, eds and trans., *When God Is a Customer: Telugu Courtesan Songs by Kṣetrayya and Others* (Berkeley: University of California Press, 1994); *The Collected Poems of A.K. Ramanujan* (Delhi: Oxford University Press, 1995); A.K. Ramanujan, *A Flowering Tree and Other Oral Tales from India*, eds S. Blackburn and A. Dundes (Berkeley: University of California Press, 1997); and *The Collected Essays of A.K. Ramanujan*, ed. V. Dharwadker (Delhi: Oxford University Press, forthcoming).

3 See my 'Postcolonial cosmopolitanism: a note on A.K. Ramanujan's theory and practice of criticism and translation', *Indian Literature* 37 (2) (1994), 91–7.

4 *Essays of John Dryden*, ed. W.P. Ker, 2 vols (1900; repr. New York: Russell & Russell, 1961), 1:237.

5 Here Ramanujan quotes Dryden's *Essays*, 2:228.

6 See N. Chomsky, 'Current issues in linguistic theory', in *The Structure of Language: Readings in the Philosophy of Language*, eds J.A. Fodor and J.J. Katz (Englewood Cliffs, NJ: Prentice-Hall, 1964), pp. 50–118, esp. pp. 50–52; and R. Jakobson, 'Linguistics and poetics', in his *Language in Literature*, eds K. Pomorska and S. Rudy (Cambridge, Mass.: Belknap Press; Harvard University Press, 1987), pp. 62–94, esp. pp. 78–81.

7 Julia Kristeva's conceptions of genotext and phenotext are discussed in R. Barthes, 'Theory of the text', trans. I. McLeod, in *Untying the Text*, ed. R. Young (Boston: Routledge & Kegan Paul, 1981), pp. 31–47; see esp. p. 38.

8 See R. Tagore, *The Home and the World*, trans. S. Tagore, with revisions by the author (1919; Madras: Macmillan India, 1992). The affinity between the two sets of conceptions is striking, although Tagore may well have been unaware of the classical Tamil tradition.

9 Quoted in R. Parthasarathy, ed., *Ten Twentieth Century Indian Poets* (Delhi: Oxford University Press, 1976), pp. 95–6.

10 On *parole* and *langue*, see Chomsky, 'Current issues', pp. 52, 59–60; E. Benveniste, 'Saussure after half a century', in his *Problems in General Linguistics*, trans. M.E. Meek (Coral Gables, Fl.: University of Miami Press, 1971), pp. 29–40; and J. Culler, *Structuralist Poetics: Structuralism, Linguistics, and the Study of Literature* (Ithaca, NY: Cornell University Press,

1975), pp. 8–10. On *parole, langue* and *langage*, see M. Foucault, *The Archaeology of Knowledge*, trans. A.M. Sheridan Smith (New York: Pantheon Books, 1972), esp. pp. 21–117.

11 Walter Benjamin, 'The task of the translator: an introduction to the translation of Baudelaire's *Tableaux parisiens*', in his *Illuminations: Essays and Reflections*, ed. H. Arendt, trans. Harry Zohn (New York: Schocken Books, 1969), pp. 69–82; see p. 79. Hereafter cited in the text as 'TT'.

12 On the hermeneutic circle, see E.D. Hirsch, Jr., *Validity in Interpretation* (New Haven, CT: Yale University Press, 1967), pp. 76–7.

13 T.S. Eliot, 'Tradition and the individual talent', in *Selected Prose of T.S. Eliot*, ed. F. Kermode (New York: Harcourt Brace Jovanovich; Farrar, Straus & Giroux, 1988), pp. 37–44; see p. 38.

14 T. Niranjana, *Siting Translation: History, Post-Structuralism, and the Colonial Context* (Berkeley: University of California Press, 1992); hereafter cited in the text as *ST*.

15 *The Times of India*, 25 July 1993.

16 The various texts and editions as cited by Niranjana and Ramanujan are: S.C. Nandimath, L.M.A. Menezes and R.C. Hirenath, eds and trans., *Śūnyasampādane*, vol. 1 (Dharwar: Karnataka University Press, 1965); S.S. Bhoosnurmath and L.M.A. Menezes, eds and trans., *Śūnyasampādane*, vols 2 and 3 (Dharwar: Karnataka University Press, 1968–9); Basavaraju, ed., *Allamana Vacana Candrike* (Mysore, 1960).

17 J. Derrida, 'From "Des Tours de Babel" ' trans. F. Graham, in *Theories of Translation: An Anthology of Essays from Dryden to Derrida*, eds. R. Schulte and J. Biguenet (Chicago: University of Chicago Press, 1992), pp. 218–27; hereafter cited in the text as 'DT'.

18 The quotation within the second quotation here is from Benjamin, 'Task', p. 71.

19 The epigraph to A.K. Ramanujan, 'Is there an Indian way of thinking? An informal essay', *Contributions to Indian Sociology* n.s. 23 (1) (1989), pp. 41–58, reads: 'Walter Benjamin once dreamed of hiding behind a phalanx of quotations which, like highwaymen, would ambush the passing reader and rob him of his convictions'.

20 See, for example, A.K. Ramanujan, 'Three hundred *Rāmāyaṇas*: five examples and three thoughts on translation', in *Many Rāmāyaṇas: The Diversity of a Narrative Tradition in South Asia*, ed. P. Richman (Berkeley: University of California Press, 1991), pp. 22–49.

21 See A.K. Ramanujan, 'On translating a Tamil poem', included as ch. 11 in his forthcoming *Collected Essays*.

22 Jakobson, 'Linguistics and poetics', p. 71.

23 See J.P. Butler, *Subjects of Desire: Hegelian Reflections in Twentieth-Century France* (New York: Columbia University Press, 1987).

24 See H.K. Bhabha, *The Location of Culture* (New York: Routledge, 1994).

25 Cited in n. 6 above.

26 Another, more recent, example of 'the limits and failures of philosophical reasoning' is the debate about 'consciousness' among analytical philosophers in the 1990s; see J.R. Searle, 'Consciousness and the philosophers', *New York Review of Books*, 6 March 1997, pp. 43–50, and the subsequent exchange on the topic in the issue of 15 May 1997, pp. 60–1.

27 H. Aarsleff , 'Introduction', in W. von Humboldt, *On Language: The Diversity of Human Language-Structure and Its Influence on the Mental Development of Mankind*, trans. P. Heath (Cambridge: Cambridge University Press, 1988), pp. vii–lxv; see p. xxxvi.

28 M. Foucault, 'What is an author?', in his *Language, Counter-Memory, and Practice: Selected Essays and Interviews*, ed. D.F. Bouchard, trans. D.F. Bouchard and S. Simon (Ithaca, NY: Cornell University Press, 1977), pp. 113–38; see pp. 119–20.

Chapter 7

Interpretation as possessive love

Hélène Cixous, Clarice Lispector and the ambivalence of fidelity

Rosemary Arrojo

> I owe a live apple to a woman. A joy-apple. I owe a work of apple to a woman. I owe: a birth to the nature of a woman: a book of apples. To *Des Femmes*. I owe: the loving – the mystery of an apple. The history of this apple, and of all the other apples. Young, alive, written, awaited, known. New. Nutritious.
>
> In the translation of the apple (into orange) I try to denounce myself. A way of owning. My part. Of the fruit. Of the enjoyment. Of venturing to say that which I am not yet in a position to ensure by my own care.
>
> Hélène Cixous, *Vivre l'orange/To Live the Orange*

Tejaswini Niranjana opens her well-known book on translation with a quote from Charles Trevelyan's *On the Education of the People of India*, originally published in 1838, which is quite efficient in showing the perverse love story that often underlies the colonial encounter:

> The passion for English knowledge has penetrated the most obscure, and extended to the most remote parts of India. The steam boats, passing up and down the Ganges, are boarded by native boys, begging, not for money, but for books [. . .] Some gentlemen coming to Calcutta were astonished at the eagerness with which they were pressed for books by a troop of boys, who boarded the steamer from an obscure place, called Comercolly. A Plato was lying on the table, and one of the party asked a boy whether that would serve his purpose. 'Oh yes,' he exclaimed, 'give me any book; all I want is a book.' The gentleman at last hit upon the expedient of cutting up an old *Quarterly Review*, and distributing the articles among them.
>
> (Niranjana 1992, p.1)

In this poignant scene, in which what is at stake is not simply physical force or asymmetrical military powers, but the power of seduction which dominant cultures and languages exercise over the subaltern, we find a radical denial of translation as the boys, fascinated by English originals, demand an unmediated contact with the object of their desire. Ideally, the alluring foreignness of the dominant English has to be experienced without the mediation of the boys' own language and culture and, of course, at the cost of their own historical identity. In this sense, this brief but revealing snapshot of colonial India can also be seen as an illustration of the delusive ethics that seems to underlie most acts of reading and translating – and particularly those undertaken in asymmetrical contexts – in which it is the interpreter's labour of faithful love that is supposed to guarantee the protection of the other even if it means the denial of the interpreter's own identity and interests.

If asymmetrical relations of power have established that authorship, patriarchy and colonialism do have a lot in common, by the same token, the devoted interpreter's or translator's plight may be comparable not only to the woman's (Chamberlain 1992), but also to that of the subject of colonization. One can recall, for instance, the exemplary story of la Malinche, the daughter of an influential Aztec chief, whose main task as Cortés's translator was not merely to serve as his faithful envoy and concubine, but to persuade her own people not to resist the Spanish invaders (Delisle and Woodworth (eds) 1995, p. 148). To this day, her name is a sad reminder of the Spaniards' brutal violation of the land and the women of Mexico, 'passively open' to the invader's power and cruelly abandoned to their own fate after being used and exploited. And it is to this inaugural narrative – which is also the birth scene of Mexico as a nation literally conceived in rape and in violence – that Octavio Paz attributes, for instance, some of the most important traits of Mexican culture, largely determined by the reliance on a clear-cut opposition between the vulnerable (associated with the feminine, the open, the weak, the violated, the exploited, the passive, the insulted), and the invulnerable (associated, of course, with the masculine, the closed, the aggressive, the powerful, capable of hurting and humiliating) (Paz 1959, pp. 59–80).

Some insight into the mechanisms of these asymmetrical relationships which mingle power and fascination might be gained if we examine them from the perspective of Jacques Lacan's notion of 'the subject presumed to know'. If 'transference is the acting-out of the reality of the unconscious,' the bond that brings together the subaltern and the dominant is not merely the outcome of a violent experience, but also an emotional, and even an erotic affair. 'I deemed it necessary', writes Lacan, 'to support the idea of transference, as indistinguishable from love, with the formula of the subject presumed to know. [. . .] The person in whom I presume knowledge to exist thereby acquires my love' (quoted in Felman 1987, pp. 87, 86). In what I have described here as a paradigmatic scene of colonization, as well as in the general plot that opposes the subaltern's openness towards the dominant to the latter's impenetrability towards the former, we may say that the dominant culture plays the role of 'the subject presumed to know', the unquestioned and unquestionable 'self-sufficient, self-possessed proprietor of knowledge' (ibid., pp. 87, 84). At the same time that the subaltern culture desires the knowledge which supposedly belongs to the dominant, the latter never doubts the legitimacy of its status as the owner and guardian of such knowledge. Consequently, from such a perspective, the tragedy of the subaltern is precisely the blindness with which it devotes itself to this transferential love that only serves the interests of the dominant and feeds the illusion of 'the subject presumed to know', as it also legitimates the latter's power to decide what is proper and what is not, what is desirable and what is not.

And since this is a story of love but, first of all, also of asymmetries, the fascination which the subaltern feels towards the dominant is never truly reciprocated, at least within the colonial context. In a predictable counteractive move, it has been the explicit overall goal of post-colonial theorists to subvert and even to transform the basic asymmetrical narratives constructed by colonialism by means of the recognition and the celebration of heterogeneity. Among such theories, some trends in contemporary feminism have been particularly forceful in defending a non-violent approach to difference which allegedly offers a pacifistic alternative to the age-old models imposed by patriarchy and colonialism. The prominent French feminist Hélène Cixous's highly influential thinking largely derived from her notion of the 'feminine' as transcending the traditional biological opposition between men and women (1975) is certainly one of the best-known examples of such efforts.

The main object of this chapter is precisely one of Cixous's most ambitious projects which is a remarkable illustration of the contradictions implied by her notion of the feminine: her textual 'affair' with Clarice Lispector, the Brazilian novelist and short-story writer

whose work began to be known outside Brazil only after it was literally adopted and celebrated by her most illustrious reader.
Interestingly enough, the story of this affair began on an anniversary
of Columbus's 'discovery' of America. In a book specially dedicated
to honouring Lispector's texts, Cixous writes:

> Like a voice from a birth town, it brought me insights I once
> had, intimate insights, naive and knowing, ancient and fresh
> like the yellow and violet color of freshias rediscovered, this
> voice was unknown to me, it reached me on the twelfth of
> October 1978, this voice was not searching for me, it was writing
> to no one, to all women, to writing, in a foreign tongue. I do
> not speak it, but my heart understands it, and its silent words
> in all the veins of my life have translated themselves into mad
> blood, into joy-blood.
>
> (Cixous 1979b, p. 10)

The primary task I intend to undertake here is the examination of
the main implications of Cixous's allegedly nonaggressive 'discovery'
of Lispector and the contours of the devoted relationship which
she has established with the Brazilian writer, and which has been perceived as a reversal of the paradigm of colonial, patriarchal encounters even by a sensitive critic of Cixous's treatment of Lispector like
Marta Peixoto, for whom 'Cixous's reception of Lispector inverts the
usual colonial and post-colonial dynamic whereby Latin Americans
translate and celebrate literatures from Europe and the United
States' (Peixoto 1994, p. 40). In other words, in the Cixous/Lispector
story, it is the influential European who would be playing the role of
the seduced, faithful reader as she transforms the Brazilian writer into
the very source of her own productivity both as a writer and as a
thinker. However, as I will try to argue, Cixous's feminist approach
to reading which professes to treat the texts as well as the authorial
name of Clarice Lispector with 'extreme fidelity' and outside the
traditional opposition between dominant and subaltern, is far from
letting the alterity of Lispector's work speak as such and, in fact, ends
up serving and celebrating its own interests and goals. From such a
perspective, how to characterize the dialogue that has been taking
place between the author Clarice Lispector, her 'foreignness', the
language in which she wrote her texts; and Cixous, widely regarded
as one of the most influential thinkers of our time and the Brazilian
writer's best-known reader so far? Or, if I may state the same

question in more general terms, is it possible for a self-professed pacifistic, protective reading not to be also an interfering translation?

One of the most prevalent themes of Hélène Cixous's writing revolves around the quest to dissolve the traditional, supposedly 'masculine' dichotomy which divides all there is into categories of subject and object and which has determined our ways of relating to reality and to each other. In her relentless struggle to subvert such a comprehensive, ubiquitous opposition, which she sees as the basis of all forms of oppression, particularly patriarchy and colonialism, Cixous seeks attitudes and ways of relating to the other which could give up the pursuit of power and mastery and which would allow alterity to remain as such. This stance, which is allegedly different from that of most of her contemporaries, is identified with what Cixous calls the 'feminine', that is, a certain mode of response to the laws established by patriarchy. Within such a logic, 'feminine' and 'masculine' are different ways to relate to pleasure and to the law, already defined in 'the first fable of our first book', in which 'what is at stake is the relationship to the law':

> There are two principal elements, two main puppets: the word of the Law or the discourse of God. All this transpires in this short scene before a woman. The Book begins Before the Apple: at the beginning of everything there is an apple, and this apple, when it is talked about, is said to be a not-to-be-fruit. There is an apple, and straight away there is the law. It is the start of libidinal education, it is here that one begins to share in the experience of the secret, because the law is incomprehensible.
>
> (Cixous 1988, p. 15)

For Eve, God's words ('if you taste the fruit of the tree of knowledge, you will die') do not mean anything 'since she is in the paradisiac state where there is no death'. Between the two choices with which she is faced – the law, that is 'absolute, verbal, invisible, [. . .] a symbolic *coup de force*' and, above all, 'negative'; and the apple, 'which is, is, is' – Eve will decide for the 'present', 'visible' apple which has an 'inside' that is 'good' and that she does not fear. Thus, Cixous concludes, this very first fable already 'tells us that the genesis of woman goes through the mouth, through a certain oral pleasure, and through a non-fear of the inside [. . .] Eve is not afraid of the inside, neither her own, nor that of the other' (ibid.). On the other side of the opposition, the 'masculine' response to the law is represented, for instance, by the countryman of Kafka's story who spends his whole life waiting before the law, dominated by the fear of castration. Therefore, as Cixous's logic goes, giving is easier for women (or for anyone or anything that can be called 'feminine') while men are more prone to retaining: 'a limited, or masculine, economy is characterized by retention and accumulation. Its dialectical nature implies the negation – or death – of one of the terms, for the enhancement of the other' (Conley 1992, pp. 39–40).

These opposite ways of relating to the law produce different styles, different strategies of reading and writing as well as different modes of research. A feminine style is, for example, 'the style of live water' – echoing the title of Clarice Lispector's *Água Viva* (1973) – in which 'thirst is itself that which quenches, since to be thirsty is already to give oneself drink'. Such a style 'gives rise to works which are like streams of blood or water, which are full of tears, full of drops of blood or tears transformed into stars. Made up of phrases which spill forth dripping, in luminous parataxis'. On the other side of the dichotomy, Cixous identifies a style 'marked by the pain of reduction, a "man's style" which is at the mercy of scenes of castration' and that 'gives rise to forms which are dry, stripped bare, marked by the negative, forms of which the most striking examples are those of Kafka and Blanchot' (Cixous 1988, p. 25). The pursuit of a feminine style is also the pursuit of meaning without mediation, free from the constraints of translation, and which could be different from the 'masculine' language we have been taught, a language 'that translates everything in itself, – understands nothing except in translation, [. . .] listens only to its grammar, and we separated from the things under its orders' (Cixous 1980, p. 137; quoted in Conley 1992, p. 79). Cixous, by the way, explicitly associates translation with laziness, violence and reduction: 'in these violent and lazy times, in which we no longer live what we live [. . .] we no longer listen to what things still want to tell us, we simply translate and translate, everything is translation and reduction [. . .]' (Cixous 1979a, pp. 412–13).

A 'feminine' mode of writing involves strategies which strive to treat the other 'delicately, with the tips of the words, trying not to crush it, in order to un-lie' (Cixous 1991b, p. 134). Obviously, such a mode of research, which 'presents radical alternatives to the appropriation and destruction of difference necessitated by phallic law', has implications for the ways in which texts are approached.

Since it necessarily involves a certain blurring of the limits between author and interpreter, and between the two languages and cultures involved, translation is first of all adamantly avoided. Appropriately, reading is viewed as an act of listening to the text's otherness. As a consequence, if the text as other is not to be mastered but listened to, contemporary theories of reading which emphasize the reader's productive, authorial role are 'resisted' and leave room for 'the adoption of a state of active receptivity' in which the reader tries to 'hear' that which the text is 'consciously and unconsciously saying' (Sellers 1988, p. 7). 'Feminine' reading is, thus, 'a spiritual exercise', a form of gentle 'lovemaking', in which what is important is 'to take care of the other': 'to know how to read is to take infinite time to read; it is not to take the book for a little geometric object, but for an immense itinerary. It is knowing how to scan, to pace, how to proceed very slowly. To know how to read a book is a way of life' (quoted in Conley 1992, p. 128).

But how is Lispector brought to participate in Cixous's writing and reading projects? First of all, she has been the exclusive object of several texts by Cixous, including books such as *Vivre l'orange / To Live the Orange* (1979b), *L'heure de Clarice Lispector* (1989) and *Reading with Clarice Lispector* (1991b); as well as articles and parts of books such as *Writing Differences – Readings from the Seminar of Hélène Cixous* (1988) and *Readings – The Poetics of Blanchot, Joyce, Kafka, Kleist, Lispector, and Tsvetayeva* (1990), which have been widely translated into several languages all over the world, including in Japan where, paradoxically, there is interest in Cixous's writings about Lispector even though Lispector herself has not been translated into Japanese (Castello 1996). Besides these publications, since the late 1970s Lispector has been one of the authors systematically studied in Cixous's seminars held at the University of Paris, in France, and also in the United States (Irvine University, California), in Canada (Queen's University, Ontario), and in England (University of York) (ibid.).

As she has been given prominence in Cixous's writings and seminars, Lispector has begun to share a very select world, together with Kafka, Rilke, Rimbaud, Joyce, Heidegger, Derrida and even Freud, among other writers that she has, nevertheless, 'surpassed' since she had the advantage of writing 'as a woman' and has presented Cixous with an exemplary illustration of a feminine approach in her dealings with difference (Cixous 1991a, p. 132). In a recent interview, Cixous even compares Lispector's use of 'Brazilian' (Portuguese) to

Shakespeare's use of English. As her argument goes, even though Lispector may be difficult to read, her privileged style, like Shakespeare's, makes her work 'infinite' and 'inexhaustible' (Castello 1996). Obviously, owing to her allegedly meticulous devotion to the letter and the style of Lispector's work, Cixous plainly rejects any published translation of the Brazilian writer's texts which would prevent readers from having access to that which she finds so essential in Lispector. In such circumstances, how does one teach an author whose texts are written in Brazilian Portuguese to students who are not familiar with this peripheral language? According to Cixous, by means of a careful 'word for word' translation strategy which she undertakes with students in her seminars (Cixous 1991a), and which seems to follow a similar rationale as current post-colonial textual strategies such as Tejaswini Niranjana's option for 'literalness' in order to avoid 'homogenizing' the original (ibid., p. 185) and Lawrence Venuti's conception of foreignizing translation aimed at preventing the process from 'overpower[ing] and domesticat[ing] the foreign text, annihilating its foreignness' (ibid., p. 305).

Obviously, particularly from Cixous's perspective, the plot of this productive encounter between a reader and a writer has a lot in common with a successful love affair. After having 'wandered ten years in the desert of books – without encountering an answer' (Cixous 1979b, p. 10), Cixous found in Lispector's texts all that she had apparently lost and could not quite see anywhere else. It is a myriad of all the positive feelings which such a joyous 'discovery' brought to the French thinker that is emotionally expressed in the recurring, lyrical metaphors of the apple and the orange particularly developed in *Vivre l'orange*, a lengthy, loving celebration of this fertile encounter between two women, a reader and an author, happily brought together allegedly to undo all the evils of patriarchy. The 'apple' which Cixous finds in Lispector comprises not only references to Eve's fruit and all its implications for the relationship between women and the law, but also to one of Lispector's novels, *A Maçã no Escuro* (1961). It is the finding of such an affirmative, feminine 'apple' that allows Cixous to recover (and to rewrite) a long-lost 'orange', which synthesizes references to her very origins and individuality – her birth town (Oran, Algeria), combined with the personal pronoun *Je* – and to all the associations related to the flowing, life-giving elements that she has identified with a 'feminine' approach to reality (Shiach 1989, p. 160). This apple turned into an orange which has brought fruition to Cixous's writing, saving her 'deserted hands', is, therefore, also the outcome of her learning experience 'at the school of Clarice', 'a woman with athletic eyes' who 'should teach us how to think in the direction of a thing, a rose, a woman, without killing another thing, another woman, another rose, without forgetting' (Cixous 1979b, p. 98).

What Cixous claims to find in Clarice Lispector is the 'opening of a window', 'an unveiling', 'a clariseeing' that reaches the inside of things, beyond their mere appearance (ibid., p. 74). The 'clarice radiance' leads Cixous 'outside. Outside of the walls. Outside of the ramparts of our towns', outside 'the fortified castles that our demons and aberrations have edified for themselves'. Away from 'the dead who inhabit our own homes', 'the Clarice hand gives back to us [the] spaces inhabited by the sole living-ones. In the profound and humid inside of the outside' (ibid., p. 102). And to this woman whose 'orange-colored accents' could 'rub the eyes of [Cixous's] writing which were arid and covered with white films' (ibid., p. 14), Cixous declares her (apparently) unconditional love:

> To have the fortune – little sister of joy – to have encountered the joy clarice, or the joy gh or l or anna, and since then to live in joy, in her infinitely great arms, her cosmic arms, dry and warm, tender, slim – The too great fortune? – to be in her arms, she holds me, being in her space, for days and days, and summer nights, and since then, to live, a little above myself, in a fever, a suspension, an inner race.
>
> (ibid., pp. 54–6)

This idyllic dialogue between reader and writer, far from the alleged violence and inequalities of the masculine world, which also suggests an ideal, homosexual union between soulmates, actually blurs the distinction between Cixous and Lispector, particularly in the international scenario in which the latter became known in the late 1970s. As Cixous's readings have transformed Lispector into an exemplary sample of feminine writing, most of the interest expressed in Lispector – outside Brazil and the rather limited international circle of specialists in Brazilian literature – has also dwelt on how Lispector is 'compatible' with Cixous and, most of all, on how the Brazilian author might be instrumental in illustrating 'feminine' ways of spending. In such a narrative, Lispector has been literally 'used' by Cixous as a means to negotiate this difficulty: to push 'women' and 'the feminine' together, and place them clearly within political struggle and within history. [Cixous] is not talking about the real Clarice Lispector, a Brazilian left-wing modernist writer who died in 1977, but rather exploring the power of 'Lispector' as a symbol, and seeing the sort of connections Lispector's writing allows her to make. Cixous had found 'women' as a political problem, and 'feminine writing' as a political solution. In Lispector she tries to construct the unity of these two terms.

(Shiach 1989, p. 161)

In this context, Cixous and Lispector are not merely a reader and an author but a pair, or a couple, in which Lispector's position as a major, internationally recognized writer has been almost totally subject to Cixous's reading and writing. Thus, Lispector's 'value' as a major writer basically depends on the degree to which her texts can illustrate and validate Cixous's theories, functioning as a key to the understanding of feminine writing and as 'an indication of the further development of Cixous's own texts' (Ambruster 1983, p. 155).

In the kind of 'dialogue' which Cixous establishes with Lispector, Cixous's self-attributed 'privileged critical discourse' about the Brazilian author 'ultimately gives the false impression that Lispector is a sort of Cixousian twin' (Peixoto 1994, p. 42). Thus, for Susan R. Suleiman, Cixous and Lispector are 'two authors who are not one, but who are very, very close' (Suleiman 1991, p. xv). As a consequence, one can find unexpected references to Lispector – who never wrote a single paragraph on theory – even in introductory textbooks such as Sarup's *An Introductory Guide to Post-Structuralism and Postmodernism*, whose chapter on 'French Feminist Theories' devotes a few lines to Lispector which appropriately synthesize the peculiar role she has been made to play in contemporary critical thought:

Having established the political importance of feminine writing for women, Cixous found a woman practising such a writing. This is really quite remarkable. Having theorized the limitations and dangers of dualist thought, of subjectivity based on the obliteration of the Other, Cixous discovered another woman writer who was exploring the *same issues* in fictional form: Clarice Lispector. To understand this fully, one has to remember that Cixous's theorization of feminine writing had taken place almost

entirely in terms of the texts of canonical male writers such as
Joyce, Kleist or Hoffmann. And her theoretical vocabulary had
been largely derived from male theorists such as Lacan and
Derrida. And then, suddenly, she came across a writer who was
largely unknown in France, who was Jewish, who was a woman
and who shared many of her philosophical and stylistic preoc-
cupations. [. . .] Lispector embodies many of the ideas which
Cixous had propagated. [. . .] Like Lispector, Cixous wants
to reject the constraining masks of social identity in favor of a
Heideggerian notion of the multiple and temporal experience
of Being.

(Sarap 1993, pp. 113, 114)

It is certainly revealing that the only dissenting voices among
commentators of Cixous's singular 'collaboration' with the Brazilian
writer so far have come from those whose readership of Lispector's
texts is not limited to an interest in French theories of feminine
writing. Marta Peixoto and Anna Klobucka, for instance, effectively
point to the basic contradictions between Cixous's conception of
feminine research and her own readings of Lispector. Most of all,
they point to the paradoxical circumstances which have turned
Lispector into an emblem of the care with which one is supposed
to handle difference while in fact she has been violently absorbed
by the French feminist's powerful reading and writing. Both Peixoto
and Klobucka convincingly argue that for those who have read
Lispector outside the theoretical grounds of French feminine writing,
Cixous's alleged 'extreme fidelity' to Lispector's otherness cannot
stand even the most superficial exam. This peculiar brand of 'fidelity'
turns out to be a true intervention, a rewriting, in which what
belongs to the author and to the reader is literally shaded by omissions and misquotations, and in which Lispector's Portuguese is often
disregarded or taken to be a perfect translation of French. As Peixoto
points out, in *Vivre l'orange*, which is precisely about the importance
of Lispector's text for Cixous's own work, there are 'a number of
blurred quotations, in which Cixous paraphrases recognizable
passages from Lispector without acknowledging her move, and what
might be called simulated quotations, in which the words set off in
italics might seem to be Lispector's, but are Cixous's own paraphrases and conflations of several Lispector texts' (Peixoto 1994,
p. 44). This ambivalent handling of Clarice Lispector's work often
affects the very language in which she wrote her texts. As Peixoto

has shown, Cixous's apparent knowledge of Portuguese does not exactly entrust her to make specific comments on Lispector's use of words and grammatical structures. In her comments on Lispector's omission of the first-person subject pronoun we can find a clear example of Cixous's contradictory 'dedication' to the Brazilian author's originals, as the following fragment shows: 'Clarice writes in order to dissolve through a certain chemistry, through a certain magic and love, that which would be retention, weight, solidification, an arrest of the act of writing. That is why she ends by dropping the subject pronoun and saying: What am I saying? Am saying love' (Cixous 1990, p. 69; quoted in Peixoto 1994, p. 49). What Cixous sees as a meaningful deviation, as a special device used by Lispector is nothing but the norm in Portuguese. Therefore, as Lispector's text is forced to mean that which Cixous sees in it, Portuguese has to behave as if it were French or English.

As in the case of the Indian boys begging for English texts, the Cixous/Lispector affair can be understood from the perspective of the Lacanian notion of 'the subject presumed to know'. If transference cannot be distinguished from that which we generally call 'love' and from the main gestures that constitute any act of interpretation, Cixous's treatment of Lispector's texts is certainly exemplary of the radical revision of the reading plot as proposed by Felman via psychoanalysis (Felman 1987, p. 86). In her 'therapeutical' encounter with Lispector's work, Cixous invests the Brazilian writer with the authority and prestige of 'the subject presumed to know', of the one whose writing harbours all the answers and all the insights that could validate the defence of a feminine way of spending. As in any successful psychoanalytical encounter, the dialogue between Cixous and her 'subject presumed to know' allows the former to recover her long-lost 'orange', that is, to reread herself and to translate that which she already knew and was able to rediscover into a new productivity and a new writing. It is certainly appropriate that, for Cixous, 'the subject presumed to know' is also a positive 'mother figure'. As Toril Moi points out, in Cixous's writings, the mother as the source of good is 'clearly what Melanie Klein would call the Good Mother: the omnipotent and generous dispenser of love, nourishment and plenitude' that is obviously endowed with 'infinite power' (Moi 1985, p. 115). In Cixous's association of this power with writing, Lispector becomes the one who not only has the strength to 'unveil us' and 'to open our windows' (Cixous 1979b, p. 98), but also the capacity to find the essential meaning of every word, as Cixous declares in her very first text about the Brazilian writer, '*L'approche de Clarice Lispector*' (Cixous 1979a, pp. 412–13).

However, in order for Lispector to be invested with such authority and prestige and with such power to nurture and even to cure, she has to be 'saying' precisely that which Cixous needs and wants to hear. In this truly asymmetrical dialogue, while Cixous practically does all the 'talking', Lispector is inevitably forced not only to be saying 'the same thing everywhere', as Cixous explicitly declares in an essay on *Água Viva*, but also to agree unconditionally with her powerful reader: 'if Clarice herself reread *Água Viva*, she would reread it the way she wrote it and as we read it, without a gathering point of view that allows to carry one and only one judgment' (Cixous 1991b, p. 14). If what Lispector has written must coincide with what Cixous reads into it, there is no room for any other point of view, in an exclusive relationship that consistently ignores not only all other readers of Lispector but everything that in her texts does not comply with the principles of feminine writing. Moreover, it also requires the protection of Lispector's texts and image even from the author herself, as well as 'from her historical context and her class' (Peixoto 1994, p. 52). In a passage from an earlier version of 'Extreme fidelity', for instance, Cixous unabashedly declares:

> I would never have another seminar if I knew that enough people read Clarice Lispector. A few years ago when they began to divulge her, I said to myself: I will no longer have a seminar, you only need to read her, everything is said, it's perfect. But everything became repressed as usual, and they have even transformed her in an extraordinary way, embalmed her, stuffed her with straw in the guise of a Brazilian bourgeoise with polished fingernails. So I continue to accompany her with a reading that watches over her.
>
> (Cixous 1987, p. 26; quoted in Peixoto 1994, p. 52)

The transformation of the bourgeoise Lispector – whose pictures actually show a very attractive woman obviously wearing makeup and nail polish – into an androgynous Cixousian twin points to the other side of Cixous's passionate love for the Brazilian writer's work. Instead of a supposedly feminine, non-violent approach to difference, Cixous's transferential relationship with Lispector's texts shows that there is definitely more to this textual affair than sheer admiration or gratitude. The celebration of the text that is chosen as 'the subject presumed to know' implies not only love but also a violent desire to possess that which allegedly belongs to such a privileged authority. Using Cixous's own imagery, we may say that the daughter/reader, nurtured by the mother/author's milk/writing inevitably wants to be in the mother/author's position. In 'Coming to writing', for example, as she describes her early passionate dedication to the texts she 'ate, sucked, suckled, kissed' (Cixous 1991a, p. 12), Cixous confesses her 'transgressive' desire to be in the mother's position: 'Write? I was dying of desire for it, of love, dying to give writing what it had given to me. What ambition! What impossible happiness. To nourish my own mother. Give her, in turn, my milk? Wild imprudence' (ibid.).

In order for such an appropriation to be consummated, the dialogue with the text must obviously take place without its author's potential opposition, a practice which seems to be typical of Cixous's reading habits. As Verena A. Conley points out, living female writers are conspicuously absent from Cixous's reading enterprises:

> Cixous is not often kind to living women or contemporary women writers. Their works are singularly absent from her seminars and texts. As she puts it herself in *L'ange secret*, she wishes she could write on the living with the same talent and ease with which she writes on the dead. Neither Heidegger nor Lispector talks back. Other proper names can be associated with them without any sign of protest.
>
> (Conley 1992, p. 83)

Borrowing from Roland Barthes's theorization, we could say that Cixous's productive reading not only involves the 'death' of the author but turns her into a ghostly guest that is rarely invited to the scene of interpretation (Barthes 1977). From such a perspective, how can one possibly reconcile Cixous's explicitly transformative reading practice with her own proposal that contemporary theories of reading as production be 'resisted' in order to leave room for 'the adoption of a state of receptivity', in which the reader is supposed to carefully 'hear' that which the text is saying (Sellers 1988, p. 7)?

In Cixous's undoubtedly powerful and highly influential project, which presents itself as an 'ongoing quest for affirmation of life over death and power in all its forms, including those of academic institutions and practices' (Cixous 1990, p. xii), the construction of a

Cixousian Lispector compromises that which in Lispector's texts is perfectly distinguishable not only from Cixous's but also from the Brazilian writer's proper name. Although Cixous's transformation of Lispector's first name into a noun, a verb, an adjective or an adverb that is repeatedly interwoven into her own writing has been viewed as a feminine strategy 'to avoid both patronymic and paternal genealogy' (Conley 1994, p. 83), it certainly suggests the ultimate appropriation, i.e. the transformation of Lispector or, rather, of 'clarice' into a mere sign within Cixous's own text, as the following excerpts from *Vivre l'orange* (Cixous 1979b) clearly show: 'To make a smile beam just once on a beloved mouth, to make a clarice smile rise one time, like the light burst of an instant picked from eternity' (p. 74); 'It's a matter of an unveiling, clariseeing: a seeing that passes through the frames and toils that clothe the towns' (ibid.); 'Where does the clarice radiance lead us? – Outside. Outside of the walls' (p. 102); 'How to call forth claricely: it's a long and passionate work for all the senses' (p. 104).

If authority is ultimately a form of writing, as we can conclude with Felman (1982, p. 8), in the textual affair that has brought Cixous and Lispector together, it is Cixous who has had the upper hand, it is Cixous who gets to keep a 'proper', authorial name and who has had the (also academic) power to create authority and to write it her own way. Ultimately, in this plot it is Cixous who is 'the subject presumed to know', particularly for those who are blindly devoted to her texts and who have transformed her into the author (and the authority) that she is today within the broad area of cultural studies.

In her readings of Lispector, Cixous's feminine approach to evade the violence of translation and the mediation of patriarchal language turns out to be just another instance of the same relationship between subject and object that she so vehemently rejects. To use one of her most recurrent metaphors, we could say that in Cixous's handling of Lispector's work the translation process that takes place is radically transformative, as if the 'apple' in Lispector's texts had been thoroughly transformed into an 'orange' – or, more precisely, into an Oran-*je* – which betrays a reading which is first and foremost a rewriting shaped by specific interests. It is not, however, a mere instance of 'miscommunication', as Anna Klobucka puts it (Klobucka 1994, p. 48), nor of a 'mistranslation', as Sharon Willis might call it (Willis 1992). In this context, the notions of 'mistranslation' or 'miscommunication' might imply that one could read

Lispector without intervening in her work, that a reading could actually avoid transference and capture her supposedly original apple, as Cixous herself set out to do. However, even though any act of reading necessarily implies appropriation and the double bind of transference, what is peculiar about Cixous's readings of Lispector is the circumstances which have brought together an influential, academically powerful reader and an author who had hardly been read outside the limits of her marginal context and language. One could ponder, for instance, on the fact that Cixous does not turn Kafka's or Joyce's proper names into common nouns as she does with Lispector's, or, to put it another way, one could consider that, since Kafka and Joyce are undoubtedly recognized as internationally canonical writers, it would not be feasible to completely ignore their long-established authority as writers, or the authority of the readership that has been developed around it.

In this sense, the structure which Cixous's power and influence have been able to weave in her relationship with Lispector's texts can also remind us of another well-known narrative. We might say that Cixous's 'discovery' of Lispector's work, which coincidentally took place on an anniversary of Columbus's 'discovery' of the new continent, also repeats the basic strategies and reasoning of the European conquest of America. First of all, as in the so-called 'discovery' of America, Cixous's encounter with Lispector's work is a 'discovery' between quotation marks, a 'discovery' that is also an invasion, a taking-over which has to ignore, disregard or even destroy whatever was already there. Secondly, it is a 'discovery' which is also a transformation and, of course, a renaming that is done primarily in the interest of those who are in a position to undertake such an ambitious enterprise. From this perspective, we could say that Cixous's reading of Lispector is also a form of 'colonization', in which whatever or whoever is subject to foreign domination not only has to adopt the interests of the colonizer but also comes under the latter's complete control.

As the main scenes of the encounter between Cixous and Lispector illustrate the impossibility of treating otherness 'delicately, with the tips of the words', or with 'extreme fidelity', particularly in asymmetrical contexts, this is a lesson which we can appropriately find in Lispector herself. In one of her most impressive, complex narratives, *A Paixão segundo G.H.* (1964), we are invited to follow the narrator G.H.'s tortured reflection on herself and the human condition the morning after her maid leaves her post. A middle-class, sophisticated, financially independent sculptor, G.H. lives 'in cleanliness' and in 'semi-luxury' in an elegant, spacious penthouse, from where 'one can overpower a city'. As the narrative begins, we find her dressed in white, having breakfast, and planning to visit the maid's room – something she had not done in the six months the woman had worked for her – in order to make sure that every-thing is in order before the new maid arrives. It is in this small room – 'the portrait of an empty stomach', 'the opposite' of that which she created in her own home, conveniently separated from the main living area and close to the service entrance, and which has the 'double function' of squeezing in the maid's skimpy bed and her mistress's discarded 'rags, old suitcases, old newspapers' – that Lispector's G.H. develops her reflection which culminates with her alleged transformation 'into herself'.

As she approaches the room, G.H. finds her most radical other in her blurred recollections of the black maid who has just left, but whose name and appearance she has difficulty in remembering. As she enters the surprisingly clean room – which she was expecting to find dusty and untidy – G.H. is confronted with her own 'inex-plicable' rage towards the way in which the maid, with a boldness appropriate only for the actual owners of apartments, had actually taken possession of the space that did not belong to her, not only by keeping it in order, but also by having drawn a mural in black charcoal, which G.H. sees as a sort of writing on one of the white walls. The enraged G.H., who is a sculptor precisely because she likes to arrange things with her own hands in order to take possession of her surroundings, sets out to reconquer the room. As she feels like 'killing something', G.H. violently begins 'to erase the maid's traces' from the usurped room in order to reinstate the familiar oppositions she constructed within her own world (in which the maid is of course to be kept in her subaltern place and perfectly distinguishable in every possible way from her mistress and oppo-site). The vehemence of G.H.'s anger as she attempts to repossess the room finally makes her recall (without any pleasure) the maid's 'silent hatred', her facial features – 'fine and delicate like a queen's' – and her proud posture. Frenetically moving furniture around, G.H. is all of a sudden faced with an even more radical version of otherness: a cockroach. The vision of the insect coming from behind the maid's bed triggers a different trail of ambivalent feelings divided between the disgust the narrator feels towards the cockroach, and a certain admiration for the resilient insect's ancient 'wisdom' which allows it to 'concentrate on living in its own body'. After a long, tortured struggle 'to depersonalize herself', and, implicitly, to acquire that which constitutes the cockroach's wisdom, G.H. kills it and finally manages 'to transform herself into herself' by swallowing the white substance issuing from the crushed insect.

Having dared to simplify Lispector's narrative to its bare bones, I shall not even try to go into its complex metaphysical implications and I will limit myself to commenting on Cixous's reading of the 'same' text. First of all, after reading Cixous, it is not difficult to imagine why she would find Lispector's work so appealing. We can definitely recognize echoes of Cixous's idealized conception of the feminine in the independent and sophisticated G.H. Like Cixous's Eve, who is not afraid of tasting 'the fruit of the tree of knowledge', and who does not fear the inside of the forbidden fruit, G.H. finds the courage to taste the cockroach's inside in order to absorb its wisdom. Furthermore, also following a Cixousian path, we could probably interpret G.H.'s final awareness of the fact that her maid did in fact have an identity and even a need to express herself artistically as the former's peculiar, belated recognition of otherness. What is difficult, if not impossible, to imagine, however, is how Cixous could possibly justify her interpretation of G.H.'s narrative as a story about 'extreme fidelity' to difference, and the exhilarating possibility of a perfect communion (and communication) with otherness which could do away with mastery, supposedly teaching us that 'the other must remain absolutely strange within the greatest possible proximity' and 'must be respected according to its species, without violence, with the neutrality of the Creator, the equal and undemonstrative love with regard to each being' (Cixous 1991a, p. 171).

It seems quite clear that what Cixous's reading of G.H.'s quest significantly cannot account for is precisely the same basic elements to which she is utterly oblivious in her own treatment of Lispector's work and authorial figure: violence and asymmetry. Lispector's detailed description of the asymmetrical relationship which G.H. establishes with her black maid is not only completely ignored by Cixous, but could also be instrumental in deconstructing Cixous's tirelessly repeated notion that there is something intrinsically good or pacifistic in her proposal that otherness must be respected at all costs. As Lispector's plot undeniably indicates, what moves G.H. in her violent attempt to 'erase' the maid's traces and 'writing' from the room which did not belong to her and, ultimately, what triggers G.H.'s final revelation about the cockroach's true wisdom is exactly the outrage she feels towards the fact that the maid somehow refused to stay put in her subaltern role. In this particular instance, the respect which should be paid to otherness – or the 'extreme fidelity' allegedly owed to difference – is undoubtedly also a violent effort to keep the subaltern as the true opposite of the dominant. Similarly, it is the same ambiguous proposal of a supposedly pacifistic, feminine economy which seems to allow Cixous to consider G.H.'s killing and absorption of the insect as a 'perfect communion' with otherness. However, considering the actual plot of Lispector's text, which seems to suggest precisely the impossibility of a perfectly harmonic coexistence with the other, how can we possibly learn from G.H.'s undoubtedly aggressive relationship with her maid and with the cockroach that the other 'must be respected according to its species, without violence, with the neutrality of the Creator'?

If we compare the main scenes of the Cixous/Lispector affair to the one that depicts the boys from Comercolly begging for English books, it seems quite clear that the illusive fascination exercised by 'the subject presumed to know' does not by any means institute authority. If authority is ultimately a form of writing, it certainly belongs to those who have the means not only to write but, most of all, to impose a certain attitude and a certain reading upon this writing. As Gayatri C. Spivak elaborates on her well-known argument according to which 'the subaltern cannot speak', 'even when the subaltern makes an effort to the death to speak, she is not able to be heard, and speaking and hearing complete the speech act' (Spivak 1996, p. 292). In the asymmetrical 'dialogue' that takes place between G.H. and the cockroach, or G.H. and the black maid, for instance, the establishment of authority has been clearly and directly dependent on the dominant's power to decide what to do both with the insect's alleged wisdom and with the maid's unwelcome writing on the wall. In G.H.'s elegant penthouse, the absent maid and the wise but helpless cockroach will not be adequately, or pacifically, heard no matter how and what they 'speak'. Therefore, in G.H.'s exemplary 'colonial' space, the asymmetrical relationship which she establishes with her subaltern prevents her from actually 'learning' from the insect, her bizarre 'subject presumed to know', in a non-aggressive manner, or even from 'collaborating' with it. In such a context, if the dominant G.H. wants something from the other, she does not hesitate to destroy it in order to take possession of that which she desires. Similarly, in the perverse 'dialogue' which Cixous establishes with Lispector, who conveniently cannot talk back, the Brazilian author will not really 'speak' no matter how and what she wrote in her marginal language, because the completion of her 'speech act' – at least within the boundaries of this 'dialogue' – has been entirely dependent on Cixous's power not only of deciding what Lispector is in fact allowed to say but, most of all, of being heard and taken seriously, no matter what *she* says. Thus, far from demonstrating the possibility of undoing the basic 'masculine' oppressive dichotomy between subject and object, which she appropiately associates with patriarchy and colonialism, Cixous's textual approach to Lispector's work is in fact an exemplary illustration of an aggressively 'masculine' approach to difference.

References

Ambruster, C. (1983) 'Hélène-Clarice: nouvelle voix', *Contemporary Literature* 24 (2): 155.

Barthes, R. (1977) 'The death of the author' and 'From work to text', *Image. Music. Text*, trans. S. Heath (New York: Hill & Wang, 1977).

Castello, J. (1996) 'Francesa divulga mistérios de clarice', *O Estado de São Paulo*, 27 Oct.

Chamberlain, L. (1992) 'Gender and the metaphorics of translation', *Rethinking Translation: Discourse, Subjectivity, Ideology*, ed. L. Venuti (New York and London: Routledge), 57–74.

Cixous, H. (1975) 'Le rire de la meduse', *L'arc* 61: 39–54.

— (1979a) 'L'approche de Clarice Lispector', *Poétique* 40: 408–19.

— (1979b) *Vivre l'orange/To Live the Orange* (Paris: Des femmes).

— (1980) *Illa* (Paris: Des femmes).

— (1987) 'Extrême fidélité', *Travessia* 14: 20–31.

— (1988) *Writing Differences: Readings from the Seminar of Hélène Cixous*, ed. S. Sellers (Milton Keynes: Open University Press).

— (1989) *L'heure de Clarice Lispector* (Paris: Des femmes).

— (1990) *Readings: The Poetics of Blanchot, Joyce, Kafka, Kleist, Lispector, and Tsvetayeva*, ed. V.A. Conley (Minneapolis: University of Minnesota Press).

— (1991a) *Hélène Cixous's 'Coming to Writing' and Other Essays*, ed. D. Jenson (Cambridge, Mass.: Harvard University Press).

— (1991b) *Reading with Clarice Lispector*, ed. V.A. Conley (Minneapolis: University of Minnesota Press).

Conley, V.A. (1992) *Hélène Cixous* (New York: Harvester Wheatsheaf).

Delisle, J. and Woodsworth, J. (eds) (1995) *Translators through History* (Amsterdam and Philadelphia: John Benjamins).

Felman, S. (1982) 'To open the question', *Literature and Psychoanalysis* (Baltimore: The Johns Hopkins University Press).

— (1987) *Jacques Lacan and the Adventure of Insight: Psychoanalysis in Contemporary Culture* (Cambridge, Mass.: Harvard University Press).

Klobucka, A. (1994) 'Hélène Cixous and the hour of Clarice Lispector', *Substance* 73: 41–62.

Lispector, C. (1961) *A Maçã no Escuro* (Rio de Janeiro: Francisco Alves; repr as *The Apple in the Dark*, trans. G. Rabassa, (New York: Knopf, 1967).

— (1964) *A Paixão segundo G.H.* (Rio de Janeiro: Editora do Autor; repr. as *The Passion according to G.H.*, trans. R.W. Sousa, Minneapolis: University of Minnesota Press).

— (1973) *Água Viva* (Rio de Janeiro: Artenova; repr. as *The Stream of Life*, trans. E. Lowe and E. Fitz, Minneapolis: University of Minnesota Press, 1989).

Moi, T. (1985) *Sexual/Textual Politics* (London and New York: Methuen).

Niranjana, T. (1992) *Siting Translation: History, Post-Structuralism, and the Colonial Context* (Berkeley: University of California Press).

Paz, O. (1959) *El laberinto de la soledad* (Mexico: Fondo de Cultura Económica).

Peixoto, M. (1994) *Passionate Fictions: Gender, Narrative, and Violence in Clarice Lispector* (Minneapolis: University of Minnesota Press).

Sarup, M. (1993) *An Introductory Guide to Post-Structuralism and Postmodernism* (Athens: The University of Georgia Press).

Sellers, S. (ed.) (1988) 'Introduction', *Writing Differences: Readings from the Seminar of Hélène Cixous* (Milton Keynes: Open University Press).

Shiach, M. (1989) 'Their "symbolic" exists, it holds power – we, the sowers of disorder, know it only too well', *Between Feminism and Psychoanalysis* ed. T. Brennan (London and New York: Routledge).

Spivak, G.C. (1996) 'Subaltern talk: interview with the editors (1993–94)', *The Spivak Reader*, ed. D. Landry and G. Maclean (London and New York: Routledge), pp. 287–308.

Suleiman, S.R. (1991) 'Writing past the wall', *'Coming to Writing' and Other Essays*, ed. D. Jenson (Cambridge, Mass.: Harvard University Press).

Venuti, L. (1995) *The Translator's Invisibility: A History of Translation* (London and New York: Routledge).

Willis, S. (1992) 'Mistranslation, missed translation: Hélène Cixous' *Vivre l'orange*', *Rethinking Translation: Discourse, Subjectivity, Ideology*, ed. L. Venuti (New York and London: Routlege), pp. 106–19.

Chapter 8

Shifting grounds of exchange

B.M. Srikantaiah and Kannada translation

Vanamala Viswanatha and Sherry Simon

Like other forms of cultural traffic which follow in the wake of colonial contact, translations are objects of suspicion. As vehicles of colonial influence, as purveyors of foreign novelty to the metropolis, they travel the routes opened by conquest. But they also enter into relations of transfer whose results are not entirely predictable. It is because they are products of the interaction between cultures of unequal power, bearing the weight of shifting terms of exchange, that translations provide an especially revealing entry point into the dynamics of cultural identity-formation in the colonial and post-colonial contexts.

This chapter will highlight the work of writer/translator B.M. Srikantaiah (1884–1946). We want to look at his work with several views in mind: to understand the ways in which translation has contributed to the specific history of Kannada literature (in comparison with the experiences of Western literary cultures, as well as of other Indian literatures such as Hindi and Bengali, for instance), to consider more generally the way translations can enrich – or impede – the development of a literary identity, and to investigate the ideological grounds which condition the production and reception of translations. What are the operative political and cultural forces which, in specific contexts, determine the value given to translations? What kinds of power can translations exercise? While translations during the colonial period are often considered to be wholly derivative forms of writing whose impact was largely negative, the work and influence of B.M. Srikantaiah suggests a much more complex and productive role for translations.

The larger framework for this investigation is a concern for the paradoxical results of cultural and literary contact. On the one hand, it is known that massive influence from the West created heavily imitative forms of expression in India, as in other colonized areas; on the other, we know that this same influence also had the effect of provoking the emergence of totally new forms. For instance, the most intense point of British influence in India was in Bengal. It was the very force of this influence, however, that provided the impetus for renewed forms of Bengali narrative, and in particular the emergence of the novel in Bengali (Das, 1995, p. 41). Today, an increasingly global situation of literary exchange means that there is a drive towards uniformity and levelling of difference, but there is also a counter-force of resistance working to produce original forms of the local. Translations contribute to both of these dynamics: while often serving as the vehicle of global commonplace, they also act as catalysts in the emergence of contestatory forms of writing. Translations provoke cultural change.

This essay is a collaborative effort, coming out of our different locations and knowledges. We have constructed our narrative by combining the different perspectives from which we view this material: on the one hand, an insider's participatory grasp of the relations between Kannada and English literature; on the other, the kinds of perceptions made possible by familiarity with the interlingual situation in Canada. The presence of two strong literary cultures in Canada and the imperatives of official bilingualism have resulted in a rich tradition of literary translation as well as a well-developed sensitivity to the dissymmetries in the impact and cultural value of translations.[1]

Though the intricate weave of languages and cultures in India makes for a vastly more complex socio-linguistic ecosystem than the Canadian one, translation is in both cases a particularly sensitive indicator of cultural tensions. Using this double perspective allows us to enlarge the frame through which we can understand cultural difference as it works through translation.

We begin with the axiom that India, perhaps more fully than most other nations, is a 'translation area'. Languages and idioms are in constant interaction, whether at the level of informal daily interchange, or in the more formal registers of governmental communications or creative work. The power of English as a link language grows steadily, yet continues to coexist everywhere with the national language (Hindi) and regional languages.

The Indian literatures today carry traces of their formation through intense vectors of interaction, linguistic and cultural – from

Sanskrit and Persian, English and other Indian languages. Most Indian languages initiated their respective literary traditions through translations – either from Sanskrit or from other Indian languages.[2] And interaction between the pan-Indian 'high' literary traditions and the regional 'low' forms, the reciprocal influences among epic, folktale and other oral traditions have also stimulated the emergence of new forms of Indian writing.[3] English literature, as well, continues to be a strong presence on the Indian scene, in a 'singular case', according to Sisir Kumar Das, of the 'coexistence of literary systems' in the modern world.[4] Predictably, translation from and into English remains the most vigorous, but also the most politically contested, area of literary transactions in contemporary India.

It is impossible, therefore, to speak about Indian literature (or, the Indian literatures) without taking into account the dynamics of cultural interrelations within the various Indian languages and literary traditions, with the former colonial power and, increasingly today, with the literature produced by the Indian diaspora in Britain, North America and elsewhere. These ongoing contacts and exchanges have fostered a tradition of 'creation through rewriting' which is central to the history of Indian writing practices. Does this mean, as G.N. Devy suggests, that, unburdened by the negative Judaeo-Christian implications of the Fall, translation carries a positive cultural, historical and ethical charge in India?[5] It is certainly true that for the Western scholar, used to the literary mono-lingualism which prevails in much of the West, the Indian situation provides a dramatic contrast. Whereas in the European tradition, the commerce between languages is an accessory function, becoming a part of the process of creation only in exceptional cases (as in the great High Modernist writers Pound, Beckett, Joyce and then Nabokov), in India this relationship is foundational. Cases of literary bilingualism are common, rather than exceptional. Both Srikantaiah and the poet-translator A.K. Ramanujan (1929–1993), for instance, exemplify this polyvalence, practising the full continuum of writing functions which include Kannada poet, English writer and poet, scholar and translator.

These crucial interlinguistic dynamics have yet to be given suffi-cient attention by theoreticians of post-colonial literary relations. Some recent theoretical writing on translation in India has, however, begun this task. On the one hand, there are the programmatic texts of Aijaz Ahmad and Tejaswini Niranjana, which denounce the incapacity of Western theory to take into account the dynamics and

values of multilingualism in India. For Niranjana, Western translation theory is impervious to the power relations which drive cultural
relations between unequal partners, particularly in the case of the
orientalist project. Ahmad castigates Western scholarship for its
insensitivity to the 'civilizational complexity' of India, which cannot
be 'lived or thought through in terms of the centralizing imperatives
of the nation-state we have inherited from the European bourgeoisie'
– or from the perspective of a tradition privileging only 'High
Textuality' (Ahmad, 1992, p. 74). He reminds us of the paradox that
English has become in some sense the only truly 'national' literary
language in India, all other languages relegated to 'regional' status
(p. 78) and that English will become 'the language in which knowledge of Indian literature is produced' when the fundamental nature
of much of this work is polyglot (ibid., pp. 245–52).[6]

The writings of Sujit Mukherjee, Harish Trivedi and G.N. Devy,
on the other hand, focus on investigations into the actual practices
and contexts of translation in India. While they share many of the
assumptions of Niranjana and Ahmad, they attempt to expose the
ambiguity of values which emerge through cultural *transactions*.
Showing how translation was used by Indians to shape a response to
orientalism, Trivedi documents the cultural work of translation
through extensive studies of translations by Indian writers. These
case studies root the work of literary exchange firmly in the 'cultural
grounds' (Trivedi, 1993, p. 63) from which it emerged. Mukherjee
and Devy show how the intents and effects of translation in India
must be understood within the long tradition of rewriting, which
gives translations the authority and legitimacy of original texts. Their
studies of authors and literary movements construct a complex archi-
tecture of pressures and counterpressures, revealing the ways in
which literary exchanges have moved through a variety of phases,
each dictated by specific goals and readership, all the while actively
nourishing the literary potential of many of the Indian languages
(Devy, 1993, pp. 117–25). Far from being a tool exclusive to the
singular goals of missionaries, orientalist scholars and administrators,
translation has served a variety of uses, as complex and ambiguous
as the cultural context from which they emerged.[7] The study of these
linguistic and cultural relations remains, however, fragmentary. We
turn now to the translational relations between Kannada and
English, a rich terrain for such investigation.

The particular situation of the Kannada language within the
Indian mosaic is as follows. Kannada is one of the four Dravidian

languages of South India, spoken today in the state of Karnataka by nearly 25 million people. Kannada literary production has a history of fifteen centuries, making it second only to Tamil in the longevity and wealth of its literary tradition.

We find, in the relations between Kannada and English, strong models of the kinds of effects which translations have at specific moments in the interplay between colonizing and colonized cultures. This reading will concentrate on the work of B.M. Srikantaiah (from now on BMS) which provides such a model. He played a highly influential role as teacher, writer and translator into Kannada at the start of the century, but the source of his enormous reputation as a pioneering literary personality was his translation of sixty Romantic and Victorian poems entitled *English Geethagalu* (1926). Described as 'The Lyrical Ballads' of Kannada literature, this volume has been considered a 'guidebook for lyric poetry in Kannada'.[8] Many of the poems in the volume continue today to be prescribed as obligatory reading in high schools and colleges in Karnataka, while some are set to music and have become part of popular culture.

BEFORE BMS

Critics of Kannada literature are unanimous in describing Kannada literature of the last century as wholly derivative, drawing its sustenance from the past. There existed a large body of mythological and religious narratives, biographies of deities and stories for Yakshagana folk theatre, but there was little that was innovative in the themes or forms of expression, which had been acquired from old Sanskrit and old Kannada literature and had very little link to contemporary life. In addition, there was a gap between the highly structured nature of old Kannada and the contemporary, spoken idiom (Havanur, 1974).

Translations served to help Kannada literature break away from these traditional forms. They were first undertaken by missionaries and by administrators in the service of colonial rule. Both Ferdinand Kittel (1832–1903) and B.L. Rice (1837–1927)[9] translated Christian hymns according to the earlier metrics and the songs of Dasas, but others attempted to translate Christian texts into Kannada so that they could be sung to Western melodies. In the latter case, they were forced to modify the ancient rhyme schemes and metrical patterns in order to make their poems musically viable. For the first time in Kannada literature, the ancient rhyme schemes and metrical patterns were given up. According to Havanur, the modern Kannada short poem came into being around 1838 through the invocation poems translated by the Christian missionaries.

Another stimulus to modern Kannada literature came with the need to provide textbooks in Kannada for younger children. Many translated poems, specifically designed to provide an idiom familiar to the spoken language, were included in these textbooks. In 1873, the *First Book of Kannada Poetry*, containing poems like 'Advice to Young Girls', 'Glory to Victoria' and 'Monkey's Game', was published. This poetry was to be free of the bombast of traditional Sanskrit poetry, while aiming at simplicity and clearness compatible with the spoken dialect. S.G. Narasimhacharya published a collection of simple poems for children, as well as *Aesop's Fables*.[10] These translations were not particularly accomplished from an aesthetic point of view; they were important, rather, for their role in creating a new readership for Kannada.

By the end of the nineteenth century, under the influence of English literature, and following the Bengali and Marathi examples, new genres featuring the personal experience of the writer were introduced into Kannada literature: lyric poetry, the travelogue, the diary, the biography, the novel. Many of the new writers came from journalism (Havanur, 1974). But it was only with the work of BMS in 1921 that the lyric as a form really took hold in Kannada.

The work of BMS, largely recognized as the most fully accomplished creative use of translation at this time, is to be seen, therefore, against the backdrop of a period intensely interested in translation as a way of coming to terms with British influence and in altering the canonical forms of Kannada literature.[11] The generalized interest in issues of translation, and the seriousness with which these issues were treated, can be observed in a remarkable treatise published in English in Mysore in 1910. *The Art of Translation: A Critical Study* by R. Raghunath Rao, BA is an admirably perceptive study of translation ethics and technique, prepared for university students in Mysore and Bangalore. Apart from the clear and forthright tone of the essay, and its sharp and well-documented critique of translations of *Shakuntala* by B.L. Rice (and to some extent of Monier Williams), what is most striking about Rao's views is his awareness that translation adequacy must be judged in the light of the evolving dynamics between cultures. The degree of success of cultural transmission depends on the political and cultural forces operating at that moment.

In the Kannada milieu of that time, the nature of the forces at work were clear enough. English literature was the 'gift' of the colonizers. The obvious disparity of cultural power between English and Kannada literature was largely interpreted in one way: the wealth of English literature was to be used in the service of Kannada. In November 1907, M.D. Alasingaracharya (1877–1940), a well-known writer and scholar in Kannada and Sanskrit, wrote:

It is wrong to totally decry or accept the West. If we reject translations and stick only to our own traditions, we lose out on capitalizing on these translations. On the other hand, if we study only English and ignore our languages, the study itself will be purposeless. Therefore, if we can view both languages with an unprejudiced mind, then it will give an impetus to the development of the Kannada language. Therefore, all of us who have English education should never forget our primary aim of improving our own language and our own land. Unless we are bilingual, this is impossible.

(Ananthanarayana, 1962, pp. 28–9)

The same sentiment is echoed by A.B. Srikantaiah, yet another Kannada scholar, when in 1915 he says:

There are two ways to develop our mother tongue. Either the native language should be strong within itself. When that is not so, we have to gain this strength through translations. Therefore, all English-educated people, if you don't wake up and develop your languages and translate writing that is relevant for us today, we shall excommunicate you.

(ibid.)

THE WORK

BMS was by profession an English teacher with an MA (Eng.) from Madras University. During the early years of his career he refused to speak in Kannada, and published *A Handbook of Rhetoric* (1912) in English. Later, though, he became a fervent Kannada activist and contributed in many ways to the promotion of Kannada literature.

Using his institutional power at the University of Mysore, he helped to set up an MA in Kannada literature, organized publishing avenues and lecture tours for writers, encouraged students to engage with Kannada in different capacities. In addition, his own work as a creative writer, as a critic, and especially as a translator, was decisive. He is said to have given the Kannada language a 'way of thinking, a texture of thought'.[12]

His creative writing was limited to one collection of poems, criticism, and a series of essays on the development of the Kannada language and literature. His translations include three plays, which were all stimulated by his acute sense of the absence of tragedy in Kannada.[13] The first play, *Gadayuddha Natakam* (1926), is an adaptation of a tenth-century Kannada epic by Ranna, which, in contrast to original Vyasa Mahabharata, valorizes Duryodhana as a tragic hero. In 1927 he wrote *Ashwatthaman*, using the structure of Sophocles' *Ajax*, to force the immortal character of Ashwatthaman of the original Mahabharata to become mortal. *Parasikaru* was the third play, published in 1935; it is a translation of Aeschylus' *Persians*.

The three plays demonstrate three different translation/rewriting strategies, for which there are three different Sanskrit terms. The first play is an example of *roopa-antar* (changing the shape), in the sense that BMS has intensified the tragic dimensions of Duryodhana and transformed the epic form to the dramatic, thereby creating a new genre of tragic theatre in Kannada. The second is an *anu-vada* (something that follows after), in that BMS, by making the conventionally immortal Ashwattaman die, has subjected the Indian myth to the structures and intents of Greek tragedy and made the Indian myth subservient to the dynamics of Sophocles' play. *Parasikaru* illustrates a third strategy, *bhashanthara* (changing the language), in which BMS offers a literal translation of Aeschylus' *Persians*, choosing to retain all the cultural elements of the original intact.

Of the three strategies, the first one, the transforming mode, has become and remained the most influential. The last mode was the least successful of the three, because it was perceived as excessively alien to the culture. The second was actively resisted because it was seen as a conscious and contrived distortion of tradition – devised only to fulfil what was again perceived as an imported need for tragedy. However, as a writing strategy which enabled the Kannada literary tradition to be maintained, while introducing needed changes which came from outside that tradition – by providing a satisfying match between new literary forms and indigenous material – the first mode of translation enjoyed the greatest success.

All of these strategies are deployed in the *English Geethagalu* as well. Of the sixty-three poems published in that collection, three were original compositions and the rest translations of English Romantic and Victorian poets, the largest numbers being by Shelley (nine), Wordsworth (five), Burns (seven), Tennyson (three), Byron (two). Many of the poems were love poems; others dealt with patriotism, nature and philosophical issues. Aside from the patriotic poems, which are translated completely literally (place-names, titles, etc. simply transcribed into Kannada), the other poems all show some kind of adaptation. The naturalization is of several kinds: proper names are changed to Kannada names ('Rose Aylmer' becomes 'Paduma'; 'Bonnie Leslie' becomes 'Sundari Kamale'); natural phenomena are also adapted ('summer' becomes 'vasantha', meaning spring; 'greenwood tree' becomes 'adavimara', 'tree in the woods'). The most important changes, however, have to do with the introduction of folk expressions and traditional ballad forms, as well as rhythms of spoken Kannada which had not previously been considered part of the high poetic tradition. One of the most interesting changes occurs in the poem 'The Bridge of Sighs', where Christianity is equated with the ideals of the Aryan tradition with which the Kannada reader is familiar:

> Alas for the rarity
> Of Christian charity
> Under the sun
>
> (original)

> O, where is it hiding
> The kindness of Aryan Dharma
> The compassion of the Aryan people
> Only the burning one knows!
>
> (back-translation of BMS's version)

> My Love is like a red, red rose
> That's newly sprung in June
>
> (original)

> The girl I love is the red in the lotus
> The radiant red in the newly blossomed lotus
>
> (back-translation of BMS's version)

Like the rose, the lotus in Sanskrit and Kannada love poetry is a standard image. Again, BMS uses a well-coded and familiar device to naturalize the English text.

These two examples are among many which could be singled out from these poems, showing how BMS remains within the universe of traditional Kannada poetry even while 'translating' an alien culture. This naturalizing dynamic is made perfectly clear in BMS's preface, where he says that he has not necessarily chosen the 'best' poems in English but those that best suit the Kannada temperament, thus making translation an act of conscious appropriation.

> Through this small volume, Kannada people can learn something about English literature ... [and in this way escape] mindless traditionalism and expose ourselves to themes like war, love, death, patriotism, nature, human relations, etc. which have been universal and to see how different poets from various countries have dealt with these is necessary for us. We need to take courage and diligently review these and march forward towards progress.

His most successful and popular translated poems show, then, a perfect fit between his intention, choice of text and translation strategy. In fact, BMS's poems have completely displaced the originals as far as the Kannada reader is concerned. The poems did not open onto an engagement with English culture, but served the cause of Kannada.

BMS: CULTURAL ICON

Is it this allegiance to Kannada which explains the tremendous impact of *English Geethagalu* at the time of its publication and the continuing worship of BMS in the Kannada critical milieu? The period known as the Renaissance of Kannada literature, from 1900 to 1940, was marked by the impact of Western education, the Hindu reform movement and the Gandhian nationalist movement. There was a clear consciousness that Kannada literature needed new stimulation, such as it had received from previous contacts with Sanskrit and Persian. The English tradition – including the Classics – was seen as a new form of outside influence, which could provide challenge and nourishment for Kannada, at the same time strengthening a sense of Kannada identity in opposition to Hindi, Tamil or Marathi. But most important, certainly, is the fact that BMS sensed the need to shape a new Kannada identity which was tied down neither by a stagnant traditionalism nor by an allegiance to the English. BMS used translation in the sense of *roopantar*, transformation, as a way of countering adversaries both within and without. He employed the hegemonic voice of the colonizer to release Kannada literature from the monkey-grip of tradition which was closed in on itself, and thereby provided a liberatory impetus. On the other hand, he invoked tradition and maintained continuity with it, as an anchor against the devouring impact of colonization which threatened his project of forging a distinct Kannada identity.

The content of this Kannada identity was determined by the class and caste to which he belonged. BMS clearly declared his biases regarding what literature is and who it should reach. 'Eschewing the rural dialects, we should teach and print the clear Kannada spoken by the best caste and the educated class, to convert it into the language of our writing.'[14] Both in terms of theme and form, BMS's work established a canon which privileged male, middle-class, educated, Brahmin sensibility and the language of the Brahmin castes of the Mysore region.

Even while promoting a modern identity which included new genres and secular themes, this canon excluded other idioms and styles. Bendre (1896–1982), an outstanding Kannada poet from the region of Dharwad, used the spoken rhythms and folk idiom of the Dharwad dialect, distinctly different from the canon BMS helped establish. Being a nativist, he felt that BMS, through his translations, had used the voice of the colonizer to gain power for his own work. The example of Kuvempu (1904–1994) is also pertinent. He came from the Shudra caste, was educated at a missionary school, but adopted a style of writing poetry which is highly Sanskritized and Brahminical. His epic poem *Ramayana Darshanam* is written in a highly stylized Kannada which enjoyed poetic legitimacy.[15] His two major novels, however, are written in a local style and the language of his region. As far as his poetry was concerned, Kuvempu felt forced to fall in line with the canon established by BMS. Only Bendre was able to resist. The canonical status of BMS consecrated, then, one idiom of Kannada writing which was to remain dominant for several decades. Though productive in that it set off a wave of translations[16] and new creative work, BMS's project is certainly not without its political ambiguities, in particular with respect to his unquestioned loyalty to the maharajah of Mysore. In addition, his Kannada nationalism ignored the pan-Indian Gandhian nationalism which was so important during this time.[17]

That the success of his work was linked to the hierarchy of caste and class in Karnataka is by no means irrelevant. BMS's own struggle with English sets off, in its wake, another level of struggle within Kannada culture. That is, his translations impose *within* Kannada culture a hierarchy of idioms. A new field of divisions, inequalities and oppositional forces is at once created and revealed by these translations. Evidence for this can be seen in the Bandaya ('Protest') literary movement of 1975 which radically questioned the dominance of forms of writing favoured by the upper-caste and English-educated elite. As a result, the marginalized voices of Muslim, Dalith, women and tribal writers have become increasingly audible in Kannada writing. Translations of these writers promote the emergence of new versions of Kannada cultural identity.

SOME MODELS OF CULTURAL DIFFERENCE IN TRANSLATION

The dissymmetries between Kannada and English exist today, as they did for BMS. But the sites at which translators can express their political engagement have shifted.

BMS's story is that of the first significant encounters between Kannada and English literature in the pre-independence state of Mysore. The example of BMS underlines the paradoxal effects of imitation and mimicry, of the perverse homage which allows for a transfer of powers from the source into the receiving language.[18] For modern Kannada literature, then, translation is a truly foundational act, providing a new idiom which was immediately taken up by a new generation of writers. At the same time, this move was grounded in one primordial reality, one absolute given: the superiority of English over Kannada.

The work of the poet and immensely influential translator A.K. Ramanujan, in contrast, tells of a later constellation of cultural relations between post-independence India and the West.[19] He also used the power of English to legitimate the literary value of Kannada, but he did so by translating *into* English, participating in a configuration of influences which involved a new set of intents and suspicions. For AKR, working within an understanding of cultural worlds as potentially *equivalent*, translatability, the distance between unlike realities, was not an issue that his readers were to be constantly reminded of. Questions of translation were to be dealt with in the prefaces and introductions of his works, letting the reader then cross over into the pleasurable order of aesthetics. The hand of the translator is the heavy but invisible presence that smoothes over the unruly shapes of the original. The problems of translation could be solved through rigour, sensitivity and craftsmanship.

The contemporary translator of Kannada literature faces yet another configuration of cultural relationships, one in which the very notion of alterity is troubled. The poles which regulate translation are unstable, the categories of East and West always crumbling into fragments and yet continuing to dominate, direct and interpret activities of transfer and exchange. The work of Tejaswini Niranjana, translator and post-colonial critic, privileges the *critical* aim of translation, with the intention of distancing the reader.[20] Niranjana, much like Gayatri Spivak, will propose a 'tentative' and 'disruptive' text, in contrast to Ramanujan's finely crafted poem. This 'interventionist' mode of translation is an expression of the contemporary difficulty in conceptualizing cultural relations, of the crisis in modes of cultural exchange. Translation comes to play a crucial *cognitive* role in drawing attention to the problematic nature of transmission and transfer.

Each of these translating projects enacts a relationship of difference. Each responds to a historical and political conjuncture, embodying this response within the aesthetics of the translated text. It is tempting to see these moments as steps in a historical progression, moving from a situation of absolute hierarchy towards a more fluid and hybridized cultural relationship between Kannada and English. The translations of BMS reflect the ambiguities of the first moments of significant cultural encounter between English and Kannada, those of AKR a modernist confidence in civilizational equivalence, and the work of Niranjana a critical and oppositional understanding of cultural relations. It is less important, however, to see these projects as coming progressively closer to the truth of alterity than to be attentive to these different shapings of cultural difference – and the way they are mobilized and activated through translation.

KANNADA AND CANADA

Although the historical determinants affecting translation in Canada are very different from those in India, it is possible to observe similarities in the way translation crystallizes configurations of cultural difference. It is not the fabric of textual engagement which is comparable, but rather the way in which the translational encounter moves through stagings of difference. In both cases, there is continuity established through a long-term dialogue between cultural 'partners', but the terms of this exchange are affected by the often conflictual nature of political and economic relations.

Most of literary translation undertaken in Canada is 'intranational'. If we look at translations of novels from French into English, that is from the 'major minority language' in Canada into the dominant language,[21] it becomes clear that translation practice has been shaped by dramatic changes in conceptualizations of cultural difference. The literature of Quebec has been transmitted to English Canada through a series of frames which have provided the motivation and the manner for translation. These frames could be called *ethnographic*, *emergent* and *pluralistic*. In the first case, translation negotiates between cultural entities which are different *by nature*, separate historical worlds, between which only relations of cordial tolerance could be envisaged. In the second, difference is a result of a conscious political effort of self-fashioning, corresponding to a movement of political nationalism. And the third refers to the complex realities of the present (always more difficult to encapsulate) in which many micro-identities circulate across the barriers of national culture, making translation a reflection of the dramas of hybridity and self-doubt characteristic of much cultural expression today. Examples of translations which correspond to these frames are: W.H. Blake's translation of *Maria Chapdelaine* by Louis Hémon (the novel written in 1916, the translation published in 1921); the translations by David Homel, Betty Bednarski, Ray Ellenwood and Kathy Mezei of novels in 'joual' in the 1970s; and the contemporary translation of novels such as *Mauve Desert* by Nicole Brossard. Without attempting to present any of these episodes in detail (see Simon 1992, 1997), we can see, both through the prefatory material furnished by translators and the strategies of translation themselves, that competing conceptions of Quebec culture are at work.[22] These examples demonstrate that translation practice is always grounded in a theory of culture, in a set of assumptions about the ways in which linguistic forms carry cultural meanings. This implicit theory of culture is necessarily a reflection of the changing power relations which shape and maintain national/cultural boundaries.

Though they are often initiated through violence, translations, as forms of contact, also put into play systems of interaction whose outcomes introduce new terms of exchange. What recent post-colonial theory alerts us to is the need to restore complexity to our understanding of relations of alterity, of oppositional identities created through struggle. The heritage of imperialism, according to Edward Said, is paradoxical. Although it led people to believe that they were 'exclusively Western, or Oriental', in fact '[i]mperialism consolidated the mixture of cultures and identities on a global scale' (Said 1993: 336).[23] Stuart Hall reminds us that the movements of military and cultural conquest which established colonialism were interwoven with 'transverse linkages', disruptions and dislocations which affect both the dominated and dominating cultures. Hall argues that post-colonialism 'obliges us to re-read [these] binaries as forms of transculturation, of cultural translation', to rediscover the 'transverse movements which were always inscribed in the history of "colonisation" but carefully overwritten by more binary forms of narrativisation' (Hall 1996: p. 247, 251).

These, then, are the paradoxical logics of exchange in which translations participate. Though important vectors of colonial influence, translations, as in the case of BMS's work, made possible the creation of new kinds of literary identities. The post-colonial frame allows us to better understand the outcomes of translation by taking into account the asymmetry of languages and cultures within the evolving global context and by insisting on historically informed criticism.

Authors' Note

Vanamala Viswanatha and Sherry Simon would like to thank Vidya Vikram for permission to quote from *English Geetragalu*, 1985 (B.M. Shri Smaraka Prathishtana, Bangalore) and *Shrisahitya*, 1983 (Kannada Adhyayana Samsthe, Mysore) both by B.M. Srikantaiah.

Notes

1 See, for instance, S. Simon (ed.), *Culture in Transit: Translating the Literature of Quebec* (Montreal: Véhicule Press, 1995).

2 'Most modern Indian languages initiated their respective literary traditions with translations of works from Sanskrit, either the epics – Ramayana and Mahabharata – or philosophical texts like the Gita. During the first four centuries of their existence – thirteenth to the sixteenth centuries – there were numerous translations from one regional language to another regional language, numerous instances of literary bilingualism as well as many important translations from Indian languages to Persian and Arabic, the two languages of political domination during these centuries' (G.N. Devy, 'Indian Literature in English Translation', in Devy 1993, pp. 117–18).

3 'A Sanskrit epic like the Mahabharata contains in its encyclopedic range much folk material, like tales, beliefs, proverbs, picked obviously from folk sources, refurbished, Sanskritized, fixed forever in the Sanskritic artifice of eternity. But in a profoundly oral culture like the Indian, the Sanskrit Mahabharata itself gets returned to the oral folk-traditions, contributing the transformed materials back to the "little" traditions to be further diffused and diffracted. It gets "translated" from the Sanskrit into the regional languages; in the course of the "translations", the regional poet infuses it with his rich local traditions, combining not only the pan-Indian "great" with the regional "little", but the regional "great" with the regional "little" traditions as well. Thus many cycles of give-and-take are set in motion' (A.K. Ramanujan 1973, pp. 23–4).

4 Sisir Kumar Das points to the exceptional nature of modern Indian literary history, which, with the possible exception of the Graeco-Roman encounter, 'provides a singular case of co-existence of two literatures, one of them alien, English, and the other indigenous, an Indian literature. This co-existence of English and Indian literature became a feature of intellectual life of the English educated Indian. His political relation with England, which was becoming more and more hostile every day, did not alter the situation' (Das 1995, p. 55).

5 'The multilingual, eclectic Hindu spirit, ensconced in the belief in the soul's perpetual transition from form to form, may find it difficult to subscribe to the Western metaphysics of translation . . . . The Indian consciousness, on the other hand, and in a crude manner of differentiating, is itself a "translating consciousness" ' (G.N. Devy, 'Translation Theory: an Indian Perspective', in Devy 1993, p. 135).

6 Ahmad also warns against the limits of a purely national framework for studying translation. In this context it is worth noting that the strong moments in the history of translation theory seem to be tied to crises in the concept of the nation – from its 'birth' in the Renaissance to its consolidation during the period of the German Romantics and onward. As translation theory has served the interests of the nation, today it accompanies a questioning of national boundaries.

7 This variety is highlighted in the titles of Mukherjee's chapters: translation as new writing, as testimony, as patriotism, as perjury, as discovery.

This sensitivity is also integrated into the critical project of Meenakshi Mukherjee, who sees the birth of the Indian novel in English as an act of translation, as the result of a dialogue with Western forms involving both imitation and resistance (Mukherjee 1985). Aijaz Ahmad seems to refute this view in reference to the emergence of the novel in Urdu (Ahmad 1992, p. 116).

8 This, according to the important poet D.R. Bendre, Felicitation volume for BMS, Mysore, 1941; G.S. Shivarudrappa (ed.) (1985) *Shrinidhi*, B.M. Shri centenary volume (Smaraka Prathishtana, Bangalore: B.M. Shri).

9 Ferdinand Kittel (1823–1903) was a German, Protestant priest who studied at the Basel Mission College in Switzerland and was sent to Dharwar, Karnataka in 1853. He studied Kannada when he was in Bangalore and prepared the first Kannada–English dictionary between 1872 and 1892 (70,000 entries). He also published *Grammar of the Kannada Language* in English (1903).

   B.L. Rice (1837–1927) was born in India, educated in England and returned to Bangalore in 1860, serving as an education officer, inspector of schools and then curator, Archaelogy Department, Mysore. He is the author of *Epigraphia Karnatika*.

10 S.G. Narasimhacharya (1862–1907) was a well-known Old Kannada scholar also knowledgeable in the Sanskrit, Tamil and English traditions. He worked as a translator and textbook writer in the Education Department, and translated excerpts from Kalidasa's *Raghuvamsa* and epic poetry into Kannada. He also translated simple poems from English as well as *Aesop's Fables* and *Gulliver's Travels* into Kannada for teaching purposes.

11 This volume has been reproduced by Bhartiya Anuvad Parishad, Delhi, 1990, with a preface by Gargi Gupta.

   Rao had published a Kannada translation of *Aesop's Fables* in 1884 for the use of the girls reading in the Maharani Girls' School of Mysore. Rao provides a systematic and intelligent exploration of the problems of translation, first examining general issues and then providing detailed commentary on translations of *Shakuntala* into English, on the one hand, and Kannada, on the other. He defends free translation as the proper mode of proceeding when the realities of the two cultures are very different.

12 The following discussion is largely indebted to Kurthakoti 1992.

13 In 1941 BMS wrote a lecture on tragedy in Kannada: 'How come, in our culture, we don't have this kind of a noble picture of the deepest problems in life which makes for the greatest of literature in the West . . . . Should literature be only all sweetness? The fear of tragedy is childish, like the child's fear of darkness. These tragedies are the lode-star that shines brightly in the sky; they need to be seen only in darkness' (B.M. Srikantaiah (1983) 'Rudra Nataka', in Nayaka. Ha. Ma. (ed.) *Shrisanitya* (Mysore: Kannada Adhyyana Samsthe.)) For a full discussion of BMS's dramatic adaptations, see Kurthakoti 1992, pp. 15–20.

14 In 'Kannada Mathu Thale Ethuva Bage', Srikantaiah 1983, p. 254.
15 This poetic language is so stylized, in fact, that it has been 'translated' into a modern Kannada prose version.
16 For some thirty years after *English Geethagalu*, translations from English, in particular, were undertaken assiduously. While the 1930s and 1940s witnessed a predominant wave of translated Romantic and Victorian writers (Keats 1931, Arnold 1932, Tennyson 1936, George Eliot 1946), the 1950s saw a predominance of Russian masters (Gorky 1944, 1955, 1957, 1959), Gogol 1957, Turgenev 1957, Tolstoy 1946, 1951, 1959, 1961, Pushkin 1956, Chekhov 1962. However, the 1960s offer a more heterogeneous picture which includes the all-time favourites Wordsworth, Shelley and Byron, but also American writers (Poe, 1961, and Whitman, 1966) and Jane Austen 1961, Shaw 1963, Dickens 1960 and Hardy 1959. From: *Bibliography of Translations into Kannada* (Mysore, 1984).
17 S. Chandrashekar, *Srinidhi* (Bangalore: B.M. Shri, 1985), pp. 129–42. Chandrashekar points out that BMS was probably too close to the royalty to partake of the spirit of Indian nationalism led by Gandhi which inspired every other major writer of the time.
18 For the central creative role of imitation in the European Classical period, see Joel Weinsheimer, *Imitation* (London: Routledge & Kegan Paul, 1984).
19 A.K. Ramanujan's role within the development of Kannada literature is at once marginal and decisive. As a writer in the Kannada language, his influence is rather limited. AKR wrote poetry and short stories in Kannada, and remained an active participant on the Kannada writing scene – even if he spent much of his time in the USA. But it was not this writing which was decisive in establishing him as an important figure, nor the poetry that he wrote in English. Rather, it was his translations from Kannada and Tamil into English. These translations were from the medieval Kannada tradition (the Vacanas) in *Speaking of Siva* (1973) and from the Tamil *Poems of Love and War* (1986), but also from contemporary Kannada literature, *Samskara* by Ananthamurthy (1975), *Rotti* by Lankesh (1973), *Song of the Earth* by Adiga (1968).
20 Niranjana 1992. Niranjana has translated a number of works from Kannada including the novel *Phaniyamma*.
21 As a minority language in North America, as a culturally weak language within the Canadian confederation (until the great nationalist revival beginning in the 1960s), French was for a long time very much the dominated partner in this national dialogue. Translational relations were therefore asymmetrical, and this difference of perspective was reflected in the way translators understood their mandate. Historically, prefaces to translations of French-Canadian literature into English tend to emphasize the humanistic functions of translation, the political desirability of increased cultural interchange between the peoples of Canada; discourse on translation in Quebec has been concerned with the importance of defending the French language against the interferences of an all-powerful English-language culture.

22 Yet other kinds of considerations come into play in the translation of
    English-language literature into French. See Annie Brisset, *Sociocriticism
    of Translation* (Toronto: University of Toronto Press, 1996).
23 Edward Said: 'some notion of literature and indeed all culture as hybrid
    . . . and encumbered, or entangled and overlapping with what used to
    be regarded as extraneous elements – this strikes me as *the* essential
    idea for the revolutionary realities' (*Culture and Imperialism*, p. 317).

References

Ahmad, A. (1992) *In Theory: Classes, Nations, Literatures* (Bombay: Oxford
    University Press).
Ananthanarayana S. (1962) *Hosagannada Kaviteya Mele English Kavyada
    Prabhava* (The Influence of English Poetry on the Modern Kannada
    Poem) (Bangalore: Rajalaxmi Prakashana).
Aniketana. Journal of Kannada literature in English.
Das, S.K. (1995) *A History of Indian Literature 1911–1956* (New Delhi: Sahitya
    Akademi).
Devi, M. (1995) *Imaginary Maps*, trans. G. Spivak (New York and London:
    Routledge).
Devy, G.N. (1993) *In Another Tongue: Essays on Indian English Literature*
    (Chennai: Macmillan India Ltd).
Hall, S. (1996) 'When was the "post-colonial"? Thinking at the limit', in
    I. Chambers, and L. Curti (eds), *The Post-Colonial Question* (London and
    New York: Routledge).
Havanur, S. (1974) *Hosakannada Arunodaya* (The Renaissance in Modern
    Kannada), Mysore: Kannada Studies Centre, Mysore University.
Indian Literature 162 (Jul.–Aug. 1994) special issue: 'Remembering
    A.K. Ramanujan: On the Art of Translation'.
Indian Literature 168 (Jul.–Aug. 1995) 'Kannada Short Story Today'.
Joshi, S. (ed.) (1991) *Rethinking English: Essays in Literature, Language, History*
    (New Delhi: Trianka).
Kurthakoti, K. (1992) 'Bhashantara Matthu Punarlekhana' ('Translation
    and Rewriting') in *Bayalu-Alaya* (Hampi: Kannada University Press).
Loomba, A. and Kaul, S. (eds) (1994) *On India: Writing History, Culture, Post-
    Coloniality. Oxford Literary Review* 16 (1/2) (special issue).
Mukherjee, M. (1985) *Realism and Reality: The Novel and Society in India* (Delhi:
    Oxford University Press).
Mukherjee, S. (1994) *Translation as Discovery* (London: Sangam Books).
Niranjana, T. (1992) *Siting Translation: History, Post-Structuralism, and the
    Colonial Context* (Berkeley and Los Angeles: University of California Press).
Ramunajan, A.K. (trans.) (1973) *Speaking of Śiva* (Harmondsworth: Penguin).
— (1991) *Folktales from India* (Harmondsworth: Penguin).
Rao, R.R. (1910) *The Art of Translation: A Critical Study* (repr. by Bhartiya
    Anuvad Parishad, Delhi, n.d.).

Rice, E.P. (1921) *A History of Kanarese Literature*, 2nd edn (Calcutta: Association Press and Oxford University Press).

Said, E. (1993) *Culture and Imperialism* (New York: Knopf).

Sharma, R. (1984) 'English *Githagalu* as Transcreation', in *B.M. Shri: The Man and His Mission* (Bangalore: Prathishtana).

Simon, S. (1992) 'The language of cultural difference: figures of alterity in Canadian translation', in L. Venuti (ed.), *Rethinking Translation: Discourse, Subjectivity, Ideology* (London and New York: Routledge).

— (1997) 'Translation and cultural politics in Canada', in W. Ramakrishna, (ed.), *Translation and Multilingualism* (Delhi: Pencraft International).

— (1994) *Le Trafic des Langues. Traduction et culture dans la littérature québécoise* (Montreal: Boréal).

Singh, A.K. (ed.) (1996) *Translation, Its Theory and Practice* (New Delhi: Creative Books).

Spivak, G. (1992) 'Acting bits/identity talk', *Critical Inquiry* 18: 770–803.

— (1993) 'The politics of translation', *Outside in the Teaching Machine* (London and New York: Routledge).

Srikantaiah, B.M. (1983) *Shrisahitya* (Collected Works of BMS), ed. H.M. Nayaka (Mysore: Adhyayana Samsthe).

Trivedi, H. (1993) *Colonial Transactions: English Literature and India* (Calcutta: Papyrus).

— (1994) 'Theorizing the nation', *Indian Literature* 160 (Mar.–Apr.) (special issue: 'Literary Criticism: The New Challenges'): 31–45.

— (1995) 'The politics of post-colonial translation', in Singh (ed.) (1996).

Chapter 9

Translation and literary history

An Indian view

Ganesh Devy

'Translation is the wandering existence of a text in a perpetual exile,'
says J. Hillis Miller.[1] The statement obviously alludes to the
Christian myth of the Fall, exile and wandering. In Western metaphysics translation is an exile, a fall from the origin; and the mythical
exile is a metaphoric translation, a post-Babel crisis. Given this metaphysical precondition of Western aesthetics, it is not surprising that
literary translations are not accorded the same status as *original works*.
Western literary criticism provides for the guilt of translations for
coming into being *after* the original; the temporal sequentiality is
held as a proof of diminution of literary authenticity of translations.
The strong sense of individuality given to Western individuals
through systematic philosophy and the logic of social history makes
them view translation as an intrusion of 'the other' (sometimes pleasurable). This intrusion is desirable to the extent that it helps define
one's own identity, but not beyond that point. It is of course natural
for the monolingual European cultures to be acutely conscious of
the act of translation. The philosophy of individualism and the metaphysics of guilt, however, render European literary historiography
incapable of grasping the origins of literary traditions.

One of the most revolutionary events in the history of English
style has been the authorized translation of the Bible. It was also
the literary expression of Protestant Christianity. The recovery of
the original spirit of Christianity was thus sought by Protestant
England through an act of translation. It is well known that Chaucer
was translating the style of Boccacio into English when he created
his *Canterbury Tales*. When Dryden and Pope wanted to recover a
sense of order, they used the tool of translation. Similar attempts
were made in other European languages such as German and
French.

During the last two centuries the role of translation in communicating literary movements across linguistic borders has become very important. The tradition that has given us writers like Shaw, Yeats, Joyce, Beckett and Heaney in a single century – the tradition of Anglo-Irish literature – branched out of the practice of translating Irish works into English initiated by Macpherson towards the end of the eighteenth century. Indian English Literature too has gathered its conventions of writing from the Indological activity of translation during the late eighteenth century and the nineteenth century. Many of the Anglo-Irish and Indian English writers have been able translators themselves. Similarly the settler colonies such as Australia, Canada and New Zealand have impressive modern traditions of literature, which have resulted from the 'translation' of the settlers from their homeland to alien locations. Post-colonial writing in the former Spanish colonies in South America, the former colonies in Africa and other parts of the world has experienced the importance of translation as one of the crucial conditions for creativity. Origins of literary movements and literary traditions inhabit various acts of translation.

Considering the fact that most literary traditions originate in translation and gain substance through repeated acts of translation, it would be useful for a theory of literary history if a supporting theory of literary translation were available. However, since translations are popularly perceived as unoriginal, not much thought has been devoted to the aesthetics of translation. Most of the primary issues relating to 'form' and 'meaning' too have not been settled in relation to translation. No critic has taken any well-defined position about the exact placement of translations in literary history. Do they belong to the history of the 'T' languages or do they belong to the history of the 'S' languages? Or do they form an independent tradition all by themselves? This ontological uncertainty which haunts translations has rendered translation study a haphazard activity which devotes too much energy discussing problems of conveying the original meaning in the altered structure.

Unfortunately for translation, the various developments concerning the interdependence between meaning and structure in the field of linguistics have been based on monolingual data and situations. Even the sophisticated and revolutionary theoretical formulation proposed by structural linguistics is not adequate to unravel the intricacies of translation activity. Roman Jakobson in his essay on the linguistics of translation proposed a threefold classification of translations: (a) those from one verbal order to another verbal order within the same language system, (b) those from one language system to another language system, and (c) those from a verbal order to another system of signs (Jakobson, 1959, pp. 232–9). As he considers, theoretically, a complete semantic equivalence as the final objective of a translation act – which is not possible – he asserts that poetry is untranslatable. He maintains that only a 'creative translation' is possible. This view finds further support in formalistic poetics, which considers every act of creation as a completely unique event. It is, however, necessary to acknowledge that synonymy within one language system cannot be conceptually identical with synonymy between two different languages. Historical linguistics has some useful premises in this regard. In order to explain linguistic change, historical linguistics employs the concept of semantic differentiation as well as that of phonetic glides. While the linguistic changes within a single language occur more predominantly due to semantic differentiation, they also show marked phonetic glides. However, the degree of such glides is more pronounced when a new language comes into existence. In other words, whereas linguistic changes within a single language are predominantly of a semantic nature, the linguistic differences between two closely related languages are predominantly phonetic. Technically speaking, then, if synonymy within one language is a near impossibility, it is not so when we consider two related languages together.

Structural linguistics considers language as a system of signs, arbitrarily developed, that tries to cover the entire range of significance available to the culture of that language. The signs do not mean anything by or in themselves; they acquire significance by virtue of their relation to the entire system to which they belong. This theory naturally looks askance at translation which is an attempt to rescue/abstract significance from one system of signs and to wed it with another such system. But language is an open system. It keeps admitting new signs as well as new significance in its fold. It is also open in the socio-linguistic sense that it allows an individual speaker or writer to use as much of it as he can or likes to do. If this is the case, then how 'open' is a particular system of verbal signs when a bilingual user, such as a translator, rends it open? Assuming that for an individual language resides within his consciousness, we can ask whether the two systems within his consciousness can be shown as materially different and whether they retain their individual identities within the sphere of his consciousness. Or do such systems become a single open and extended system? If translation is defined as some kind of communication of significance, and if we accept the structuralist principle that communication becomes possible because of the nature of signs and their entire system, it follows that translation is a merger of sign systems. Such a merger is possible because systems of signs are open and vulnerable. The translating consciousness exploits the potential openness of language systems; and as it shifts significance from a given verbal form to a corresponding but different verbal form it also brings closer the materially different sign systems. If we take a lead from phenomenology and conceptualize a whole community of 'translating consciousness' it should be possible to develop a theory of interlingual synonymy as well as a more perceptive literary historiography.

The concept of a 'translating consciousness' and communities of people possessing it are no mere notions. In most Third World countries, where a dominating colonial language has acquired a privileged place, such communities do exist. In India several languages are simultaneously used by language communities as if these languages formed a continuous spectrum of signs and significance. The use of two or more different languages in translation activity cannot be understood properly through studies of foreign-language acquisition. Such theories work round the premise that there inevitably is a chronological gap and an order or a priority of scale in language-learning situations. The field is stratified in terms of value-based indicators L1 and L2, though in reality language-learning activity may seem very natural in a country like India. In Chomsky's linguistics the concept of semantic universals plays an important role. However, his level of abstraction marks the farthest limits to which the monolingual Saussurean linguistic materialism can be stretched. In actual practice, even in Europe, the translating consciousness treats the SL and TL as parts of a larger and continuous spectrum of various intersecting systems of verbal signs. Owing to the structuralist unwillingness to acknowledge the existence of any non-systemic or extra-systemic core of significance, the concept of synonymy in the West has remained inadequate to explain translation activity. And in the absence of a linguistic theory based on a multilingual perspective or on translation practice, the translation thought in the West overstates the validity of the concept of synonymy.

J.C. Catford presents a comprehensive statement of theoretical formulation about the linguistics of translation in *A Linguistic Theory of Translation*, in which he seeks to isolate various linguistic levels of translation. His basic premise is that since translation is a linguistic act any theory of translation must emerge from linguistics: 'Translation is an operation performed on languages: a process of substituting a text in one language for a text in another; clearly, then, any theory of translation must draw upon a theory of language – a general linguistic theory' (Catford, 1965, p. vii). The privileged discourse of general linguistics today is closely interlinked with developments in anthropology, particularly after Durkheim and Lévi-Strauss. During the nineteenth century, Europe had distributed various fields of humanistic knowledge into a threefold hierarchy: comparative studies for Europe, Orientalism for the Orient, and anthropology for the rest of the world. In its various phases of development modern Western linguistics has connections with all these. After the 'discovery' of Sanskrit by Sir William Jones, historical linguistics in Europe depended heavily on Orientalism. For a long time afterwards linguistics followed the path of comparative philology. And after Saussure and Lévi-Strauss, linguistics started treating language with an anthropological curiosity. When linguistics branched off to its monolingual structuralist path, comparative literature still persisted in its faith in the translatability of literary texts. Comparative literature implies that between two related languages there are areas of significance that are shared, just as there may be areas of significance that can never be shared. Translation can be seen as an attempt to bring a given language system in its entirety as close as possible to the areas of significance that it shares with another given language or languages. All translations operate within this shared area of significance. Such a notion may help us distinguish synonymy within one language and the shared significance between two related languages.

The translation problem is not just a linguistic problem. It is an aesthetic and ideological problem with an important bearing on the question of literary history. Literary translation is not just a replication of a text in another verbal system of signs. It is a replication of an ordered sub-system of signs within a given language in another corresponding ordered sub-system of signs within a related language. Translation is not a transposition of significance or signs. After the act of translation is over, the original work still remains in its original position. Translation is rather an attempted revitalization of the original in another verbal order and temporal space. Like literary texts that continue to belong to their original periods and styles *and* also exist through successive chronological periods, translation at once approximates the original and transcends it.

The problems in translation study are, therefore, very much like those in literary history. They are the problems of the relationship between origins and sequentiality. And as in translation study so in literary history, the problem of origin has not been tackled satisfactorily. The point that needs to be made is that probably the question of origins of literary traditions will have to be viewed differently by literary communities with 'translating consciousness'. The fact that Indian literary communities do possess this translating consciousness can be brought home effectively by reminding ourselves that the very foundation of modern Indian literatures was laid through acts of translation, whether by Jayadeva, Hemcandra, Michael Madhusudan Dutta, H.N. Apte or Bankim Chandra Chatterjee.

We began our discussion by alluding to the Christian metaphysics that conditions reception of translation in the Western world. Let us allude to Indian metaphysics in conclusion. Indian metaphysics believes in an unhindered migration of the soul from one body to another. Repeated birth is the very substance of all animate creations. When the soul passes from one body to another, it does not lose any of its essential significance. Indian philosophies of the relationship between form and essence, structure and significance are guided by this metaphysics. The soul, or significance, is not subject to the laws of temporality; and therefore significance, even literary significance, is ahistorical in Indian view. Elements of plot, stories, characters, can be used again and again by new generations of writers because Indian literary theory does not lay undue emphasis on originality. If originality were made a criterion of literary excellence, a majority of Indian classics would fail the test. The true test is the writer's capacity to transform, to translate, to restate, to revitalize the original. And in that sense Indian literary traditions are essentially traditions of translation.

Note

1   I have quoted here from my notes of a lecture given by Professor J. Hills Miller at the IX Centenary Celebration Symposium of the University of Bologna, Italy, in October 1988. I have quoted his words without any changes.

References

Catford, J.C. (1965) *A Linguistic Theory of Translation* (London: Oxford University Press).

Jakobson, R. (1959) 'On linguistic aspects of translation', in R.A. Brower, (ed.), *On Translation* (Cambridge, Mass.: Harvard University Press).

Bibliography

Achebe, C. [1959] *Things Fall Apart*, New York: Fawcett Crest, 1991.
—— [1966] *A Man of the People*, New York: Doubleday, 1989.
Ahmad, A. *In Theory: Classes, Nations, Literatures*, Bombay: Oxford University Press, 1992.
Ambruster, C. 'Hélène-Clarice: nouvelle voix', *Contemporary Literature* 24 (2) (1983): 155.
Anand, M.R. 'Pigeon Indian: some notes on Indian English writing', in M.K. Naik ed., *Aspects of Indian Writing in English: Essays in Honour of Professor K.R. Srinivaa Iyengar*, Madras: Macmillan, 1979.
Ananthanarayana *Hosagannada Kaviteya Mele English Kavyada Prabhava* (The Influence of English Poetry on the Modern Kannada Poem), Bangalore: Rajalaxmi Prakashana, 1962.
Andrade, O. de 'Manifesto antropófago', in A. Candido and J.A. Castello, *Presença da Literatura Brasileira*, vol. 3, São Paulo: Difusão Européia do Livro, 1968, pp. 68–74.
Ashcroft, B., Griffiths, G. and Tiffin, H. *The Empire Writes Back: Theory and Practice in Post-colonial Literature*, London and New York: Routledge, 1989.
Barthes, R. 'The death of the author' and 'From work to text', *Image. Music. Text*, trans. S. Heath, New York: Hill & Wang, 1977.
—— 'Theory of the text', trans. I. McLeod, in Robert Young ed., *Untying the Text*, Boston: Routledge & Kegan Paul, 1981.
Basavaraju, ed., *Allamana Vacana Candrike*, Mysore, 1960.
Bassnett, S. *Translation Studies*, rev. edn, London: Routledge, 1991.
Bassnett, S. and Lefevere, A. eds, *Translation History and Culture*, London: Cassell, 1995.
Benjamin, W. 'The task of the translator: an introduction to the translation of Baudelaire's *Tableaux parisiens*', in *Illuminations: Essays and Reflections*, ed. H. Arendt, trans. H. Zohn, New York: Schocken Books, 1969, pp. 69–82.
Benveniste, E. 'Saussure after half a century', in *Problems in General Linguistics*, trans. M.E. Meek, Coral Gables, Fl.: University of Miami Press, 1971.

Bhabha, H.K. 'DissemiNation: time, narrative, and the margins of the modern nation', in H.K. Bhabha ed., *Nation and Narration*, London and New York: Routledge, 1990, pp. 291–322.

—— 'Interrogating identity: the postcolonial prerogative', in D.T. Goldberg ed., *Anatomy of Racism*, Minneapolis: University of Minnesota Press, 1990.

—— *The Location of Culture*, London and New York: Routledge, 1994.

Bhoosnurmath, S.S. and Menezes, L.M.A. ed. and trans., *Śūnyasāmpadane*, vols 2 and 3, Dharwar: Karnataka University Press, 1968–9.

Bourdieu, P. *Outline of a Theory of Practice*, trans. R. Nice, Cambridge: Cambridge University Press, 1977.

Brault, J. *Poèmes des quatre côtés*, Saint-Lambert: Editions du Noroît, 1975.

—— 'Entretien' avec A. Lefrançois, *Liberté* 100 (17) (Jul.–Aug. 1975).

—— 'Quelques remarques sur la traduction de la poesie', *Ellipse* 21 (1977): 10–35.

—— *Agonie*, Montreal: Boréal Express, 1984.

—— *La poussière du chemin*, Montreal, Boréal,1989.

Brennan, T. 'The national longing for form', in H.K. Bhabha ed., *Nation and Narration*, London and New York: Routledge, 1990, pp. 44–70.

Brisset, A. *Translation and Sociocriticism*, Toronto: University of Toronto Press, 1996.

Brockington, J.L. 'Warren Hastings and Orientalism', in G. Cornall and C. Nicholson eds, *The Impeachment of Warren Hastings: Papers from a Bicentenary Commemoration*, Edinburgh: Edinburgh University Press, 1989.

Brossard, N. *Le Désert mauve*, Montreal: L'Hexagone, 1987.

—— *Mauve Desert*, trans. S. de Lotbinière-Harwood, Toronto: Coach House, 1990.

Butler, J.P. *Subjects of Desire: Hegelian Reflections in Twentieth-Century France*, New York: Columbia University Press, 1987.

Cairns, D. and Richards, S. *Writing Ireland: Colonialism, Nationalism and Culture*, Manchester: Manchester University Press, 1988.

Cannon, G. *Oriental Jones: A Biography of Sir William Jones 1746–1794*, London, 1964.

Castello, J. 'Francesa divulga mistérios de Clarice', *O Estado de São Paulo*, 27 Oct. 1996.

Catford, J.C. *A Linguistic Theory of Translation: An Essay in Applied Linguistics*, London: Oxford University Press, 1965.

Chamberlain, L. 'Gender and the metaphorics of translation', in L. Venuti ed., *Rethinking Translation – Discourse, Subjectivity, Ideology*, New York and London: Routledge, 1992, pp. 57–74.

Cheyfitz, E. *The Poetics of Imperialism: Translation and Colonization from The Tempest to Tarzan*, New York and Oxford: Oxford University Press, 1991.

Chomsky, N. 'Current issues in linguistic theory', in J.A. Fodor and J.J. Katz eds, *The Structure of Language: Readings in the Philosophy of Language*, Englewood Cliffs, NJ: Prentice-Hall, 1964, pp. 50–118

Cixous, Hélène 'Le rire de la meduse', *L'arc* 61 (1975): 39–54.

—— 'L'approche de Clarice Lispector', *Poétique* 40 (1979): 408–19.

—— *Vivre l'orange/To Live the Orange*, Paris: Des Femmes, 1979.

—— *Illa*, Paris: Des Femmes, 1980.

—— 'Extrême fidélité', *Travessia* 14 (1987): 20–31.

—— *Writing Differences: Readings from the Seminar of Hélène Cixous*, ed. S. Sellers, Milton Keynes: Open University Press, 1988.

—— *L'Heure de Clarice Lispector*, Paris: Des Femmes, 1989.

—— *Readings: The Poetics of Blanchot, Joyce, Kafka, Kleist, Lispector, and Tsvetayeva*, ed. V.A. Conley, Minneapolis: University of Minnesota Press, 1990.

—— *Hélène Cixous's 'Coming to Writing' and Other Essays*, ed. D. Jenson, Cambridge, Mass.: Harvard University Press, 1991.

—— *Reading with Clarice Lispector*, ed. V.A. Conley, Minneapolis: University of Minnesota Press, 1991.

Clifford, J. *The Predicament of Culture*, Cambridge, Mass.: Harvard University Press, 1988.

Conley, V.A. *Hélène Cixous*, New York: Harvester Wheatsheaf, 1992.

Culler, J. *Structuralist Poetics: Structuralism, Linguistics and the Study of Literature*, Ithaca, NY: Cornell University Press, 1971.

Das, S.K. *A History of Indian Literature 1911–1956*, New Delhi: Sahitya Akademi, 1995.

de Campos, H. 'Da tradução como criação e como crítica', *Tempo Brasileiro*, 4–5 (Jun.–Sept. 1963); repr. in de Campos 1992, pp. 31–48.

—— *Oswald de Andrade: Trechos Escolhidos*, Rio de Janeiro: Agir, 1967.

—— *Morfologia de Macunaíma*, São Paulo: Perspectiva, 1973.

—— *Deus e o Diablo no Fausto de Goethe*, São Paulo: Perspectiva, 1981.

—— 'Da razão antropofágica: diálogo e presença na cultura Brasileira', *Colóquio/Letras* 62 (Jul. 1981); repr. in de Campos 1992, pp. 231–55.

—— 'The rule of anthropophagy: Europe under the sign of devoration', trans. M.T. Wolff, *Latin American Literary Review* 14 (27) (Jan.–Jun. 1986): 42–60.

—— *Qohélet = O-que-sabe: Eclesiastes: poema sapiencial*, trans. H. de Campos with the collaboration of J. Guinsburg, São Paulo: Perspectiva, 1991.

—— *Metalinguagem & Outras Metas: Ensaios de Teoria e Crítica Literária*, 4th rev. and enlarged edn, São Paulo: Perspectiva, 1992.

—— *O Arco-Íris Branco: Ensaios de Literatura e Cultura*, Rio de Janeiro: Imago Editora, 1997.

Delisle, J. and Woodsworth, J. eds, *Translators through History*, Amsterdam and Philadelphia: John Benjamins, 1995.

Derrida, J., 'Des Tours de Babel', in J. Graham ed., *Difference in Translation*, Ithaca, NY: Cornell University Press, 1985.

Devi, M. *Imaginary Maps*, trans. G. Spivak, New York and London: Routledge, 1995.

Devy, G.N. *In Another Tongue: Essays on Indian English Literature*, Madras: Macmillan India, 1993.

Dharwadker, V. 'Postcolonial cosmopolitanism: a note on A.K. Ramanujan's theory and practice of criticism and translation', *Indian Literature* 37 (2) (1994): 91–7.

Dharwadker, V. and Ramanujan, A.K. eds, *The Oxford Anthology of Modern Indian Poetry*, Delhi: Oxford University Press, 1994.

Dingwaney, A. and Maier, C. eds, *Between Languages and Cultures: Translation and Cross-Cultural Texts*, Pittsburgh and London: University of Pittsburgh Press, 1995.

Dyson, K.K. 'Forging a bilingual identity: a writer's testimony', in P. Burton, K.K. Dyson and S. Ardener eds, *Bilingual Women: Anthropological Approaches to Second Language Use*, Oxford: Berg, 1993.

Eliot, T.S. 'Tradition and the individual talent', in *Selected Prose of T.S. Eliot*, ed. F. Kermode, New York: Harcourt Brace Jovanovich; Farrar, Straus & Giroux, 1988, pp. 37–44.

Emecheta, B. *The Joys of Motherhood*, New York: George Braziller, 1979.

Even-Zohar, I. 'Polysystem studies', *Poetics Today* 11 (1) (1990), special issue.

Felman, S. 'To open the question', *Literature and Psychoanalysis*, Baltimore: The Johns Hopkins University Press, 1982.

——— *Jacques Lacan and the Adventure of Insight: Psychoanalysis in Contemporary Culture*, Cambridge, Mass.: Harvard University Press, 1987.

Fitzgerald, E. Letter to Cowell, 20 March 1857, cited in S. Bassnett, *Translation Studies*, London: Routledge, 1991.

Flood, G. *An Introduction to Hinduism*, Cambridge: Cambridge University Press, 1996.

Foucault, M. *The Archaeology of Knowledge*, trans. A.M. Sheridan Smith, New York: Pantheon Books, 1971.

——— 'What is an author?', in *Language, Counter-Memory, Practice: Selected Essays and Interviews*, ed. D.F. Bouchard, trans. D.F. Bouchard and S. Simon, Ithaca, NY: Cornell University Press, 1977.

——— 'Nietzsche, genealogy, history', in P. Rabinow ed., *The Foucault Reader*, Harmondsworth: Penguin, 1986.

Fuentes, C. *Aura*, London: André Deutsch, 1990.

Gagnon, D. *La Fille à marier*, Montreal: Editions Leméac, 1985.

——— *The Marriageable Daughter*, Toronto: Coach House Press, 1989.

Gates, H.L., Jr. 'Afterword: Zora Neale Hurston: "A Negro Way of Saying" ', in Hurston 1990 pp. 185–95.

Haafner, J. 'Lotgevallen en vroegere zeereizen van Jacob Haafner', ed. C.M. Haafner (Amsterdam, 1820); repr. in *De Werken van Jacob Haafner*, vol. 1, ed. J.A. de Moor and P.G.E.I.J. van der Velde, Zutphen: De Walburg Pers, 1992, pp. 41–160.

Haren, O.Z. van 'Agon, Sultan van Bantam', *Leven en werken van W. en O.Z. van Haren*, ed. J. van Vloten, Deventer: A ter Gunne, 1874, pp. 232–55.

Havanur *Hosakannada Arunodaya* (The Renaissance in Modern Kannada), Kannada Studies Centre, Mysore University, 1974.

Heaney, S. 'The interesting case of John Alphonsus Mulrennan', *Planet: The Welsh Internationalist* 41 (Jan. 1978): 34–40.

Hermans, T. ed. *The Manipulation of Literature: Studies in Literary Translation*, New York: St Martin's Press, 1985.

Hirsch, E.D., Jr. *Validity in Interpretation*, New Haven, CT: Yale University Press, 1967.

Hollanda, H.B. de and Gonçalves, M.A. *Cultura e Participação nos Anos 60*, 7th edn, São Paulo: Brasiliense, 1989.

Holmes, James S. *Translated! Papers on Literary Translation and Translation Studies*, 2nd edn, Amsterdam: Rodopi, 1994.

Hulme, P. *Colonial Encounters*, London and New York: Routledge, 1986.

Hurston, Z.N. [1937] *Their Eyes Were Watching God*, New York: Harper & Row, 1990.

Indian Literature 162 (Jul.–Aug. 1994), special issue: 'Remembering A.K. Ramanujan: on the art of translation'.

Indian Literature 168 (Jul.–Aug. 1995), special issue: 'Kannada short story today'.

Ivir, V. 'Procedures and strategies for the translation of culture', *Indian Journal of Applied Linguistics*, 13 (1987), 2.35–46.

Jakobson, R. 'On linguistic aspects of translation', *On Translation*, ed. R.A. Brower, Cambridge, Mass.: Harvard University Press, 1959, pp. 232–39.

—— 'Linguistics and poetics', in K. Pomorska and S. Rudy eds, *Language in Literature*, Cambridge, Mass.: Belknap Press, Harvard University Press, 1987, pp. 62–94.

Johnson, R. 'Tupy or not tupy: cannibalism and nationalism in contemporary Brazilian literature', in J. King ed., *Modern Latin American Fiction: A Survey*, London and Boston: Faber & Faber, 1987, pp. 41–59.

Joshi, S. ed. *Rethinking English: Essays in Literature, Language, History*, New Delhi: Trianka, 1991.

Kachru, B. *The Indianization of English: The English Language in India*, New Delhi: Oxford University Press, 1983.

—— *The Alchemy of English: The Spread, Functions and Models of Non-native Englishes*, New Delhi: Oxford University Press, 1989.

Kachru, Y. 'The Indian face of English', *Seminar* 391 (Mar. 1992).

Ker, W.P. ed. *Essays of John Dryden*, 2 vols, 1900; repr. New York: Russell & Russell, 1961.

Klobucka, A. 'Hélène Cixous and the hour of Clarice Lispector', *Substance* 73 (1994): 41–62.

Kramtsch, C. 'The second-language student', *PMLA* 112 (3) (1997).

Kurthakoti, K. 'Bhashantara matthu punarlekhana' ('Translation and rewriting'), in *Bayalu-Alaya*, Kannada University, Hampi, 1992.

Kÿaalmÿaan, G.C. 'Some borderline cases of translation', *New Comparison* 1 (1986): 117–22.

Lakoff, G. and Johnson, M. *Metaphors We Live By*, Chicago: University of Chicago Press, 1980.

Lal, P. *Transcreations: Seven Essays on the Art of Transcreation*, Calcutta Writers' Workshop, 1996.

Lane, E. *The Thousand and One Nights*, London, 1859.

Lefevere, A. *Translating Literature: the German Tradition*, Assen/Amsterdam: Van Gorcum, 1977.

—— 'Slauerhoff and "Po Tsju I": three paradigms for the study of influence', *Tamkang Review* 10 (1979): 67–77.

—— 'Why waste our time on rewrites? The trouble with interpretation and the role of rewriting in an alternative paradigm', in Hermans 1985, pp. 215–43.

—— *Translation, Rewriting, and the Manipulation of Literary Fame*, London and New York: Routledge, 1992.

—— *Translating Literature: Practice and Theory in a Comparative Literature Context*, New York: Modern Language Association, 1992.

—— 'Introductory comments II', in Cross Cultural Transfers: Warwick Working Papers in Translation, University of Warwick: Centre for British and Comparative Studies, 1994.

Lefevere, A. and Jackson, K.D. eds, 'The art and science of translation', *Dispositio* 7 (1982), special issue.

Lester, J. [1969] *Black Folktales*, New York: Grove Press, 1970.

Lispector, C. *A Maçã no Escuro*, Rio de Janeiro: Francisco Alves, 1961. *The Apple in the Dark*, trans. G. Rabassa, New York: Knopf, 1967.

—— *A Paixão segundo G.H.*, Rio de Janeiro: Editora do Autor, 1964. *The Passion according to G.H.*, trans. R.W. Sousa, Minneapolis: University of Minnesota Press, 1988.

—— *Água Viva*, Rio de Janeiro: Artenova, 1973. *The Stream of Life*, trans. E. Lowe and E. Fitz, Minneapolis: University of Minnesota Press, 1989.

Loomba, A. and Kaul, S. eds, 'On India: writing history, culture, postcoloniality', *Oxford Literary Review* 16 (1–2).

Marre, J. de *Batavia*, Amsterdam: Adriaan Wor en de Erve G. onder de Linden, 1740.

McGuirk, B. *Latin American Literature: Symptoms, Risks and Strategies of Post-structuralist Criticism*, London and New York: Routledge, 1997.

Mehrez, S. 'Translation and the postcolonial experience: the francophone North African text', in L. Venuti ed., *Rethinking Translation: Discourse, Subjectivity, Ideology*, London: Routledge, 1992.

Moi, T. *Sexual/Textual Politics*, London and New York: Routledge, 1985.

Monier-Williams, Sir Monier, *A Sanskrit-English Dictionary Etymologically and Philologically Arranged*, Delhi: Motilal Banarsidass, 1997 [1899].

Morrison, T. [1977] *Song of Solomon*, New York: Signet, 1978.

Mukherjee, M. *The Twice Born Fiction*, New Delhi: Heinemann, 1971.

—— *Realism and Reality: The Novel and Society in India*, Delhi: Oxford University Press, 1985.

Mukherjee, S. [1981] *Translation as Discovery*, London: Sangam Books, 1994.

Naik, M.K. *A History of Indian English Literature*, New Delhi: Sahitya Akademi, 1982.

—— ed., *Aspects of Indian Writing in English: Essays in Honour of Professor K.R. Srinivasa Iyengar*, Madras: Macmillan, 1979.

Nandimath, S.C., Menezes, L.M.A. and Hirenath, R.C., eds. and trans., *Śūnyāsampadane*, vol. 1, Dharwar: Karnataka University Press, 1965.

Narayan, R.K., 'English in India: some notes on Indian English writing', in Naik ed. 1979.

Nepveu, P. *L'Ecologie du réel: Mort et naissance de la littérature québécoise*, Montreal: Boréal, 1988.

Ngãugãi wa Thiong'o [1967] *A Grain of Wheat*, rev. edn, Oxford: Heinemann, 1986.

—— *Moving the Centre: The Struggle for Cultural Freedoms*, London: James Currey, 1993.

Nida, E.A. *Toward a Science of Translating: With Special Reference to Principles and Procedures Involved in Bible Translating*, Leiden: E.J. Brill, 1964.

Niranjana, T. *Siting Translation: History, Post-structuralism and the Colonial Context*, Berkeley: University of California Press, 1992.

Parthasarathy, R., ed., *Ten Twentieth Century Indian Poets*, Delhi: Oxford University Press, 1976.

Paz, O. *El laberinto de la soledad*, Mexico: Fondo de Cultura Económica, 1959.

—— trans. I. del Corral, 'Translations of Literature and Letters', in R. Schulte and J. Biguenet eds, *Theories of Translation from Dryden to Derrida*, Chicago: University of Chicago Press, 1992, pp. 152–63.

Peixoto, M. *Passionate Fictions: Gender, Narrative, and Violence in Clarice Lispector*, Minneapolis: University of Minnesota Press, 1994.

Pratt, M.L. *Imperial Eyes: Travel Writing and Transculturation*, London and New York: Routledge, 1992.

Pym, A. *Translation and Text Transfer: An Essay on the Principles of Intercultural Communication*, Frankfurt: Peter Lang, 1992.

Rafael, V. *Contracting Colonialism: Translation and Christian Conversion in Tagalog Society under Early Spanish Rule*, Ithaca, NY: Cornell University Press, 1988, p. 213.

Ramanujan, A.K. 'Is there an Indian way of thinking? An informal essay', *Contributions to Indian Sociology*, n.s., 23 (1) (1989).

—— 'Where mirrors are windows: toward an anthology of reflections', *History of Religions* 28 (3) (1989): pp. 187–216.

—— 'Three hundred *Rāmāyaṇas*: five examples and three thoughts on translation', in P. Richman ed., *Many Rāmāyaṇas: The Diversity of a Narrative Tradition in South Asia*, Berkeley: University of California Press, 1991, pp. 22–49.

—— *The Collected Poems*, Delhi: Oxford University Press, 1995.

—— *A Flowering Tree and Other Oral Tales from India*, eds. S. Blackburn and A. Dundes, Berkeley: University of California Press, 1997.

—— *The Collected Essays*, ed. V. Dharwadker, Delhi: Oxford University Press, forthcoming.

—— trans., *The Interior Landscape: Love Poems from a Classical Tamil Anthology*, Bloomington: Indiana University Press, 1967.

—— trans., *Speaking of Śiva*, Harmandsworth: Penguin, 1973.

—— trans., *Samskara: A Rite for a Dead Man*, by U.R. Anantha Murthy, Delhi: Oxford University Press, 1976; corrected edn, 1978; new paperback edn, New York: Oxford University Press, 1989.

—— trans., *Hymns for the Drowning: Poems for Viṣṇu by Nammālvār*, Princeton: Princeton University Press, 1981.

—— ed. and trans., *Poems of Love and War: From the Eight Anthologies and the Ten Long Poems of Classical Tamil*, New York: Columbia University Press, 1985.

—— *Folktales from India: A Selection of Oral Tales from Twenty-two Languages*, New York: Pantheon Books and Harmondsworth: Penguin, 1991.

Ramanujan, A.K., Rao, V.N. and Shulman, D., ed. and trans., *When God is a Customer: Telugu Courtesan Songs by Ksetrayya and Others*, Berkeley: University of California Press, 1994.

Rao, R.R. [1910] *The Art of Translation: A Critical Study* repr. Delhi: Bhartiya Anuvad Parishad, n.d.

—— *Kanthapura* [1938] New Delhi: Orient, 1971.

Rice, E.P. *A History of Kanarese Literature*, 2nd edn, Calcutta: Association Press and Oxford University Press, 1921.

Robin, R. *Le roman mémoriel*, Longueuil: Editions du Préambule, 1990.

Rushdie, S. [1981] *Midnight's Children*, New York: Penguin, 1991. London: Picador, 1982.

—— *Imaginary Homelands*, New Delhi: Penguin and Granta, 1991.

Sabin, M. *The Dialect of the Tribe: Speech and Community in Modern Fiction*, New York: Oxford University Press, 1987.

Schwab, R. *The Oriental Renaissance: Europe's Discovery of India and the East 1680–1880*, New York: Columbia University Press, 1984.

Said, E. *Orientalism*, New York: Pantheon, 1978.

Santiago, S. *Uma Literatura nos Trópicos: Ensaios de Dependência Cultural*, São Paulo: Perspectiva, 1978.

Sarup, M. *An Introductory Guide to Post-Structuralism and Postmodernism*, Athens: The University of Georgia Press, 1993.

Schwartzwald, R. *Institution littéraire, modernité et question nationale au Québec de 1940 à 1976*, Doctoral thesis, Laval University, 1985.

Schwarz, R. 'Nacional por subtração', in *Tradição Contradição*, Rio de Janeiro: Jorge Zahar Editor/Funarte, 1987.

—— *Misplaced Ideas: Essays on Brazilian Culture*, trans. and ed. J. Gledson, London and New York: Verso, 1992.

Sellers, S. ed. 'Introduction', *Writing Differences: Readings from the Seminar of Hélène Cixous*, Milton Keynes: Open University Press, 1988.

Sengupta, M. 'Translation, colonialism, and poetics: Rabindranath Tagore in two worlds', in S. Bassnett and A. Lefevere eds, *Translation, History and Culture*, London and New York: Cassell, 1995, pp. 56–63.

Sharma, R. '*English Githagalu* as transcreation', in *B.M. Shri: The Man and His Mission*, Bangalore: Prathishtana, 1984.

Shiach, M. 'Their "symbolic" exists, it holds power – we, the sowers of disorder, know it only too well', in T. Brennan ed., *Between Feminism and Psychoanalysis*, London and New York: Routledge, 1989.

Sidhwa, B. [1988] *Cracking India*, Minneapolis: Milkweed, 1991.

Simms, N. 'Three types of "touchy" translation', *Pacific Quarterly Moana*, 8 (2) (1983): 48–58.

Simon, S. 'The language of cultural difference: figures of alterity in Canadian translation', in L. Venuti ed., *Rethinking Translation: Discourse, Subjectivity, Ideology*, London and New York: Routledge, 1992.

—— *Le Trafic des langues: Traduction et culture dans la littérature québécoise*, Montreal: Editions du Boréal, 1994.

—— ed. *Culture in Transit: Translating the Literature of Quebec*, Montreal: Véhicule Press, 1995.

—— 'Translation and cultural politics in Canada', in S Ramakrishna ed., *Translation and Multilingualism*, Delhi: Pencraft International, 1997.

Singh, A.K. ed. *Translation, Its Theory and Practice*, New Delhi: Creative Books, 1996.

Singh, K. 'Indish', *Seminar* 321 (May 1986).

Snell-Hornby, M. 'Linguistic transcoding or cultural transfer? A critique of translation theory in Germany', in S. Bassnett and A. Lefevere eds, *Translation, History and Culture*, London and New York: Cassell 1995, pp. 79–86.

Sommer, D. 'Resistant texts and incompetent readers', *Latin American Literary Review*, 20 (1992): 40.104–8.

Souza, E.M. de 'A crítica literária e a tradução', in *I Seminário Latino-Americano de Literatura Comparada, 1986*, Porto Alegre: Universidade Federal do Rio Grande do Sul, 1986, pp. 181–6.

Spivak, G.C. 'Acting bits/identity talk', *Critical Inquiry* 18 (1992): 770–803.

—— 'The politics of translation', in *Outside in the Teaching Machine*, New York and London: Routledge, 1993.

—— 'Subaltern talk: interview with the editors 1993–94', in D. Landry and G. Maclean eds, *The Spivak Reader*, London and New York: Routledge, 1996, pp. 287–308.

Srikantaiah, B.M. *Shrisahitya* (Collected Works of BMS), ed. H.M. Nayaka, Mysore: Kannada, Adhyavana Samsthe, 1983.

Steiner, G. *After Babel: Aspects of Language and Translation*, Oxford: Oxford University Press, 1975.

Suleiman, S.R. 'Writing past the wall', in *Hélène Cixous' 'Coming to Writing' and Other Essays*, ed. D. Jenson, Cambridge, Mass.: Harvard University Press, 1991.

Tagore, R. [1919] *The Home and the World*, trans. S. Tagore, with revisions by the author, Madras: Macmillan India, 1992.

Thelwell, M. 'Introduction', in A. Tutuola, *The Palm-wine Drinkard and My Life in the Bush of Ghosts*, New York: Grove Press, 1994, pp. 177–90.

Tonkin, E. 'Engendering language difference', in P. Burton, K.K. Dyson and S. Ardener eds, *Bilingual Women: Anthropological Approaches to Second Language Use*, Oxford: Berg, 1993.

Toury, G. 'A rationale for descriptive translation studies', in T. Hermans ed. *The Manipulation of Literature*, New York: St Martin's Press, 1985, pp. 16–41.

—— *Descriptive Translation Studies and Beyond*, Amsterdam: John Benjamins, 1995.

Trivedi, H. *Colonial Transactions: English Literature and India*, Manchester University Press, 1993

—— 'The politics of post-colonial translation', in A.K. Singh ed. *Translation, Its Theory and Practice*, New Delhi: Creative Books, 1996.

—— 'Theorizing the nation', *Indian Literature* 160 (Mar.–Apr. 1994), special issue: 'Literary criticism: the new challenges': 31–45.

Trivedi, H. and Mukherjee, M. (eds) *Interrogating Post-colonialism: Theory, Text and Context*, Shimla: Indian Institute of Advanced Study, 1996.

Tymoczko, M. *The Irish 'Ulysses'*, Berkeley and Los Angeles: University of California Press, 1994.

—— 'The metonymics of translating marginalized texts', *Comparative Literature*, 47 (1995): 1.11–24.

Venuti, L. 'Simpatico', *Sub-Stance* 65 (1991): 3–20.

—— ed. *Rethinking Translation: Discourse, Subjectivity, Ideology*, London and New York: Routledge, 1992.

—— *The Translator's Invisibility: A History of Translation*, London and New York: Routledge, 1995.

Vieira, E.R.P. 'Por uma teoria pós-moderna da tradução', unpub. PhD thesis, Belo Horizonte: Universidade Federal de Minas Gerais, 1992.

—— 'A postmodern translation aesthetics in Brazil', *Translation Studies: An Interdiscipline*, Amsterdam: John Benjamins, 1994.

—— 'New registers in translation for Latin America', in K. Malmkjaer and P. Bush eds, *Literary Translation and Higher Education*, Amsterdam: John Benjamins, 1997.

von Humboldt, W. *On Language: The Diversity of Human Language-Structure and its Influence on the Mental Development of Mankind*, trans. P. Heath, Cambridge: Cambridge University Press, 1988.

Wall, R. *An Anglo-Irish Dialect Glossary for Joyce's Works*, Gerrards Cross: Colin Smythe, 1986.

Washington, M.H. 'Foreword', in Hurston 1990, pp. vii–xiv.

Willis, S. 'Mistranslation, missed translation: Hélène Cixous' *Vivre L'Orange*', in L. Venuti ed., *Rethinking Translation: Discourse, Subjectivity, Ideology*, New York and London: Routledge, 1992, pp. 106–19.

Wisnik, J.M. 'Algumas questões de música e política no Brasil', in A. Bosi ed., *Cultura Brasileira: Temas e Situações*, São Paulo: Ática, 1987, pp. 114–23.

Name Index